MW01226050

Critical Perspectives on Canadian Theatre in English

General Editor Ric Knowles

PLAYWRIGHTS CANADA PRESS

Aboriginal Drama and Theatre

Critical Perspectives on Canadian Theatre in English
volume one

Aboriginal Drama and Theatre

Edited by Rob Appleford

Playwrights Canada Press
Toronto • Canada

Playwrights Canada Press
202-269 Richmond Street West, Toronto, ON M5V 1X1
416.703.0013 • info@playwrightscanada.com • www.playwrightscanada.com

Playwrights Canada Press acknowledges that we operate on land, which, for thousands of years, has been the traditional territories of the Mississaugas of the New Credit, the Huron-Wendat, the Anishinaabe, Métis and the Haudenosaunee peoples. Today, this meeting place is still home to many Indigenous people from across Turtle Island and we are grateful to have the opportunity to work and play here.

We acknowledge the financial support of the Canada Council for the Arts—which last year invested $153 million to bring the arts to Canadians throughout the country—the Ontario Arts Council (OAC), the Ontario Media Development Corporation and the Government of Canada for our publishing activities.

 Canada Council Conseil des arts
for the Arts du Canada

 ONTARIO ARTS COUNCIL
CONSEIL DES ARTS DE L'ONTARIO
an Ontario government agency
un organisme du gouvernement de l'Ontario

 Canada

 Ontario
Ontario Media Development
Corporation

Cover image: Jin-me Yoon, *between departure and arrival,* 1996/1997.
Partial installation view, Art Gallery of Ontario.
Video projection, video montage on monitor, photographic mylar scroll, clocks with 3-D lettering, audio. Dimensions variable.
Courtesy of the artist and Catriona Jeffries Gallery, Vancouver.
Typesetting/Cover Design: JLArt

Library and Archives Canada Cataloguing in Publication

Aboriginal drama and theatre / edited by Rob Appleford.

(Critical perspectives on Canadian theatre in English ; v. 1)
Includes bibliographical references.
ISBN 978-0-88754-792-8

1. Canadian drama (English)--Native authors--History. 2. Native peoples in literature. 3. Theater--Canada--History. I. Appleford, Robert, 1966- II. Series.

PS8163.A26 2005   C812.009'897   C2005-902761-4

First edition: May 2005

Table of Contents

General Editor's Preface

Critical Perspectives on Canadian Theatre in English sets out to make the best critical and scholarly work in the field readily available to teachers, students, and scholars of Canadian drama and theatre. In volumes organized by playwright, region, genre, theme, and cultural community, the series publishes the work of scholars and critics who have, since the so-called renaissance of Canadian theatre in the late 1960s and early 1970s, traced the coming-into-prominence of a vibrant theatrical community in English Canada.

Each volume in the series is edited and introduced by an expert in the field who has selected a representative sampling of the most important critical work on her or his subject since circa 1970, ordered chronologically according to the original dates of publication. Where appropriate, the volume editors have also commissioned new essays on their subjects. Each volume also provides a list of suggested further readings, and an introduction by the volume's editor.

It is my hope that this series, working together with complementary anthologies of plays published by Playwrights Canada Press, Talonbooks, and other Canadian drama publishers, will facilitate the teaching of Canadian drama and theatre in schools, colleges, and universities across the country for years to come. It is for this reason that the titles so far selected for the series—*Aboriginal Drama and Theatre, African-Canadian Theatre, Judith Thompson, George F. Walker, Theatre in British Columbia, Feminist Theatre and Performance, Space and the Geographies of Theatre, Environmental and Site Specific Theatre,* and *Queer Theatre*—are designed to work as companion volumes to a range of Canadian drama anthologies recently published or forthcoming from the country's major drama publishers that complement them: *Staging Coyote's Dream: An Anthology of First Nations Drama in English* (Playwrights Canada, 2003); the two volumes of *Testifyin': Contemporary African Canadian Drama* (Playwrights Canada, 2000, 2003); *Judith Thompson: Late 20th Century Plays* (Playwrights Canada, 2002); the various collections of plays by George F. Walker published by Talonbooks; *Playing the Pacific Province: An Anthology of British Columbia Plays, 1967-2000* (Playwrights Canada, 2001), and other projected volumes. I hope that with the combined availability of these anthologies and the volumes in this series, courses on a variety of aspects of Canadian drama and theatre will flourish in schools and universities within Canada and beyond its borders, and scholars new to the field will find accessible and comprehensive introductions to some of the field's most provocative and intriguing figures and issues.

Finally, the titles selected for *Critical Perspectives on Canadian Theatre in English* are designed to carve out both familiar and new areas of work. It is my intention that the series at once recognize the important critical heritage of scholarly work in the field and attempt to fill in its most significant gaps by highlighting important work from and about marginalized communities, work that has too often been neglected in courses on and criticism of Canadian drama and theatre. In its nationalist phase in the late 1960s and 70s, English-Canadian theatre criticism tended to neglect work by women, by First Nations peoples and people of colour, by Gay, Lesbian, Bi- or Trans-sexual artists, and by those working in politically, geographically, or aesthetically alternative spaces. While respecting, honour-ing, and representing important landmarks in Canadian postcolonial theatrical nationalism, *Critical Perspectives on Canadian Theatre in English* also sets out to serve as a corrective to its historical exclusions.

Ric Knowles

Acknowledgements

All of the essays included here are published with permission of the copyright holder.

Tomson Highway's "On Native Mythology" was first published in *Theatrum* 6 (Spring 1987): 29-31; Sheila Rabillard's "Absorption, Elimination, and the Hybrid: Some Impure Questions of Gender and Culture in the Trickster Drama of Tomson Highway" was first published in *Essays in Theatre/Études Théâtrales* 12.1 (November 1993): 3-27; Floyd Favel Starr's "The theatre of orphans/Native languages on stage" was first published in *Canadian Theatre Review* 75 (Summer 1993): 8-11; Alan Filewod's "Receiving Aboriginality: Tomson Highway and the Crisis of Cultural Authenticity" was first published in *Theatre Journal* 46 (1994): 363-73; Reid Gilbert's "'Shine on us, Grandmother Moon': Coding in Canadian First Nations Drama" was first published in *Theatre Research International* 21.1 (Spring 1996): 24-32; Drew Hayden Taylor's "Alive and well: Native theatre in Canada," was first published in *Journal of Canadian Studies* 31.3 (Fall 1996): 29-37; Floyd Favel Starr's "The artificial tree: native performance culture research, 1991-1996," was first published in *Canadian Theatre Review* 83 (Spring 1997): 83-85; Robert Nunn's "Hybridity and Mimicry in the Plays of Drew Hayden Taylor," was first published in *Essays on Canadian Writing* 65 (Fall 1998): 95-119; Yvette Nolan's "Selling Myself: the Value of an Artist," was first published in *Zeitschrift Für Kanada-Studien* 19.1 (1999): 74-84; Ric Knowles' "Translators, Traitors, Mistresses, and Whores: Monique Mojica and the Mothers of the Métis Nations," was first published in *Siting the Other: Re-visions of Marginality in Australian and English-Canadian Drama*, ed. Marc Maufort and Franca Bellarsi (Brussels: P.I.E. Peter Lang, 2001), 247-65; Geraldine Manossa's "The Beginning of Cree Performance Culture," was first published in *(Ad)dressing Our Words: Aboriginal Perspectives on Aboriginal Literatures*, ed. Armand Garnet Ruffo (Penticton, B.C.: Theytus Books, 2001), 169-80; Daniel David Moses' "Of The Essence: about Tomson Highway's *The Sage, The Dancer and The Fool*," "Tricky Rabbit: about Beatrice Mosionier's *Night of the Trickster*," "A Bridge Across Time: about Ben Cardinal's *Generic Warriors and No Name Indians*," and "The Lady I Saw You with last Night: about Floyd Favel's *Lady of Silences*" were first published in *CanPlay* 18.4-19.2, his "Flaming Nativity: about Billy Merasty's *Fireweed*," was first published in *Gatherings: The En'owkin Journal of First North American Peoples* 12 (2001), 26-30; Rob Appleford's "Daniel David Moses: Ghostwriter With a Vengeance" was originally written for publication in *Daniel David Moses*, ed. David Brundage and Tracey Lindberg (Toronto: Guernica, 2005); and Armand Garnet Ruffo's "*A Windigo Tale*: Contemporizing and Mythologizing the Residential School Experience" is published here for the first time, with the permission of the author.

Acknowledgement also goes to graduate student Ross Langager who did some work scanning documents and looking for sources.

Introduction: Seeing the Full Frame

by Rob Appleford

[When the people emerged from the Underworld it was dark, so they made stars and told the War Twins to go place them properly.] Coyote said to himself, "I will go with the two boys." They put the seven together, the Pleiades, in a good position, and those six, Orion, they put them together, and the biggest one they put towards the east, and another they put on the south side, and another on the west side, and another on the north side. Then they put up the dipper [...] Just when they had put all these up, Coyote said to himself, "It is a big job!" He said to the boys, "We shall never finish this work, we shall all die first, why can't we do this?" He took the stars and threw them in every direction, improperly [...] Then [the people] saw stars scattered all over the sky. The people said, "Bad Coyote, did you do that?"—"Yes," he said.—"If you had not gone with them, all the stars would be well placed. But you are bad Coyote; you scattered them all over the sky." They were very angry. Coyote said, "That's all right, it's a lot of work to put them all into good positions, better to scatter them around."

—Parsons 239-40

Once a grizzly bear, coming down a narrow mountain trail, met a mouse coming up the trail. The mouse stood up and looked the grizzly bear in the eyes. Then he said, "Is your name Kak?" The bear got so agitated at being called such a silly name that he fell off the mountain. (I got that story from reading Claude Lévis Strauss.) Your name really *is* Kak. You will not fall down just by me saying it, but if millions of us say it over and over maybe you will fall down, and that would be very good for you. I want to say my own things to the world, and so, of course, given history, part of "my own things" is that you don't let me say things. Another part is that your name is Kak. You may think these are the main things I have to say; you probably think I am *your* mouse. You think I am *your* Other.

—Durham, "The Ground Has Been Covered" 103

When looking at the variety and success of what we call "Aboriginal drama" [1] or "Aboriginal theatre" in Canada, I am struck that this body of work's greatest strength lies in the delight of the unforeseen, the audience's wondering of what will happen next. Will the play tell us a traditional story, provide a critique of this story, reflect upon current events, incorporate a motif from Greek mythology, or demand a slapstick pratfall? All seem equally possible, and equally exciting. I was reminded of this delight of the unforeseen in 1997 when I was asked by two undergraduate students to provide a short scene from an Aboriginal play for them to perform for their Aboriginal Literatures class. At the time, I was working on the third chapter of my dissertation on Aboriginal theatre, and had been savouring what I had seen to be the controlled irony of Métis playwright Yvette Nolan's short piece entitled *Child.* They took to the work immediately and mounted a performance of it for the class, and I was invited to watch. During this performance, I experienced "the moment of the trickster" that Marie Annharte Baker has described, the point at which "we trip up and over our very limited human undertakings" (48). In my analysis of the piece, I had focused on its message of cross-cultural understanding, and had seen its effect largely in terms of its carefully distanced language. I hadn't foreseen the intensely emotional affect of the work in performance, its evocation of an Aboriginal child's experience of being lost and found. The performance left the audience (including myself) intensely moved and grateful for the passionate rendering given by its performers, and I was reminded quite graphically of the power of Aboriginal drama to combine emotional honesty with self-conscious critique in surprising ways. Kathleen Shannon, the pioneering feminist-documentary filmmaker with the National Film Board, relates a similar instance in her career helping an Aboriginal community make a film about itself:

> I worked on a film that a crew of young Native people had shot and we'd taken the rushes for that film around to a number of Native communities. There was one shot [...] that I would have gotten rid of because to my eye, it looked like a repetition of the shot that was previous to it. But in Native communities that shot always got a laugh [...] Finally I said to someone "What's going on in that shot that's so funny?" He said "Oh, it's that policeman who loses his hat." [...] I looked at it closely, and there was something happening a way up in the corner of the frame and I had not noticed it in the hundreds of times that I had seen that shot. Yet an audience of Native people had seen that the first time 'round. [...] I was taught [...] to look at what's relevant, discard what's not part of the action [...] the fact was, I had not seen the full frame.

In drama and theatre, the unforeseen encompasses both the unpredictability of the narrative's focus, and the theatrical means through which this focus is effectively rendered. But it also encompasses the unstable fields of identity and reception, less a delight in this context than an anxious necessity.

In his Introduction to *Performing Canada: The Nation Enacted in the Imagined Theatre* (2002), Alan Filewod cautions that "'Canadian theatre' has always been a difficult and problematic term, less a definition of a thing than a site of debate and contestation. It summons two historically unstable terms to create a third site of crisis" (x). If we substitute the term "Aboriginal" for "Canadian" in Filewod's warning, we can readily perceive the aptness of such a reminder. In this context, the "crisis" that Filewod suggests is produced by (and productive of) the conflation of nation and performance, marked by the at once mutually constitutive and obscuring relation between Aboriginal political identities and the "voice" these identities are allowed (in fact forced) to adopt. The critical reception of Aboriginal theatre and drama has, from the beginning, risked conflating political utility with artistic practice, and has typically placed undue pressure on Aboriginal playwrights and performers to adopt a voice which can be judged as inherently unified, homogeneous, and political.

That these two fields—political identity and voice—are intertwined is easily demonstrated by a consideration of the early critical responses to one of the first and most successful Aboriginal playwrights, Tomson Highway. In a review of an Alberta Theatre Projects' 1990 production of Highway's *The Rez Sisters*, Martin Morrow sets up an implied and highly political standard of value which is used to judge Highway's play:

> With the Mohawks at the barricades and the Peigans at the bulldozers this summer [references to the Oka and Old Man Dam (Alberta) standoffs respectively], Alberta Theatre Projects' production of *The Rez Sisters* couldn't have come at a better time. [...] A wry, insightful slice of Native life without any overt messages, this is a story, not about issues, but about human beings. (D1)

In this light, Morrow's own problematic reading of *The Rez Sisters* makes particular sense, given its political context. In Canada, the political manoeuvring in the aftermath of the Oka Crisis (1990) revealed how the issue of heterogeneity in Aboriginal communities could be vital in the struggle to resolve Aboriginal issues. Thomas Siddons, then Minister of Indian Affairs, refused to begin land negotiations with the Quebec Mohawks until they "got their act together" and established consensus over grievances and demands (Thompson). Frustrated by the factionalism he found in the Kanesatake Mohawks (factionalism for which he blamed the escalation of the crisis itself [Fraser "Native system" A1]), the minister characterized the indigenous political system of the Mohawks as promoting instability in the community. In response, Kanesatake Grand Chief George Martin charged that Siddons and his ministry were engaged in a divide-and-conquer strategy in order to transfer the blame for breakdowns in the talks onto the Mohawks (Kuttenbrouwer A5). In her questioning of Siddon's handling of the affair, Liberal MP Ethel Blondin underlined the irony of Siddon's depiction of Mohawk government as inherently unstable by pointing out that since 1986 "the turnover of ministers of Indian affairs has been almost as great as that of chiefs in Kanesatake" (Fraser A4).

This fear of heterogeneity (and the desire for homogeneity) affects not only non-Aboriginal observers of the political process, but also Aboriginal activists who seek to intervene in this process, who often feel they must present the provisional appearance of a unified front to the mainstream public in order to be taken seriously. Jana Sequoya, an American Chickasaw-identified writer of mixed descent, articulates the problematic nature of solidarity amongst Native Americans seeking change:

> it is one of the paradoxes of democratic government that without
> the appearance of a homogeneous political identity—an identity
> constituted in terms of the dominant system of representation—the
> issues crucial to Native American survival as regionally diverse peo-
> ples cannot be heard. (455)

In the case of Highway, supposedly unreflexive and therefore universal Aboriginal
narratives are set against those which are seen to communicate "overt messages,"
messages which remind the audience that Aboriginal peoples have unique political and social concerns which need to be urgently addressed. By being explicitly
championed by critics like Morrow in opposition to the mobilized activists of Oka
and Old Man Dam, Highway becomes a sign of a homogenized public ethnicity
with an attendant teleological slant; rather than idiosyncratic, exploratory exper-
iments in cultural (re)construction, his plays become transformed into static and
reified templates for ethnic identity. Filewod's "third site of crisis" here becomes
the site of the Aboriginal speaking subject, either evacuated or (pre)occupied.

   Thus, for critics, it is not a question of disentangling Aboriginal drama and theatre from its perceived political affect. Instead, it becomes necessary to understand
how political affect filters, mitigates, and complicates what can be apprehended
when Aboriginal drama and theatre is staged. Kathleen Shannon's anecdote about
missing the policeman's hat when watching the film footage, and thereby not seeing
"the full frame," suggests two related fields of inquiry which bear directly upon the
analysis of Aboriginal drama and theatre in Canada. The first involves the denat-
uralizing of the audience's gaze (both Aboriginal and non-Aboriginal) in order to
foreground the cultural and political premises that determine the (mis)apprehen-
sion of the "full frame," or in other words, the investigation of how things are seen.
The second involves a consideration of how the footage's "joke" reflects certain
aspects of Aboriginal culture and community, or in other words, the investigation
of what is on view. The essays in this collection deal in various ways with these two
areas of inquiry, and their conclusions attempt to make the apprehension of "the
full frame" of Aboriginal drama and theatre possible.

   The pieces by Yvette Nolan, Ric Knowles, Alan Filewod, and Rob Appleford
all focus on the problematic of the field of reception, how pre-existent notions of
Aboriginality—and of Western canonical texts and the tools of analysis they promote—help prevent a resistant Aboriginal drama from being effectively staged.
Nolan argues that expectations about Aboriginal images and content directly
influence how her plays are received and, by extension, what kind of plays she
feels able to write. Although she refuses to capitulate to the homogenizing force of
the marketplace, she admits that "the names you are given often stick a lot harder
than the ones you choose." While acknowledging the institutional pressures and
presuppositions that reinscribe colonial relations within the academy, Knowles
attempts to let the counter-discursive work of playwright Monique Mojica help
him consider "the cultural work which [it] might perform in shifting power relationships within contemporary Canadian and "American" (in the broadest sense)

societies." Rather than attempting to contain Mojica's work within a generic category of feminist or postcolonial resistance, Knowles explores the "sources, inspirations, genealogies and intertexts" in Mojica's work in order to reveal the specific resistance her work enacts. In opposition to Knowles' cautious optimism, Filewod argues, in his discussion of the 1991 revival of Highway's *Dry Lips Oughta Move to Kapuskasing* at Toronto's Royal Alexandra Theatre, that the entrenched hegemony of western realist dramaturgy forestalls any thoroughgoing transformation of Canadian theatre reception. Instead, Filewod argues that "voices of cultural affirmation and resistance are received by White critics as a testament of authentic and unmediated reality, which, in critical response, disallows the agency of resistance itself." Appleford pushes this skepticism further in his discussion of Daniel David Moses' work, in that he makes a case for reading Moses as a "ghost writer," one who, rather than presenting authentic Aboriginal speaking subjects on stage, instead rehearses the "return of the living dead," where ghosts represent "an occulted subjectivity, based on secrets, mysteries, and the concealment of the body (material and politic) by another interposed in the line of vision." While these writers come to different conclusions regarding the efficacy of challenging institutionalized conceptions of Aboriginal identity, and how theatre can mount or forestall such a challenge, the importance of understanding how the field of perception underwrites both artistic expression and critical interpretation is made plain.

Although the above-mentioned writers investigate the "third site of crisis" created by the conjunction of political sign and voice, there is another persistent strain of analysis in criticism of Aboriginal drama and theatre which focuses on the "third site of crisis" in light of Homi K. Bhabha's notion of the "third space," where

> a willingness to descend into that alien territory [...] may open the way to conceptualizing an *inter*national culture, based not on the exoticism of multiculturalism or the *diversity* of cultures, but on the inscription and articulation of culture's *hybridity*. (38)

Bhabha's "third space" challenges us to consider Aboriginal drama and theatre not as being either seen or not seen—in the sense of being "truly" understood by a "clear-eyed" audience—but rather as creating a volatile hybrid space where cultural signs from several traditions are mediated and collisioned; this allows critics such as Sheila Rabillard, Robert Nunn, and Reid Gilbert to explore the uncertainty such a hybrid space authorizes. For Rabillard, Highway's work "offers an account of colonial and postcolonial cultural expression that confounds the aesthetic with the political" and through the hybrid's "transform[ation] of the foreign," allows the audience to celebrate and critique the traditionally "feminine" qualities adhered to Aboriginal women and Aboriginal cultures in general. Similarly, Nunn's exploration of Drew Hayden Taylor's plays argues that the unstable and shifting relationships between traditional Aboriginal storytelling, mainstream pop culture references, and sitcom format allows the playwright to resist the homogenizing pull of political "voicing" through the difference asserted "in not *adopting* mainstream cultural forms but *mimicking* them. The hybrid thus created [...] is not evidence of being half-way towards absorption, but on the contrary is a powerful form of resistance to absorption." Gilbert considers several

Aboriginal playwrights in light of their "writing text at the intersection of discourses with quite different political and historical markers and, in the process, bringing those discourses together to form a new typology of signs." The "overlapping signification and forced recognition" of what Gilbert calls "translucent icons" in this hybrid theatre causes him to ask, "do they somehow reform the national consciousness?" All three writers attempt to understand the ways in which, as Bhabha suggests, "terms of cultural engagement, whether antagonistic or affiliative, are produced performatively" (2).

The other major field of inquiry explored by the writers in this collection involves the role of traditional Aboriginal stories in contemporary drama and theatre. There is a pronounced movement, in this context, from valorizing the content of traditional Aboriginal stories and mythologies in drama and theatre, to examining the potential of these stories and mythologies to radically transform both the formal characteristics of Canadian drama and theatre and the performer-audience relationship. In an important sense, the Aboriginal playwright acts not simply as a conduit between traditional and contemporary identities, but as a translator who must reevaluate how each identity can speak to the other, as Monique Mojica and Ric Knowles suggest:

> One of the tasks of First Nations theatre artists [...] *is* translation, broadly understood: translation between cultures and world views; translation between the unseen and the material worlds; translation between interior and exterior realities; translation between languages and discourses, including the values ideologies they embody; and translation of the ways in which First Nations peoples navigate identity. (v)

As a "translator," Tomson Highway affirms the continuity between oral traditions and contemporary theatrical performance; for Highway, "it's like taking the 'stage' that lives inside the mind, the imagination, and transposing it—using words, actors, lights, sound—onto the stage in a theatre." He also affirms the primacy of traditional Aboriginal mythologies in drama and theatre, in hopes that "the dreamlife of this particular people, this particular landscape, can achieve some degree of exposure among general audiences." Similarly, Drew Hayden Taylor's essay on Aboriginal theatre argues that oral traditions present a continuing, multivalent model for theatrical performance, where the story, like drama itself, "was like an onion, you could always peel away more and more to get to the core of the story." While neither Highway nor Taylor presume an effortless cross-pollination between identities and forms of expression, Armand Garnet Ruffo leads us through the difficult process of finding traditional Aboriginal spiritual motifs that can articulate contemporary trauma. His experience forcefully reminds us that the relationship between oral traditions and contemporary expression must be worked for, not simply assumed, and that "the potential to draw on traditional oral sources to tackle contemporary issues and create provocative theatre (as well as other forms of cultural expression) is only beginning to be realized."

Floyd Favel Starr's and Geraldine Manossa's explorations of "Native Performance Culture," and Daniel David Moses' personal meditations on four Aboriginal plays in performance, focus on the transformational power of traditional knowledges in Aboriginal drama and theatre. Starr explores "indigenous 'creative structures'" that can be isolated and used to re-map Aboriginal performance forms, thus creating "not a synthesis or fusion of the 'traditional and contemporary'" but rather "an upstream journey to the source of the river of our culture, country and ourselves." Similarly, Manossa sees the sharing of multilayered information from "listener and listener" and "storyteller to listener" as "the core of contemporary Native theatre." Her intimate description of a traditional storytelling event provides insight into how traditional stories create a necessary space for creative self-performance. Moses' reflections on four Aboriginal performances staged at Native Earth Performing Arts in Toronto exemplify how the myriad indeterminacies of performance and tradition must be grounded in the spectator's imagination in order for the "full frame" to be seen. For Moses, the performances permit a creative indwelling, "a spiral that contains the centre of the world, the eternal moment where each of us lives." In various ways, these writers ask vital questions about the risk and necessity of translating between identities, worlds, and performance modes. They remind us, as anthropologist Edward W. Bruner does, that "rather than ask what culture is, ask how culture is achieved, produced, and made believable" (324).

Of course, the process of compiling such a collection as this must also remind me of what is not here, what has yet to be discussed and theorized. I would have liked to include critical analysis of Margo Kane's work, especially her ongoing collaborative multimedia project *The River – Home,* or Maria Campbell's substantial post-*Jessica* playwriting career. The Aboriginal "invasion" of the Fringe circuit, exemplified by Sheldon Elter's successful one-man show *Metis Mutt,* bears reflection, as does *As Long As The Sun Shines* (Christina Grant and Doug Dunn), a play which dramatizes the 1899 signing of Treaty 8 in Grouard, Alberta, performed in 1999 with a cast of more than twenty who were descendants of the original treaty signatories. The Centre for Indigenous Theatre in Toronto, the plays of Ian Ross, Tawakin Theatre's cross-cultural exploration in Siberia, and the list goes on. The vibrancy of this field beggars the critical analysis applied to it thus far, which is as it should be. There is much to discuss, and this collection marks only a beginning in the process of watching, studying, and understanding the complexity and liberative possibilities of Aboriginal drama and theatre in Canada. As Daniel Mesguish comforts us, "the book to come is a theater" (118), which is also as it should be.

(2005)

Note

[1] Understandably, the issue of naming is highly complex. For example, attempts have been made by Indigenous peoples to renovate the term "Indian" and posit an original Latin derivation *in deo* ("of God") which they believe was mistakenly assumed by later historians to refer to Columbus' professed destination. Even more recently, the term "Indian" has morphed into the homonym-acronym "NDN," thus maintaining the oral circulation of the term as a signifier within indigenous communities without privileging its colonial pedigree. Noel Dyck argues that the term "Native" is a product of the nation-state's centric ideology of assimilation, and its generic quality serves to efface the fundamental differences which help strengthen Indigenous groups both culturally and politically (36-38). For my part, I have chosen to employ the term "Aboriginal" in my own work because of its widespread acceptance in Indigenous communities and its inclusivity. The authors included in this collection have employed various terms to refer to Indigenous peoples, and their terms have been preserved.

Works Cited

Baker, Marie Annharte. "An Old Indian Trick is to Laugh," *Canadian Theatre Review* 68 (Fall 1991): 47-48.

Bhabha, Homi K. *The Location of Culture*. New York: Routledge, 1994.

Bruner, Edward M. "Epilogue: Creative Persona and the Problem of Authenticity." *Creativity/Anthropology*. Ed. Smadar Lavie, Kirin Narayan, and Renato Rosaldo. Ithaca, NY: Cornell UP, 1993. 321-34.

Durham, Jimmie and Jean Fisher, "The Ground Has Been Covered." *Artforum International* (Summer 1988): 101-2.

Dyck, Noel. "Indian, Métis, Native: Some Implications of Special Status." *Canadian Ethnic Studies* 12.1 (1980): 34-46.

Filewod, Alan. *Performing Canada: The Nation Enacted in the Imagined Theatre. Textual Studies in Canada* 15 (Spring 2002).

Fraser, Graham. "Native system blamed for violence at Oka." *The Globe and Mail* 20 Feb 1991: A1+.

Kathleen Shannon. Interview. *Harpur's Heaven and Hell.* Vision TV, Toronto. 19 October 1992.

Kuttenbrouwer, Peter. "Ottawa hedging on its promise to give us land, Oka chief says." *Vancouver Sun* 2 October 1990: A1+.

Mesguich, Daniel and Gervais Robin. "The Book to Come is a Theater." *Sub-Stance* 18/19 (1977): 113-19.

Mojica, Monique and Ric Knowles, ed. "Introduction." *Staging Coyote's Dream: An Anthology of First Nations Drama in English.* Toronto: Playwrights Canada, 2003. iii-ix.

Morrow, Martin. "The Rez Sisters: ATP has trouble with wonderful play by Tomson Highway." *Calgary Herald* 22 Sept 1990: D1.

Parsons, E.C. *Pueblo Indian Religion.* Chicago: U of Chicago P, 1939.

Sequoya, Jana. "How (!) Is An Indian?: A Contest of Stories." *New Voices in Native American Literary Criticism.* Ed. Arnold Krupat. Washington: Smithsonian Institution P, 1993, 455-62.

Thompson, Elizabeth. "Talks to settle Oka land won't start until natives unite factions: Siddon." *Montreal Gazette* 17 Oct 1990: A5.

On Native Mythology

by Tomson Highway

"Native theatre"—for lack of better terminology—has been around for only about ten years, if that. By "Native theatre," I mean theatre that is written, performed and produced by Native people themselves and theatre that speaks out on the culture and the lives of this country's Native people.

The Indian painters made their first big statement in the early 1960s with the explosion onto the Canadian scene of such names as Norval Morrisseau, Daphne Odjig and others. This event—and particularly in the case of Morrisseau—marked the first time Indian people made available for public consumption their mythology, a mythology considered too sacred, by their own people, for this purpose and, in fact, so potent in its meaning that Christian missionaries did all they could to replace this mythology with their own. Twenty years later, it appears the writers are now finally ready to take the step taken earlier by the visual artists.

If Canada, as a cultural entity, is slowly succeeding in nurturing a literary tradition that has a distinctly and uniquely Canadian voice—albeit, one fashioned out of the melding of any number of other traditions—then the Indian people of this country have a literary tradition that goes back thousands of years. As a people, we are very much aware of the fact that there were mythologies that applied—and applied in a very powerful manner—to this specific landscape since long before the landmark year of A.D. 1492. But this literary tradition is an oral tradition, not a written one and these ancient stories were passed down generation to generation—in Cree, in Ojibway, Mohawk—until they reached us, the present generation, the first, as a group, to have a reasonable grasp of the English language.

But why not write novels? Why not short stories? Why the stage? For me, the reason is that this oral tradition translates most easily and most effectively into a three dimensional medium. In a sense, it's like taking the "stage" that lives inside the mind, the imagination, and transposing it—using words, actors, lights, sound—onto the stage in a theatre. For me, it is really a matter of taking a mythology as extraordinary and as powerful as the human imagination itself and re-working it to fit, snugly and comfortably, the medium of the stage.

The only thing is, this mythology has to be re-worked somewhat if it is to be relevant to us Indians living in today's world. The way these stories go to date, they were meant for a people who lived in a forest environment; we—our family—were all born in tents, grew up travelling by dog-sled and canoe, etc. But, today, as an adult, I am urban by choice. In order for these myths to be relevant to my life, to my own system of spiritual beliefs, I have to apply these myths, this mythology to the realities of city living. So, "Weesageechak" the trickster figure who stands at the very centre of Cree mythology and who is a figure as important to Cree culture as Christ is to Western culture, still hangs round and about the lakes and forests of northern Manitoba, yes, but he also takes strolls down Yonge Street, drinks beer, sometimes passes out at the Silver Dollar and goes shopping at the Eaton Centre. You should have seen him when he first encountered a telephone, an electric typewriter, a toaster, an automobile. I was there. Greek drama fascinates me because I feel that the basis for much of that drama is the mythology of that culture: the creatures, beings, the gods and events that inhabit the spiritual world of the Greeks play a central role. In much of Western literature, Christian mythology acts as a central under-pinning. And I believe that for "Native literature" to achieve any degree of universal resonance or relevance, any degree of permanence, Indian mythology must lie at its very root.

The difficulty Native writers encounter as writers, however, is that we must use English if our voice is to be heard by a large enough audience: English and not Cree. The Cree language is so completely different and the world view that that language engenders and expresses is so completely different—at odds, some would say—that inevitably, the characters we write into our plays must, of necessity, lose some of their original lustre in the translation. So, of necessity again, we are very conscious of the fact that we are working with a language that we must reshape to our own particular purpose. I suppose it's a little like trying to imagine what Chekhov's *The Three Sisters* must look and sound and feel like in the original Russian performed by a Russian company of actors and then seeing it performed in "Oxford" English. We get the general drift, maybe more, but I don't think we get the total reality of it, in the end. At any rate, the English language, as any language does, is changing constantly and we have a say in the changing of that language, it will be interesting to see where we get with it in the next few decades.

Indian mythology is filled with the most extraordinary events, beings and creatures. These lend themselves so well to visual interpretation, to exciting stage and visual creation: the cannibal spirit Weetigo (Windigo in Ojibway) who devours human flesh (in one show, we had him dining out at a Yuppie restaurant in Yorkville); the young man Ayash who encounters a village populated by women with teeth in their vaginas and has to deal with them as part of his vision quest, the woman who makes love to a thousand snakes; and so on and so forth. Not only are the visuals powerful, the symbolism underlying these extraordinary stories is as basic and as direct as air. And they come from deep, deep within the flesh and blood of a people who have known this particular landscape since time immemorial and who are so close to it they have become an integral part if it, like rock.

A recent Toronto production provides a good example. In *The Rez Sisters*, the story, essentially, is of the lives of these seven extraordinary Ojibway women, their passions, their tragedies, their exhilarations and of their bizarre and fantastical adventure with a game called bingo, a game otherwise as tawdry and mundane as laundry day on an Indian reservation (the "Rez" to us Indian folk). But on a larger scale, the story is of the Trickster, Nanabush—the Ojibway equivalent of the Cree Weesageechak—and his adventure with these women, the fun he has in "monitoring" the spiritual dimension of their lives. As this spirit figure is the one who straddles the consciousness of Man and that of God, the intermediary between the Great Spirit and his people—he informs the cancer victim among this group of women, Marie-Adele Starblanket, that "it is almost time for you to come with me", all the while disguised as a seagull who shits on Marie-Adele's lawn, swings from her clothesline as she does laundry, etc. Marie-Adele, in some dark corner of herself, knows somehow that she is dying and sort of, though not quite, recognizes the spirit inside the beckoning bird.

Later, as the women are in the van, driving down the highway to Toronto to take part in "the biggest bingo in the world", they stop for a flat tire. In the darkness, Nanabush, now in the guise of a nighthawk, makes another appearance. And he and Marie-Adele have this violent confrontation through which Marie-Adele realizes, for certain now, that she is going to die soon. When the women get to the bingo palace, Nanabush appears to Marie-Adele for the last and final time, this time in the guise of the bingo master—"the master of the game", as Marie-Adele now addresses him—who finally takes her hand at the climax of the game and proceeds to escort her into the spirit world. The other six women, who meanwhile have had varying degrees of awareness with this creature throughout, are left weeping and mourning at her grave. The Trickster has played his "trick" and he chortles. The play, in fact, becomes the tale of small and petty doings of men/women on this earth while only half-aware of some grander, larger "design" that rules their lives.

The mythology of a people is the articulation of the dreamworld of that people; without that dreamlife being active in all its forms—from the most extreme beauty to the most horrific and back—the culture of that people is dead, it is a dead culture and it is, in effect, a dead people we speak of. And, ironically enough, with the threat of nuclear annihilation facing us square in the face, we could be a dead culture and a dead people sooner than we think.

So, I suppose that we Indian people writing for the stage ultimately want to be heard so the dreamlife of this particular people, this particular landscape, can achieve some degree of exposure among general audiences. They just may learn, we keep hoping, something new and something terribly relevant and beautiful about that particular landscape that they too have become inhabitants of.

(1987)

Absorption, Elimination, and the Hybrid: Some Impure Questions of Gender and Culture in the Trickster Drama of Tomson Highway

by Sheila Rabillard

I

In his classic study of Winnebago Trickster tales, Paul Radin recounts the following story:

> Trickster [Wakdjunkaga] now took an elk's liver and made a vulva from it. Then he took some elk's kidneys and made breasts from them. Finally he put on a woman's dress. In this dress his friends enclosed him very firmly. The dresses he was using were those that the women who had taken him for a raccoon had given him. He now stood there transformed into a very pretty woman indeed. Then he let the fox have intercourse with him and make him pregnant, then the jaybird and, finally, the nit. After that he proceeded toward the village.
>
> Now, at the end of the village, lived an old woman and she immediately addressed him, saying, "My granddaughter, what is your purpose in travelling around like this? Certainly it is with some object in view that you are travelling!" Then the old woman went outside and shouted, "Ho! Ho! There is someone here who has come to court the chief's son." This, at least, is what the old woman seemed to be saying. Then the chief said to his daughters, "Ho! This clearly is what this woman wants and is the reason for her coming; so, my daughters, go and bring your sister-in-law here." Then they went after her. She certainly was a very handsome woman. The chief's son liked her very much. Immediately they prepared dry corn for her and they boiled slit bear-ribs. That was why Trickster was getting married, of course. When this food was ready they put it in a dish, cooled it, and placed it in front of Trickster. He devoured it at once. There she (Trickster) remained. (22-23)

To this Radin appends a commentary:

> This episode like the preceding ones is well known; no trickster cycle omits it. The reason generally given is that Trickster does it to avenge some insult. The change of sex is played on an oversexed individual in order to show to what lengths such a person will go, what sacred things he will give up and sacrifice to satisfy his desires.

Such is its role in one of the most famous of all North American Indian trickster cycles, that of *Wisaka* of the Fox tribe. But here in the Winnebago cycle it is not to avenge an insult but ostensibly to obtain food that the transformation of sex has occurred.

Taken in conjunction with the sex episodes which have preceded and the two incidents that follow, its meaning becomes clear. It is part of Wakdjunkaga's sex education. This must begin by sharply differentiating the two sexes. It is as if Wakdjunkaga were being told: this is the male; this, the penis; this is cohabitation; this is the female organ; this is pregnancy; this is how women bring children into the world. Yet how can Wakdjunkaga, with his generalized sexual organs, arranged in the wrong order and still living distinct from him in a receptacle on top of his body, how can he be expected to understand such matters? For that reason Wakdjunkaga's sex life, indeed, his whole physical life, is for him still something of a wild phantasmagoria. (137-38)

Radin goes on to note that when the mother-in-law discovers the trickery, Wakdjunkaga, who usually mocks those he/she has fooled, instead runs away. "Too many taboos have been broken," Radin remarks, particularly those forbidding any joking between mother-in-law and son-in-law, and the raconteur expresses this shock by bringing his narrative to a full stop. "Suddenly, and for the first time in the cycle, [Trickster] is pictured as a normal man with a wife to whom he is legally married, and a son for whom it is still necessary to provide. In short, he is suddenly represented as a good citizen, as a thoroughly socialized individual." This interlude does not last, however; soon he wanders on to further adventures and, in Radin's words, "the biological education of Wakdjunkaga is now to be resumed" (139).

I begin my discussion with Radin's anthropological study not because I suppose there to be a uniform "Indian" culture that would allow one to read Tomson Highway's use of Nanabush in terms of the Winnebago Trickster[1] (as I will argue, "Indian" as a category seems to derive its power from its usefulness in defining the White for him/herself) but because Radin's 1956 study demonstrates the desire for purity, boundary, and definition that exercises the dominant culture in relation to the colonized Native North Americans, a desire that Highway's drama cycle, I shall argue, thwarts. My argument is informed by Homi K. Bhabha's theory of the hybrid text which evades the rigid definition and division of cultures and their hierarchical ordering. Drawing upon both deconstructive and psychoanalytic theory, Bhabha uses the term "hybrid" to specify the space of colonial discourse in which "the insignia of authority becomes a mask, a mockery," a space "which has been systematically denied by both colonialists and nationalists who have sought authority in the authenticity of 'origins.' It is precisely as a separation from 'origins' and 'essences' that this colonial space is constructed" ("Signs Taken for Wonders" 103).[2] The hybrid offers an account of colonial and post-colonial cultural expression that confounds the aesthetic with the political and provides a means of describing the transgressive power of Highway's drama. Radin's commentary on the Winnebago Trickster becomes a point of departure for this study because it demonstrates so vividly the structure of authority, origins, and essences from which Highway's hybrid drama separates itself.

In his commentary on the tales Radin strives for a species of fixity—specifically, the fixing of sexual and gender boundaries. This effort is particularly remarkable given the fantastical nature of the Trickster's sexual exploits: in other episodes he carries his enormous penis in a box on his back, sends it swimming on its own to couple with a woman he sees bathing, has it partially eaten away by a chipmunk. Despite the fact that, as Radin records, tellers of Trickster tales often varied the order of incidents according to their sense of style and occasion, and that sexual adventure is by no means the chief topic of the tales which deal with a variety of other tricks and follies, the anthropologist specifies what seem to him the core tales and their order—a sequence of stories dealing with sexual organs and with intercourse and sex change—and argues that the sequence is "part of Wakdjunkaga's sex education". [3] The unfamiliar phantasmagoria of the tales' sexual materials is seen, first of all, as central to establishing an essential "nature and meaning" for the myths, one having to do with the basis of human sexual identity; and this phantasmagoria, furthermore, is perceived as a disorder implying and indeed requiring its opposite—ordered and strictly delimited sexual identities and gender roles.

As Radin presses these tales to yield essential and clear-cut boundaries of gender and sexual identity, he also takes considerable pains to establish their provenance in terms of a particular conception of cultural purity as guarantor of authenticity. He avers that:

> the text is authentic, obtained in an authentic manner, is adequately translated and that it represents an accepted version of the Trickster myth as it was to be found among the Winnebago in 1912. We can safely assume, moreover, that it had the same form one hundred years ago as it had then. (112)

Radin assures the reader that his reporter, Sam Blowsnake, added nothing of his own style to the narratives (even though he admits elsewhere that the Winnebago audiences of these tales appreciated a skilled raconteur and that the teller often tried to add his own emphasis to the drama of the telling) and that the source for the tales is not Blowsnake's father, who converted to "the new semi-Christian Peyote cult," but rather another unidentified narrator (112). His search for authenticity is strongly coloured by what has been called the "ethnographic present"—the hypothesized pure culture that the ethnographer tries to extract from what are considered the adulterating influences of contact with other, chiefly White, cultures. It is now commonplace to acknowledge that the study of the "ethnographic present" requires a deliberate setting aside of the present with its complex interaction and intermingling of cultures, including the interaction of the ethnographer with his or her interlocutors, and reveals a strong need to conceive of cultures (and by extension, races) in essentialist terms. Such essentializing manifests a desire for cultural and racial purity: the Indian culture is, ideally, the culture before contact with Whites, for the real Indian and the real White are defined by their difference from one another. The colonized people are made to serve the colonizers, thus, by enabling them to affirm their own pure identity.[4] This search for purity of definition, through its nostalgic narrative structure, works to sustain the twinned stereotypes of noble savage and degraded Indian.[5] Both stereotypes, of course, along with the location of essential "Indianness" in the past, contribute to the politically convenient and sentimentally soothing notion of the vanishing Indian who is, by definition, on the way to extinction.[6] Radin, then, attempts to partition White from Native North American culture, excluding any influence of the recent hybrid Peyote Christianity and pushing the source of the tales as far into the past as he can— not to pre-contact times, perhaps, but at least to 1812.[7]

Against this backdrop of Radin's search for cultural expression of an essential and definitive purity we can begin to understand Highway's dramas as hybrid, impure—to paraphrase Bhabha, as works that articulate the knowledges of cultural authority with forms of "native" knowledges and confront them with discriminated subjects that they rule but can no longer represent ("Signs Taken for Wonders" 99). In what follows, I discuss Highway's plays in the light of the analysis of Orientalism in which Bhabha's theory is grounded and locate one source of their power in their transgression of boundaries and definitions in which the authority of the dominant culture is invested. The discussion opens with an analysis of the fluidity of gender in *The Rez Sisters* and *Dry Lips Oughta Move to Kapuskasing* and in particular their challenge to traditional conceptions of the female. After a brief examination of the evidence that First Nations peoples have been constructed—in a North American version of Orientalism—as a fixed and "feminized" Other, I argue that Highway's plays disrupt such fixities not by laying claim to their opposite (and thus sustaining the "masculine" strengths of the dominant culture) but through celebration of qualities that have traditionally been considered "female," both in moving and comic imagery and in resilient, adaptive characters.[8] My argument will be complicated by an essentialist cast in many of Highway's comments. I suggest, however, that the structure of Highway's projected drama cycle and the relationship between the first two plays of the sequence imply the permeability of the boundaries of gender and culture, and that his polemical statements invoke a strategic essentialism. The final section of the paper examines more directly the hybrid's challenge to psychic and political stabilities. Focussing chiefly, though not exclusively, on *Dry Lips*, it explores the range of cultural materials that Highway has amalgamated in the motifs and the form of his texts, and the ways in which this bursting of categories manifests itself as well in the circumstances of performance: cast, acting style, theatre, audience. The complexity of *Dry Lips* allows me to extend the notion of the hybrid to the theatrical event and to examine the transgressive energies of a work that flirts openly with the dangers of assimilation.

II

The Rez Sisters is a two-act play of considerable power and a certain deliberate roughness. It has a cast of seven Native North American women, ranging from the senior Pelajia Patchnose, fifty-three, who repairs her own roof and speculates on what she would do to improve the Reserve if she were chief, through her sister, three half-sisters, and sister-in-law Veronique, to the youngest, Veronique's mentally disabled adopted daughter, twenty-four-year-old Zhaboonigan Peterson. The eighth character, who is played by a male dancer, is the spirit Nanabush. He appears in three guises as the Seagull (in white feathers), the Nighthawk (in black feathers), and the Bingo Master of the biggest bingo in the world to which the seven rez sisters are inevitably drawn. Act One is set on the (fictional) Wasaychigan Hill Indian Reserve, Manitoulin Island, Ontario; amid much gossip, news is heard of THE bingo game in Toronto, and one rez sister, Marie-Adele, learns she has to go to Toronto for cancer treatment. The women drop their bickering and determine to raise the $1400.00 needed to get them all to the city, combining medical and bingo trips. Act Two falls into four sections: a mime of the fundraising; a sequence of driving all night in a van to Toronto, during which the women talk about their hopes and their past lives; a phantasmagorical bingo game which transforms not just the stage but the entire theatre into the Toronto bingo palace, where the ailing Marie-Adele waltzes with the Bingo-Master; and, finally, the aftermath of the excursion back on the Wasaychigan Hill Reserve. Only six women remain: Marie-Adele has died of cancer, leaving fourteen children cared for by the barren Veronique; and Pelajia's sister Philomena, the sole bingo winner, has spent her $600.00 prize on a wonderful new bathroom. Since its 1986 production by the Native Earth Performing Arts Company, *The Rez Sisters* has become part of a developing cycle initially conceived as a trilogy but recently described by Highway as a seven-play sequence.[9]

In *The Rez Sisters* the female is the locus of an interplay between absorption and elimination—a counterpoint that has both physical and cultural dimensions. Women's bodies in this drama are open, vulnerable to penetration by the male in sometimes brutal sex acts; open to the breaking force of blows; defenseless against the proliferation of cancer cells overthrowing the body's internal boundaries and hierarchies; open to the allure of a culture that offers consumer come-ons like "The Biggest Bingo Game in the World." But this body which can be penetrated can also swallow and—more significantly—eliminate. Void. Defecate. Among the tempered and qualified joys of the conclusion is Philomena's purchase of a long-desired toilet suite. The harsh and bitterly comic energies of the play not only enthrone this one woman on her porcelain seat but ally the sisters as a group with the elusive, somewhat malign, but inevitably triumphant power of the trickster figure, Nanabush, who has appeared earlier in the drama as a gull-like creature who shits amazingly and where he wills, usually to the frustration of specific human wishes and the general desire for order.

If, as Edward Said and others have argued, the assigning of conventionally female characteristics to peoples perceived as Other by a dominant and patriarchally-configured society is a way of usefully pressing them into an inferior mould, here Highway suggests some of the resources of strength to be recouped from the association of a culture with the female. In the seven reservation women he celebrates female flexibility and fluidity, the ability to take in the foreign body, the strange and the threatening; and the mysterious female powers associated with flux, elimination, releasing and expelling which allow woman both apparent transformation and miraculous survival. This allusion to Said's well-known work on imperialism reminds us that a number of studies—some predating Said's work, some more recent and often indebted to him—have suggested the validity of an analysis of the European and Euro-American representation of Native North Americans analogous to his analysis of Orientalism. [10] Jeannette Armstrong, for example, issues a protest to the dominant culture in which her anger and frustration testify to the pervasiveness of Eurocentric representation of Native North Americans:

> Imagine interpreting for us *your own people's* thinking toward us, instead of interpreting for us, our thinking, our lives and our stories. We wish to know, and you need to understand, why it is that you want to own our stories, our art, our beautiful crafts, our ceremonies, but you do not appreciate or wish to recognize that these things of beauty arise out of the beauty of our people. (143-44)

It is not the structures of knowing and representing alone that lend the European authority, however, but the network of related generalizations regarding the subject peoples as well; prominent among these generalizations applied to "Orientals" and, as I argue, to "Indians," are a cluster of characteristics that are considered in Eurocentric societies markedly female and thus—given the cultural inferiority of women—markers of the "naturally" subservient role of the colonized. Said, for instance, describes the scholarly attitude that fostered the image of the "learned male Westerner surveying as if from a peculiarly suited vantage point the passive, seminal, feminine, even silent and supine East, then going on to articulate the East" (*Orientalism* 137-38). Nerval, he notes, recognizes the Orient as a land of dreams which everywhere "conceal[s] a deep, rich fund of female sexuality" (*Orientalism* 182). In "Orientalism Reconsidered," Said himself draws the analogy between Orientalism and patriarchy:

> We can now see that Orientalism is a praxis of the same sort, albeit in different territories, as male gender dominance, or patriarchy, in metropolitan societies: the Orient was routinely described as feminine, its riches as fertile, its main symbols the sensual woman, the harem, and the despotic—but curiously attractive—ruler. (23)

If Said's study suggests that we might expect to find the Native North American similarly described by a discourse that objectifies, subjects, "feminizes" the Other, Mariana Torgovnick's *Gone Primitive* gives us another way of understanding the dominant culture's forging of a link between subjected peoples and "female" characteristics. In her study of the means by which the modern world defined and used "the primitive" she writes that she discovered in all her material

> that gender issues always inhabit Western versions of the primitive. Sooner or later those familiar tropes for primitives become the tropes conventionally used for women. Global politics, the dance of colonizer and colonized, becomes sexual politics, the dance of male and female. (17)

It is scarcely surprising, for instance, that we find a literary figure like Duncan Campbell Scott, an influential civil servant in the Department of Indian Affairs, gain-ing renown as a poet at the turn of the century for writing of Native American subjects chiefly as stoic, mysterious, distanced women who evoke from him meditations on suffering and loss. The once-fashionable anthology pieces "Onandaga Madonna" and "The Forsaken" are characteristic: in the latter, an old Chippewa woman is abandoned by her family on a lonely island. She "Composed her shawl in state,/Then folded her hands ridged with sinews and corded with veins,/Folded them across her breasts spent with the nourishing of children," and after three days and nights of waiting "without pain, or dread, or even a moment of longing," she dies beneath a blanket of snow that literally incorporates her into the landscape (30). In such poems, Scott conforms to certain Eurocentric habits of mind discerned by David Murray in a similar cultural context:[11] indulgence in the frisson evoked by a modernist version of the sublime, i.e. an encounter with the untranslatable, unrepresentable Other (such as Scott imagines in the unimaginable stoicism of the old woman); and Romanticist melancholy at the prospect of the supposedly inevitable extinction of the Noble Savage (the "Onandaga Madonna" is described as "This woman of a weird and waning race" [230]). Scott both mourned this passing in his poetry and planned for it in his government reports projecting the complete assimilation of the Native peoples.

This typical literary strategy may also be seen as extending into considerations of language. Stephen Greenblatt makes the telling point that European superiority to the Native North American was once expressed in the notion that Indians did not even possess a language: when Columbus kidnapped several inhabitants of the continent he recorded that the abduction was committed in order "that they may learn to speak" (562). According to David Murray, the Native North American was further denied the tool of language through the accounts of missionaries, and the histories that used these as sources, which routinely omitted virtually all acknowledgement of the linguistic mastery shown by Native American translators and intermediaries (5-13). In such instances, Native North Americans are doubly feminized: not only the passive objects of knowledge, unable to represent themselves, but strongly associated with the feminine side of the traditional Western division between reason and emotion, between the rational, language-using mind and the irrational body.

Given this history of "double" feminization, it seems a neatly comic turning of the tables for Highway to open his dramatic cycle with a play in which this feminized silence and passivity is broken by a rush of linguistic exuberance from the mouths of seven female characters. (Nanabush has a monologue near the close of the drama as the Bingo Master, but the only other speech from a male character—the chief's response to the rez sisters' request for travel money—is merely indicated by percussion sounds.) Annie Cook in particular talks so quickly that the other women scarcely understand her ("She talks faster than she walks" [16]), but the rest of the women are far from quiet—Veronique, the most pious and supposedly meek conservative among them, is in fact the most enthusiastic gossip. The variety and richness of the vocal performances induce in the audience a heightened awareness of the play as a bravura display of the possibilities of speech: there are country-and-western songs, confessions, monologues meditative and declamatory, rhyming word-games, quick inter-cut dialogue, and an epic slanging match in which the lines of the characters overlap and battle for dominance. The voices of Annie Cook and her rez sisters rise against a silencing knowledge—historical, anthropological, poetic, linguistic.

Whether female muse to male poet, or feminized subject people to be studied by those whose presumed business it is to know and rule, the Native American is figured as passive, childlike, emotional rather than analytical, identified with the land and the biological, with mere female being rather than with virile doing. Thus, when Highway chooses to devote the first drama of his trilogy to seven reservation women, the female-dominated stage imagery he creates cannily puts in play—and opens to question—a complex of connections among gender, culture, and colonializing discourse. The rez sisters, far from passive, analyze their situation and get things done.

The first figure we see is Pelajia Patchnose, alone on the roof of her house, in faded blue denim men's cover-alls ("You gotta wear pants when you're doing a man's job" [7]), nailing shingles. She complains that for years "the old chief's been making speeches about getting paved roads 'for my people' and still we got dirt roads all over," and vows when she wins the bingo jackpot to "put that old chief to shame and build me a nice paved road right here in front of my house" (7-8). Most memorably, the seven women engage in an organized fury of fundraising in order to scrape together the $200 each that they carefully estimate is needed to go to the biggest bingo game in the world. (Emily Dictionary taunts them with being "welfare cases," and Marie Adele reminds them that none of them have any money—although Veronique thinks Pelajia has a little put aside; clearly the money does not come easily.) Their fund drive is staged shortly after the opening of Act Two, allowing the scene of frenzied, concerted effort to balance the "full scale riot" (44) near the close of Act One in which the women let loose the jealousies and antagonisms that have built up in their circumscribed community. If the positioning of the interlude of mimed labours suggests that we see it as a corrective of the uncontrolled passions unleashed in the previous Act, so too does the structure of the scene: as the fight gradually intensified—"*All talk at the same time, quietly at first, but then getting louder and louder until they are all screaming*" (44)—so now does the energy of work: "*The drive is underlined by a wild rhythmic beat from the musician, one that gets wilder and wilder with each successive beat…. The movement of the women covers the entire stage area, and like the music, gets wilder and wilder, until by the end it is as if we are looking at an insane eight-ring circus*" (70). Even though the money-making activity rises to a manic and comic intensity, so that Annie's garage sale sells off Pelajia's basement furniture, and the basement setting on stage "*simply dissolves into the madness of the fundraising drive*" (71), the passion here is clearly directed toward a communal aim and the audience is made to feel the emotionality of the women as creative rather than destructive; active rather than passive; part of their ability to seize and shape the direction of their own lives.

Indeed, even within the course of the first act, the seriocomic rage of the "riot" scene is tempered by reason and mutual concern. Thus, several events arrest the flow of anger in Act One; after the peak of vituperation has been reached stage directions indicate that the battling women freeze and the lights go down on their fight while Zhaboonigan, who has run in fright from the melee, tells Nanabush how she was raped; as she stops speaking the women engage in verbal combat again, but at a less intense pace, speaking now in sequence rather than simultaneously, and the slackening suggests an unspoken concern for the emotional distress of Zhaboonigan. Then, as cancer-stricken Marie-Adele suddenly reels from a flash of pain and weakness brought on by the effort of trying to punch Veronique, the women keep silent for a moment in sympathy. The insults resume, but the complete antagonism of all versus all is diluted as Annie expresses admiration for Emily's toughness; and finally the battle dissolves completely when Annie's letter confirms the existence of the special $500,000 Toronto bingo and the women put aside all irritations to focus on their common goal. Consultation on strategy follows, financial analysis, a brief set-back but no slackening of resolve when the Chief refuses a loan. Although the women's aim seems trivial and almost misguided—after all their efforts, a $1,400 expenditure will gain a mere $600 in winnings for one woman—Highway makes a drama of their longing, planning, resilience, endurance, their incurable activism.

There is one important qualification that must be made to the argument that Highway counters the Orientalizing association of the Native North American with the feminine, and it is clearly implied by Richard Hill's "Savage Splendor: Sex, Lies and Stereotypes." Hill discovers in the dominant culture's depiction of Native North Americans images of masculine savagery and aggression—particularly, sexual aggression versus White women—in addition to more generalized depictions of childish and/or feminized passivity and primitivism. Hill points out that such appeals to deep and inchoate sexual insecurities of White males offered them a seeming emotional justification for the untrammeled savagery of conquest, and this surely is the case; there is a masculine stereotype, then, in addition to the feminized Other. As I shall argue, however, this sexually threatening stereotype of the Indian male also has a role to play in an examination of what I have called the "impurity" of Highway's theatre, his challenge to gender and culture boundaries; for it speaks of a profound fear of miscegenation. [12]

III

Perhaps the most powerful questioning of the colonializing bonds of sharply demarcated genders and cultures is effected in *The Rez Sisters* through the interplay of absorption and elimination. It is imagery that focuses the audience's attention inescapably upon the female body and, moreover, upon its most taboo aspects: its fluxes, flows, and unstable boundaries, the features that have seemed perhaps most fearful and foreign to a male-dominated culture and that, consequently, have been most firmly associated with feminine inferiority, vulnerability and even uncleanness. The second play of the cycle, *Dry Lips Oughta Move to Kapuskasing*, makes more explicit what is implied in *The Rez Sisters*: Pierre St. Pierre recollects that Dickie Bird Halked was born on the floor of a bar because Big Joey was too afraid to intervene: "And Big Joey, may he rot in hell, he was the bouncer there that night, when he saw the blood, he ran away and puked over on the other side of the bar, the sight of all that woman's blood just scared the shit right out of him" (93).

The processes of absorption, indeed, seem at first evidence of the women's weaknesses. Emily Dictionary boasts that her first husband's beatings taught her to fight back, that she left him to join a motorcycle gang of rez women in San Francisco and to become the lover of their leader, Rose: "Man, us sisters could weave knuckle magic" (51). But in Act One she has come back to the rez and got "hooked" by Big Joey; she is "all wedged up with that hunk" (52) and her eye is black from one of Joey's punches she absorbed during a jealous fight with another of his women. Her body is "hooked," "wedged," penetrated, bruised, and she seems vulnerable to him, for all her pride in independence. And it is not only the penetrability of the women's bodies; their culture, too, seems open to foreign influences that surround them. Annie Cook is mightily impressed by her daughter's living with a French guy in Sudbury, and repeatedly tells all who will listen that his name must be pronounced with the correct accent, Ray*mond.* She is also infatuated with a Jewish country singer known as Fritz the Katz, and so convinced white guys "are nicer to their women.... White guys don't make you do things to them. You just lie there and they do it all for you" (86-87) that Emily taunts her with "Apple Indian Annie. Red on the outside. White on the inside" (86). But Annie isn't the only rez sister apparently vulnerable to the seductions of the dominant culture. They all fantasize about THE BIGGEST BINGO IN THE WORLD: when Annie wins she will buy a huge record player and all of Patsy Cline's records; Veronique will shop for "a brand-new stove. In Toronto. At the Eaton Centre," and "write a cookbook called *The Joy of Veronique St. Pierre's Cooking*" (36-37). (Perhaps the one note of resistance to the beguilements of the White consumer culture is sounded by the cancer-stricken Marie-Adele who wants to buy an island in the North Channel of Lake Huron, an island with lots of trees and sweetgrass.)

More ominously, the imagery of fluid boundaries, the women's openness to penetration bodily and culturally, takes on undertones of potential destruction. Zhaboonigan, the mentally disabled girl and the only one besides the dying Marie--Adele who can see the seagull/Nanabush, tells him how a few years ago she was picked up by some White boys in a car, raped with a screwdriver, and left in the bush, bleeding and naked. "Everybody calls me Zhaboonigan. Why? It means needle. Zhaboonigan. Going-through-thing. Needle Peterson. Going-through thing Peterson. That's me. It was the screwdriver" (47-48).[13] Halfway through Act Two, and shortly after another appearance of Nanabush, this time in the guise of the Nighthawk, Emily recalls the death of her lover Rose, who literally could not bear to yield any longer. "Cruisin' down the coast highway that night. Rose in the middle. Me and Pussy Commanda off to the side. Big 18-wheeler come along real fast and me and Pussy Commanda get out of the way. But not Rose. She stayed in the middle. Went head-on into that truck like a fly splat against a windshield" (97).

With absorption, however, comes elimination. In a virtually alimentary figure, openness to what is outside, penetrability, becomes an aspect of encompassing, digesting; transforming the foreign. It is not just wounds that the women receive but food and semen which they incorporate, make their own, and re-produce as strength and life. The waste, of course, is voided—a comic triumph—and throughout the play the women's most exuberant and forceful language (yet another species of outflowing) is liberally dotted with excremental expletives and references, from the opening pages: "You were born here. All your poop's on this reserve" (3), to Philomena's closing paean to her new porcelain:

> [M]y absolute most favorite part is the toilet bowl itself. First of all, it's elevated, like on a sort of... pedestal, so that it makes you feel like... the Queen... sitting on her royal throne, ruling her Queendom with a firm yet gentle hand. And the bowl itself—white, spirit white—is of such a shape, such an exquisitely soft, perfect oval shape that it makes you want to cry. Oh!!! And it's so comfortable you could just sit on it right up until the day you die. (117-18)

Allied with this closing celebration of the ability to transform what has been incorporated is Emily's pregnancy by Big Joey. Her baby, shortly to be expelled into the world, will be the triumphant product of past penetration, vulnerability turned to evidence of the transformative strength of the women before us. With her swelling belly and breasts, Emily's actions underline her power as she heaves cases of Carnation milk in the store and roughly comforts Zhaboonigan. According to Highway, the strength of Emily Dictionary celebrates the strength of one of his sisters, long victim of an abusive husband. He described her "soul glowing," and her husband in his sixties a "hollow shell" no longer able even to bully. He spoke of crimes shriveling their perpetrators, linking these observations to the occasion of his address, the anniversary of Columbus' arrival in North America (Talk, U of Victoria).

Highway, thus, neither rejects the identification of Native North American culture with the "female," nor engages in a simple re-valuation of the gendered characteristics assigned by the dominant culture, but evokes through theatrical and verbal imagery a complex interplay of vulnerability and incorporative power. This paradoxical conjunction of apparent weakness and strength is most plain, perhaps, in the women's encounters with Nanabush. As the sole "male" on stage—the seagull that shits on Marie-Adele's picket fence despite her efforts to chase him away, the intoxicating Bingo Master of chance and wealth, the Nighthawk who prepares cancer-stricken Marie-Adele for her death—the spirit-creature seems a figure for everything the women must deal with, the uncontrollable things that test their spirits, and form the material present, both boundary and mediation between them and the spirit world. Part of what they encounter, of course, is the dominant White culture; but we note that this too is figured by Nanabush (most explicitly as the Toronto bingo impresario), and thus encompassed within the Native culture in yet another act of absorption and transformation. When, at the close of the play, Nanabush lands behind Pelajia Patchnose, who is still mending her roof, and dances to the beat of her hammer he seems to mock and celebrate her at the same time; he is a figure for the women's—and a culture's—pain and strength.

IV

Highway's focus on women's experience in the first play of his cycle, I suggest, gives evidence of his awareness of the power of the colonizers' discourse to fix the conquered culture in feminized, de-valued terms; he is engaged in a process more radical, however, than a simple reversal of the values of terms set by White society for his drama mounts a challenge to such categories of knowledge as "masculine" and "feminine." One of the indications of the fluidity of the genders in Highway's dramatic world is the performative, presentational mode in which they are defined. Gender distinctions take on a playfulness in both *Rez Sisters* and *Dry Lips* as defining physical characteristics are given an exaggeration that hints at role, provisionality. In the earlier play, Big Joey never appears but his attractions take on legendary dimensions as the rez sisters gossip, joke, and quarrel. Pelajia teases Philomena, "You got your skirt ripped on a nail and now you can see your thighs. People gonna think you just came from Big Joey's house" (7). Emily Dictionary reports that she fought with Gazelle Nataways over him (her black eye was acquired accidentally in the struggle) and Annie Cook warns that if Emily goes on the trip to Toronto she'll lose Big Joey and with him all her juicy womanhood: "and then whose thighs will you have to wrestle around with in the dead of night? You'll dry up, get all puckered up and pass into ancient history" (57). Gender is put in play even more overtly in *Dry Lips*, a drama which in many respects offers explicit commentary on the more lightly-worked patterns of *The Rez Sisters*. In the dumb-show that opens the second play of the sequence, Gazelle Nataways (who, like all but one of the play's four female characters appears only as a manifestation of Nanabush) puts on a gigantic pair of false, rubberized breasts over her own bare breasts; an iconic life-size poster of Marilyn Monroe presides over the action. Patsy Pegahmagahbow/Nanabush also appears with a prosthetic—this time a huge bum; and the unseen, role-reversing all-women's hockey team meets a temporary setback when the puck is lost—so Pierre St. Pierre the referee reports—down Gazelle Nataways's V-necked hockey sweater:

> Down the crack. Right down that horrendous, scarifyin' Nataways bosom crack.... They say that puck slid somewhere deep, deep into the folds of her fleshy, womanly juices... and it's lost. Disappeared. Gone. Phhht! Nobody can find that puck. (81)

The title of the third of the dramas signals that Highway employs similarly destabilizing touches of exaggeration in *The Large Tit*.

The critique of gender is more powerfully evident when we look at Highway's plays as part of a cycle, whether a trilogy or a series of seven dramas. From this perspective, the role of the Trickster becomes more prominent as well as the continuity between the dramas which taken in sequence comment upon and complicate one another. It is worth quoting at length from his prefatory "A Note on Nanabush" in the published version of *Dry Lips Oughta Move to Kapuskasing*:

> The most explicit distinguishing feature between the North American Indian languages and the European languages is that in Indian (e.g.

Cree, Ojibway), there is no gender. In Cree, Ojibway, etc.... the male-female-neuter hierarchy is entirely absent. So that by this system of thought, the central hero figure from our mythology—theology, if you will—is theoretically neither exclusively male nor exclusively female, or is both simultaneously. Therefore, where in *The Rez Sisters*, Nanabush was male, in this play—"flip-side" to *The Rez Sisters*—Nanabush is female (12). [14]

The inadequacy of the mainstream perception of gender, at least as far as the Trickster is concerned, is underlined at one point during *Dry Lips* when Simon Starblanket addresses Nanabush: "If God, you are a woman/man in Cree but only a man in da Englesa, then how come you still got a cun..." and Nanabush/Patsy corrects him: "...a womb" (113). In a 1990 talk at the University of Western Ontario, Highway spoke of the importance of Nanabush—both in his dramatic cycle and, under various names, in the cultures of the Native North American peoples—as a figure who combines masculine and feminine. He stressed the difference between the Christian religion, which would separate male from female, Christ from the Virgin Mary, and a religion where Nanabush—trickster, transformer, and something of a Christ-figure as inter-mediary between humanity and the world of the spirit—includes both of the genders that the dominant culture would divide. Highway noted that in the next play of the cycle, *Dry Lips*, the pattern of *Rez Sisters* reverses, with seven male characters and a female spirit figure; and in the final drama of the trilogy that he then projected, he intended that Nanabush would be at once male and female. Highway's acknowledged homosexuality added a significant frame to his refusal to confine the gender possi-bilities of Nanabush. In short, the presiding spirit of Highway's plays is inimical to boundaries, polarities, and binary oppositions:

> The dream world of North American Indian mythology is inhabited
> by the most fantastic creatures, beings and events. Foremost among
> these beings is the "Trickster," as pivotal and important a figure in
> our world as Christ is in the realm of Christian mythology.... [T]
> his Trickster goes by many names and many guises. In fact, he can
> assume any guise he chooses. (*Dry Lips* 12)

One could go further, and suggest that there is a political edge to Highway's critique of the polarized genders. At least in *Dry Lips*, Highway more than hints at an association between opposition of the sexes and White oppression. *Dry Lips* establishes its darker tone in contrast to *The Rez Sisters* with an epigraph, a quo-tation from Lyle Longclaws: "before the healing can take place, the poison must first be exposed." The play which follows exposes antagonism between male and female in a harsher fashion and in a way that stresses its presence within rez life. Where *The Rez Sisters* has Zhaboonigan Peterson recall her rape by White boys passing in a car, for example, *Dry Lips* stages the rape of Patsy Pegahmagahbow by Dickie Bird Halked as his natural father, Big Joey, looks on. The words of Big Joey when he calls the debut of the women's hockey league—"Wounded Knee Three! Women's version!"—first make an explicit association between political domination and male/female antagonism (63). The connections in his mind are revealed more clearly in Act Two when two of his rez brothers, Zachary and Spooky, demand to know why he did not intervene to stop the rape; he responds in a speech that links Wounded Knee and a masculine wounding with the fearfulness of woman's blood and the birth of his illegitimate, alcohol-damaged son Dickie Bird:

> Wounded Knee, South Dakota, Spring of '73. The FBI. They beat us to the ground. Again and again and again. Ever since that spring, I've had these dreams where blood is spillin' out from my groin, nothin' there but blood and emptiness. It's like... I lost myself. So when I saw this baby comin' out of Caroline, Black Lady... Gazelle dancin'... all this blood... and I knew it was gonna come... I... I tried to stop it... I freaked out. I don't know what I did... and I knew it was mine... (119-20)

Zachary asks again, "Why did you let him do it?" and the answer finally comes: "Because I hate them! I hate them fuckin' bitches. Because they—our own women—took the fuckin' power away from us faster than the FBI ever did" (120). Big Joey appears to assert that the women—who, offstage, have intruded into an exclusively male sport—and the agents of White domination both emasculate. But the verbal imagery of his speech, and the theatrical images of rape and public, drunken childbirth that surround it counteract any sense that women should be seen as victimizers and impress upon the audience, rather, a pervasive wounding in which the mutual enmity of male and female seems most closely allied with the self-inflicted wounds of alcohol, a species of self-division induced by a state of pain and oppression. In short, the drama seems to invite the audience to see the opposition between the genders as a hurtful condition analogous to—if not the product of—the sufferings brought about by White colonization.

I have argued that Highway's drama moves towards a dissolution of divisions of gender and in so doing not only subverts the definition of the Native North American as passive, female, inferior but disrupts the Orientalizing system of knowledge itself by means of this challenge to one of the basic categories on which the strategy is based. My argument is complicated, however, by the fact that the depth of this challenge to gender and the Other is not fully evident until one considers the patterns of the play cycle: the reversal of focus from female to male characters as *Dry Lips* follows *The Rez Sisters*, the Trickster's evasion of gender categories when one takes the longer view of his/her role in the sequence of plays. Within the dramatic world of *The Rez Sisters*, in other words—despite verbal and visual imagery that dwells on permeability and flux—it is possible to feel in the celebration of the strength of the rez women an acknowlegement of the persistence of the categories of gender. Similarly, it may disturb the tidiness of this thesis to note that as Highway explains the ungendered nature of Nanabush he does so in terms that seem to imply an essential or rather essentialist division between Native North American and White. It appears that at least to some degree Highway acquiesces in the essentialist categories that, in the systems of knowledge of the dominant culture, construct both the female and the feminized Other of non-White culture. Without imposing a false consistency, however, it may be possible to account for the complexity of Highway's stance by observing the polemical cast of the statements about his work which for the most part are made in interviews, public speeches, or the prefatory notes to his plays—contexts in which he may well be concerned to define the social and political purposes of his work and to stress its difference from the usual dramatic fare. In one interview, for instance, he asserts that he wants to replace Shakespeare and Greek and Christian mythology in the minds of his people with "our own incredible times of heroism and tragedy and incredible comedy. Because until that day arrives we are going to continue to be colonized" ("Another Glimpse" 9). In short, I suggest that Highway (consciously or not) employs a strategic essentialism in his more politicized assertions, what Gayatri Spivak calls "a strategic identity reactively claimed, negotiable for struggle" (241), while his dramas, particularly in performance, challenge the stability of categories that divide genders and cultures.

To juxtapose the essentialist rhetorical strategies of his public pronouncements with Highway's dramatic practice produces an almost startling contrast for in these plays one encounters flashes of Shakespeare, the Greeks, and Christian mythology although in altered form, neither familiar nor wholly alien to an audience member from the dominant culture. Indeed, although Tomson Highway in one interview repudiates motor cars, telephones, fax machines, computers, and television as colonial tools, and announces that he doesn't own a television set, he simultaneously voices his ambition to remake these cultural products in accordance with his own people's needs: "I refuse to watch "Dallas" and "Different Strokes" and "Cheers" and Arnold Schwarzenegger [sic]. We'll make our own stories, eventually later our own "Dallas" and stuff like that" ("Another Glimpse" 9-10). When asked by a member of a lecture audience how he justified his use of the cultural products of the conquering peoples he replied that he chose the good from all that he experienced (Talk, U of Victoria). The fact that such questions are raised, I suggest, demonstrates the unease generated by Highway's transgressions of cultural categories. Indeed, recent critical discussion of *Dry Lips* in particular could not avoid the question of its cultural positioning. Gitta Honegger comments on the play's status as a "commercial breakthrough of a Native writer," catalogues subtly or boldly altered elements from the dominant culture, memorably describes Nanabush as "an oddly assimilated aboriginal Lulu," and stresses that in this play "nothing is just what it seems. Resonances of Western drama and Native customs mirror each other and refract the collisions and convergences of influences in contemporary Native cultures" (91). Robert Nunn is struck by the repositioning of *Dry Lips* from the margin "towards the mainstream," revealed by its production history and asks "whether recognition by non-native cultural authorities signifies co-option of a marginal voice by the centre or the empowerment of a marginal voice." This is a crucial question, he argues, which "addresses the issue of the relation between native and non-native cultures, the very theme of the play" (223). Such pressing questions suggest that if a challenge to gender categories indirectly threatens construction of the feminized Other, a more direct and powerful challenge to the dominant culture is mounted by work which destabilizes carefully maintained boundaries between Native and White, colonized and colonizer.

V

We recall that for Paul Radin, tales of the Winnebago Trickster were the means of defining and guarding differences between male and female, and in their authentic Otherness markers of the division between White and Native North American cultures. When Highway discusses the Trickster, as we have seen, the dominant principle at work seems to be the bridging or erasure of opposition or division: a "pivotal" figure, Nanabush "straddles the consciousness of man and that of God" and is "theoretically neither exclusively male nor exclusively female, or is both simultaneously" (*Dry Lips* 12). Highway offers his several audiences neither the authentically female nor the authentically Native North American in *The Rez Sisters* and *Dry Lips*, but rather dramas employing the strategy that Bhabha terms the hybrid—in language, form, frame, even acting style, venue, and audience. [15] Bhabha advocates an ideological analysis which proposes textual signification as the articulation of the historical in the form of literary representation—in the case of the post-colonial text, the history of impure conflicts, mixing and hybridization; and he argues that hybridity is to be valued, that "the colonial text of racial and cultural otherness must be exceeded" ("Representation" 104). Above all, he proclaims the power of hybridity to disturb colonial authority and the universalizing tendency of literary criticism manifesting itself as yet another form of control via cultural institutions:

> Culture, as a colonial space of intervention and agonism, as the trace of the displacement of symbol to sign, can be transformed by the unpredictable and partial desire of hybridity. Deprived of their full presence, the knowledges of cultural authority may be articulated with forms of "native" knowledges or faced with these discriminated subjects that they must rule but can no longer represent.... Such a process is not the destruction of a cultural system from the margins of its own aporia; nor, as in Derrida's Double Session, the mime that haunts mimesis. The display of hybridity—its peculiar "replication"—terrorizes authority with the ruse of recognition, its mimicry, its mockery. ("Signs" 99)

In the essay, Bhabha goes on to argue, contra Frantz Fanon, that the psychic choice is not either to "turn white or disappear." "There is the more ambivalent, third choice: camouflage, mimicry. Black skins white masks." Quoting Lacan, he stresses that "it is not a question of harmonizing with the background but against a mottled background of being mottled" (103). Trinh T. Minh-ha, a film-maker and fellow theorist of post-colonialism, articulates what is at stake in such an argument in a way that underlines its applicability to the work of Highway:

> Today, planned authenticity is rife; as a product of hegemony and a remarkable counterpart of universal standardization, it constitutes an efficacious means of silencing the cry of racial oppression. We can no longer wish to erase your difference, we demand, on the contrary, that you remember and assert it. (89)

The real, nothing else than a code of representation, does not (cannot) coincide with the lived or the performed. This is what Vine Deloria, Jr. accounts for when he exclaims: "Not even Indians can relate themselves to this type of creature who, to anthropologists, is the 'real' Indian." (94) [16]

In what sense, then, does Highway's Trickster drama inhabit the terrain of the hybrid? One might cite, first, Highway's allusions to Michel Tremblay's *Les Belles Soeurs* in *The Rez Sisters*. The family resemblance of the titles announces that Highway is reworking a landmark Canadian drama, and one that is highly flavoured by a cultural milieu different from his own (although, to make this gesture of appropriation more complex, one that has something of a "subaltern" provenance). Both dramas also share what might be called an operatic quality in their structure, their moments of sustained monologue or chorus, and their bravura emotional passages. What defines the hybrid strategy, however, is not mere resemblance but overt gestures that draw attention to a palimpsestic over-writing of the prior text, a re-reading that is in several senses "partial," and this we find in *The Rez Sisters*—most notably in the play's central bingo motif which plainly seems to derive from the famed "Ode to Bingo" in *Les Belles Soeurs*, but takes the material of the more established playwright in a new direction. What was a choral interlude, incidental to plot if vital to the play's atmosphere, becomes central; and that means the pleasures and risk-taking, the collective energies indicated in shared song, likewise made central, take on new qualities; bingo is no longer alluded to as an off-stage and temporary compensation for the hypocrisies, repressions, sexual fears and warfare of the genders endemic to Tremblay's dramatized world. In Highway's words, bingo "a game otherwise as tawdry and mundane as laundry day on an Indian reservation" becomes on his stage "a bizarre and fantastical adventure" for his seven rez women and a vehicle for the expression of "their passions, their tragedies, their exhilarations" ("On Native Mythology" 30).

That the plays present a novel melange of elements familiar to Native North Americans and motifs from the mainstream culture seems plain: in *Dry Lips* one finds, for instance, that the family name of one of the central characters, Zachary Jeremiah Keechigeesik (it means "heaven" or "great sky" in Cree, we are told) recalls Zeus, lord of the skies while his wife's given name is Hera. But the peculiarly disturbing hybrid quality of the dramas is equally evident in their generic transgressions. Although an increasing number of contemporary productions explore the territory between drama and a variety of performance arts, or experiment with parody and pastiche, the generic and cultural complexity of Highway's plays displays the elusiveness of the hybrid rather than the canny avant-garde positioning of postmodern formal experimentation. There is a political bite to the mixed form of his dramas, in other words, as they transgress categorizations. On the one hand, as Terry Goldie has pointed out, Native actors are usually read by the dominant society as indicators of a depiction that is realistic in mode and an authentic representation of the Other (186-87); certainly this argument seems to hold true for film performances such as those in "Dances with Wolves." However, in Highway's plays, acted by members of the Native Earth Performing Arts Company, the elements which seem most non-White are often those which also markedly breach the conventions of dramatic realism: the dances of Nanabush as bird in *The Rez Sisters*, for instance, or the wonderful bustle dance of this Trickster figure in *Dry Lips*. The Native actor on stage is not to be read as a realistic depiction of the "real Indian": no material for a mainstream audience's cultural tourism.

The process of recognizing the "authentically" Native North American is further disrupted by the close alliance of Nanabush with figures from mainstream commercial culture: in one manifestation he is the Bingo Master impresario, and when she appears in *Dry Lips* as a glamorous stripper, Nanabush is clearly allied to the seductive image of Marilyn Monroe prominent in the opening scene. (Nanabush farts for the poster Marilyn at one point later in the play.) Nor have the forms of European drama escaped the process of absorption and transformation. Gitta Honegger, for instance, suggests that one can glimpse something of the comedic pattern of Shakespeare's *A Midsummer Night's Dream* in the shape of *Dry Lips*. Highway's play is framed as a dream excursion into disorder; in her manifestation as Gazelle Nataways, the rez seductress, Nanabush—like a Titania—draws Zachary Keechigeesik into confusion while his bare backside (prominently displayed in the opening scene) Honegger argues is a visual pun on Bottom (91). The comedic plot, however, has undergone a profound alteration and no longer speaks of Providential order. The Nanabush of *Dry Lips* distracts a drunk and grief-crazed Simon Starblanket, with disastrous consequences, at the crucial point when Zachary is about to persuade him to put down his gun. She appears in one scene as a mockery Jehovah, "*sitting on a toilet having a good shit*"; her voluptuous form is "*dressed in an old man's white beard and wig, but also wearing sexy, elegant women's high-heeled pumps. Surrounded by white, puffy clouds, she/he sits with her legs crossed, nonchalantly filing his/her fingernails*" (117). The play's dream world is coloured by the nightmare of alcoholism and despair, and Zachary's awakening at the close to a placid domestic realm of wife and child contrasts so strongly with the tone of the play's dreamscape as to seem itself a merely visionary hope. The drama, thus, offers a defamiliarizing comment on comedic resolution. Highway's inventive hybridization of comedic form is only one among many such adulterations in these provocative dramas. *Dry Lips* reminds Honegger of Oedipus; and the death of vivid young Simon Starblanket evokes something of the pattern of scapegoat sacrifice that underlies much of Western tragic form. But again, this must be tragedy with a difference, with the Trickster at its centre.

One could argue that Highway's deliberate flouting of decorum, his blending of borrowings from high and low White culture also serves to create the hybrid. In *Dry Lips* he combines mystic juke boxes, country-and-western hit songs, and an amateur hockey league with evocations of Greek drama and Shakespearean comedy. The strategies and forms of opera are juxtaposed in *The Rez Sisters* with the low excitements of a monster bingo. Such conjunctions of popular and elite can subtly derail the schooled responses of a mainstream audience, as can the unexpected combination of the most distressing subject matter—rape, suicide, alcoholism—with sight gags, comic fart effects, and the like. They also suggest a perspective from the margins of the dominant society—a somewhat detached point of view from which "high" and "low" might appear in a different light and with an altered value. While it could be flattering to the dominant society to see its serious cultural products sedulously aped, it is another matter entirely to find the songs of Kitty Wells on an equal footing with evocations of Shakespearean drama; certainly this is an estranging use that refuses to accept the cultural products of the dominant society according to that society's estimations.

In linguistic terms, *The Rez Sisters* mixes English with occasional passages of Cree and Ojibway. (Highway explains in a production note that they "are used, freely in this text for the reasons that these two languages, belonging to the same linguistic family, are very similar and that the fictional reserve of Wasaychigan Hill has a mixture of both Cree and Ojibway residents" [xi].) These phrases and sentences are far from negligible—they tend to occur at moments of considerable emotion, as for example when Marie-Adele confesses to Pelajia some of the pain and fear of her slow dying, and when Nanabush escorts Marie-Adele into the spirit world. Moreover, though translations are provided in footnotes to the published text of *The Rez Sisters*, on stage the spoken dialogue would have been more estranging to the ear of an audience member without Cree or Ojibway. *Dry Lips* retains in print somewhat more of the performance effect of linguistic hybridity: though translations of short passages are incorporated within parentheses in the text, two extended speeches (Big Joey's hockey play-by-play commentaries) are translated only in appendices at the end of the playtext. It can be argued that the clash of several languages presents a metonym of the cultural interaction which is imputed by the linguistic variation. [17] In performance, moreover, the English speech of the actors who appeared in Highway's Native Earth Performing Arts productions, when subtly tinged with the rhythms and inflections of a First Nations language, created its own hybrid effect. Highway has commented, "What I do now is use the English language to explore a Cree sensibility—it's like using the English language filtered through a Cree imagination" (Preston 143). Despite this essentialist statement, Highway at times seems to acknowledge the hybridity, the impurity, of languages themselves. Thus, while he writes of the difficulty of translating the Cree language and "voice" or "world view" into English—"translation" here seeming to assume a distinctive essence and sensibility belonging to each tongue—he also acknowledges that Native writers are engaged in "working with a language that we must reshape to our own particular purpose" and even, more radically, that English is not a fixed entity but rather like a fluid process, the course of which his own present intervention may influence. "At any rate, the English language, as any language does, is changing constantly and we have a say in the changing of that language" ("On Native Mythology" 30).

The mixed languages, of course, signal the possibility of several audiences and meanings that are different for each. A member of the dominant culture, thus, is reminded that he or she is not simply the Universal audience; the authoritative Subject is subtly challenged. In performance, one's awareness of the potentially different meanings of the Trickster dramas for different audiences was heightened by their presentational style, and the novelty of any play's casting of Native North

American actors. The Native Earth Performing Arts Company gave *The Rez Sisters* an almost Brechtian narrativity, perhaps in response to the number of monologues Highway provides. Highway has commented that the oral tradition of Cree, Ojibway, and Mohawk stories with which he is familiar "translates most easily and effectively" onto the stage; so one may speculate that the acting style of the company deliberately took on something of the quality of telling ("On Native Mythology" 30). Thus Toronto audience members, in part addressed by the Native player on stage, must have reacted with a powerful sense of the cultural differences (or, in a minority of cases, similarities) between actor and audience member. "First of all," Highway's brother René recalled, "they'd never seen all those Native people onstage, talking that way, sometimes in Cree" (Preston 143). Consciousness of such chasms or commonalities would of course be increased at those junctures where boundaries between stage and auditorium were broken and the audience member was brought into more direct confrontation with the actor and his or her presentation of character. Such moments occur when the bingo game of *The Rez Sisters* extends itself to encompass the whole theatre, or in *Dry Lips* during the two hockey matches when the territory beyond the edge of the stage is taken over by the reported action of the (unseen) athletic contests. For the second Toronto production of *Dry Lips* in the spring of 1991, the venue itself spoke eloquently of the hybrid—familiar and estranging. When this drama was mounted in the Royal Alexandra Theatre, a commercial theatre known for Broadway and West End productions or their Canadian counterparts, the juxtaposition of Highway's play—which had its own most disturbing and painful though certainly spectacular effects—with the Alex's restored Edwardian glamour, suggestive of decorous and decorative entertainments, created a peculiar shock. The nature of the material, the presentational performance style, seemed continually to allude to more intimate contexts in which the address of actor to audience would take place between members of the same community.

VI

An objection could be raised that while Bhabha's classic example of the hybrid is an instance of a transgressive rewriting of the dominant culture's most authoritative text, the Holy Bible, Highway talks of a projected subversion of "Dallas" and in practice reshapes such low cultural texts as bingo games and hockey matches. To be sure, Highway is profoundly concerned to transform "by the unpredictable and partial desire of hybridity" commercialized icons of sex, sport, and monetary gain. Yet, while Highway is fascinated by the power of these debased cultural texts, within the dramatic world of *Dry Lips* Highway also subverts the colonizing power of the Church. Spooky Lacroix, whose name makes a punning comment, is a figure in the grip of a tyrannical fundamentalist belief, the only alternative he has found to his addiction to alcohol. His new spiritual addiction prevents him from communicating anything but frightening sermons to Dickie Bird Halked, afflicted with fetal alcohol syndrome. (Pierre St. Pierre comments, "He's just preachifyin' at you because you're the one person on this reserve who can't argue back" [57].) The effects of Christianity and alcohol come together in an horrific image as alcohol-damaged Dickie Bird uses Spooky's crucifix to rape Patsy Pegamagahbow, a woman associated with the hopes of a new generation, and one of the manifestations of Nanabush. In a sense, then, Highway is rewriting a holy text, as *Dry Lips* rehearses its own crucifixion. In like manner, though in a somewhat lighter mood, the climactic bingo game of *The Rez Sisters* groups the seven women at a long table, the scene "*lit so that it looks like 'The Last Supper'*"; with Zhaboonigan seated at the centre, "*banging a crucifix Veronique has brought along for luck*" (102).

Highway's hybrid strategies were perhaps already hinted at in an earlier—though much briefer—tripartite cycle in which, as in the Trickster dramas, the structure is strongly influenced by the playwright's musical training.[18] This is "New Song... New Dance," a three-part performance staged in 1988. The "acculturing" experiences of Tomson and his brother René Highway in residential school lie at the heart of the piece, danced by René to Tomson's on-stage piano accompaniment. The first section, "Andante," deals with alienation in the residential school; "Largo," the second, which is based on a Cree lullaby, René Highway in an interview said was "about healing ourselves on a deep spiritual level" (Dimanno 10). The final movement, named "Kachina" after spirits revered by the Pueblos and Hopis, he described as follows: "It's about assimilating. It shows that we are able to survive, that we *have* survived. The message is to use what we've learned and experienced and to come up with a way of expressing ourselves" (Dimanno 10). Here, prefiguring the complexities of stance in the Trickster drama cycle, the means of expression found—which clearly draw on Tomson Highway's training in classical Western music as well as Cree lullaby—create what seems, in Bhabha's terms, a unique and hybrid form which René Highway proclaimed as itself the message "that we *have* survived."

René Highway's emphasis on both assimilation and survival may appear on the surface self-contradictory; but the seeming incompatibility of the terms he used, I suggest, is only superficial and their conjunction returns us to the energies of the hybrid via David Lloyd's cognate analysis of assimilation. Lloyd argues that "assimilation" is a concept which is at once a metaphor and structured like a metaphor, and that the narrative of metaphor, the process of bringing two elements into identity in such a manner that their differences are suppressed, is always hierarchical. The process of identification produces difference and

> requires that which defines the difference between the elements to remain over as a residue. Hence... the product of assimilation will always necessarily be in an hierarchical relation to the residual, whether this be defined as, variously, the primitive, the local, or the merely contingent. (72-73)

According to Lloyd, the product of assimilation—whether the public sphere, aesthetic culture, or the abstract, "universal" Subject which subtends both of these—"may be conceived as obsessionally anxious, since its very formation produces what might undo that formation" (72-73). The product of assimilation, then, is always both the dominant culture construed as universal and that which may undo it. Thus René and Tomson Highway perform a dance of assimilation *and* survival. Moreover, René Highway's delight in their collaborative creation suggests that, depending on one's perspective, there is stimulation and pleasure (as well as anxiety) to be had from the instability of the supposedly universal social and cultural sphere; and the text that exposes the process of assimilation presents us with another version of the disruptive vigour of hybridity.

In this paper I have tried to move in the precarious space between definitions, to argue that Highway's drama cannily exploits the association of Native North American cultures with the female, while at the same time acknowledging that his plays demand we re-examine the usefulness of both of these categories—both "Native North American culture" and "the female." To turn to Bhabha's notion of hybridity offers opportunity for refinement of these crude terms, but in some respects merely defers confrontation with the same perplexities; a "hybrid" is, after all, a cross between two species so distinct that the offspring of the union cannot themselves reproduce. But despite the possible dangers of this term, Bhabha's "hybridity" at least allows the critic to respond to textual signification as in some sense the articulation of the historical interaction and tangled mutual definition of cultures. Hence, my starting point in Radin's respectful but overconfident attempt to define and record the racial and cultural Otherness of the Native North American myths he studied. By contrast, I do not want to suppose that my methodology separates subject from object of study, nor do I want to discover the meaning of the Trickster figure in its usefulness in defining racial, cultural, or gender boundaries. Nonetheless, part of the point of Bhabha's coinage is to suggest that the cultural products of the colonizer reappear in the hands of the colonized hybridized, transformed into something partially familiar to the dominant culture and yet new and estranging; still other if not, perhaps, the pure and metaphysically defining Other. In place of Radin's backward-looking gesture, his attempts to purify the Trickster stories of all trace of his assistant Blowsnake, any influence of the Peyote-Christianity of Blowsnake's father, the best frame for a drama like *The Rez Sisters* thus maybe provided by Highway's playful projection into the future: some day he hopes to stage a film version of the play with Toronto's Sky Dome as the setting for the World's Biggest Bingo and in the stands "an ocean of five thousand Indian ladies from all over Ontario, clutching their Bingo cards" (Moses 88).

(1993)

Notes

1   Tomson Highway, in a prefatory note to *The Rez Sisters*, acknowledges that his figure has roots in Cree and Ojibway cultures, with family ties to other Trickster figures: "'Weesageechak' in Cree, 'Nanabush' in Ojibway, 'Raven' in others, 'Coyote' in still others, this Trickster goes by many names and many guises. In fact, he can assume any guise he chooses" (xii).

2   While Bhabha's example of Indian villagers' rewriting of the Bible focuses attention upon resistance to overt indoctrination, his argument also directs us towards an understanding of the ways in which the hybrid destabilizes the categories of subject, authority, and essence which subtend colonial domination.

3   According to Radin, Trickster shows no inner development in the sequence of tales but rather displays "a true nature" with "a single active principle, the component elements 'phallic,' 'voracious,' 'sly,' 'stupid'—the spirit of disorder, the enemy of boundaries" (185).

4   Compare the philosophical argument made by Appiah regarding the "illusion" of race, and the enormous utility of this illusion to those who can manipulate it, and see also Trinh for analysis of the political nature of the category "Native."

5   For studies of the production of the "Indian" in literary, scientific and popular discourse and analysis of its uses in the process of colonial domination, see, among others: Hill, "Savage Splendor"; Berkhofer; Murray; Bentley, "Calibanned," and "Savage"; Goldie; and Monkman.

6   On this specific use of stereotype, see Murray and Berkhofer in particular.

7   Goldie argues that literary representation, similarly, locates the Native North American at a point of originary purity and isolation from the culturally complex present: "The indigene who wishes to cross the temporal and temperate barriers, to become coeval, to become 'hot,' either dies with the prehistoric indigene or becomes no longer indigene. So whether or not the indigene in body dies, the indigene dies" (168).

8   Plainly, I disagree with Bennett's charge that Highway's plays confirm negative stereotypes of Native North American women; see the controversy surrounding her response to Preston.

9   *The Rez Sisters* was initially produced in Toronto in 1986 by the Native Earth Performing Arts Company under Highway's artistic direction; a second play set on the Wasaychigan Hill Reserve—*Dry Lips Oughta Move to Kapuskasing* (originally *The Rez Brothers*)—was co-produced by Native Earth and Theatre Passe Muraille in 1989 and a third drama, *The Large Tit*, was workshopped with the Manitoba Theatre Centre during the 1990-91 season. Highway described a trilogy as recently as the fall of 1990, during a talk delivered at the University of Western Ontario. However, in an address given 20 October 1992 at the University of Victoria, he mentioned plans

for a seven-play sequence built around the characters introduced in the first two plays and announced that he was working on *Rose*, which he called a "rez motown musical" dealing with two of the women who rode with Emily Dictionary in the motorcycle gang she recalls in *The Rez Sisters*. The two women bikers, he said, come up to Toronto and call Emily on the reservation to say "let's go on the road again."

10 See note 5, above. The related issue of the appropriation of motifs from First Nations cultures by White writers and visual artists is addressed, for example, by Hill, "One Part per Million"; Maracle; Keeshig-Tobias; Armstrong; and Kincaid.

11 Murray discusses the modernist sublime at various points, but the clearest definition is offered on page 10 where he describes it as a "use of the idea of an otherness which is not a spiritual absolute (God, Nature) but a breakdown of our ability to represent." Murray focuses chiefly on the way in which speeches by Native North Americans were interpreted by their readers or hearers. He lays bare the mechanisms whereby their statements were silenced by subsumption within the trope of the unfathomable Other or the content of the speeches—often bitter criticism and protest—was suppressed in favour of emphasis upon the mere fact of rhetorical utterance, the external gestures here contributing to the image of doomed nobility. One of Murray's most telling examples demonstrates how a political speech by Logan, a Mingo chief, was made into the centrepiece of a nineteenth-century stage play; fictional Native American characters provided equally satisfying and non-threatening swan songs, as for instance in John Augustus Stone's *Metamora*, or *The Last of the Wampanoags* (1829). See Murray 36–40.

12 There are two instances of White and Native North American sexual contact mentioned in *The Rez Sisters* (none in *Dry Lips*) and, not coincidentally, both involve varying degrees of White male aggression towards Native women: the rape of Zhaboonigan, and Philomena's affair with her boss, which is broken off abruptly when the wife intervenes, leaving Philomena to bear a child alone and put it up for adoption.

13 I do not want to diminish the image of pain conveyed here: the rape of Zhaboonigan, Highway said in his October 1992 talk at the University of Victoria, is meant to allude to the rape of Helen Betty Osborne who was penetrated fifty-six times with a screwdriver, and whose accused attackers—all but one of four—were not convicted even though the assault, reportedly, was known and discussed by many of the folk in the small Manitoba town in which it occurred.

14 It is interesting to note that Charnley makes a similar point with reference to a different linguistic group; she cites Jeannette Armstrong's assertion that "'non-sexist thinking is deeply imbedded in our cultures and must be seen from a broader perspective than the warped point of view of a culture whose orientation is always male or female oriented rather than human oriented'" (quoted from a cassette recording of a workshop, Third International Feminist Book Fair, Montreal, June 1988). Charnley then adds the comment that "This is reflected in her [Armstrong's] Okanagan language which has no pronouns to refer to he or she."

[15] Bhabha has defined this strategy chiefly in essays dealing with the literature of the Indian subcontinent, and hybridity has proven a powerful—if contested—term in subsequent discussion of post-colonial literatures. Bhabha develops the concept of hybridity and related issues in such essays as: "The Other Question" (1983); "Signs Taken for Wonders" (1985); "Representation and the Colonial Text" (1984); "Of Mimicry and Man" (1984); "Sly Civility" (1985); and "The Other Question" (1990). Objections to Bhabha's thesis have been raised most notably by JanMohamed and by Parry.

[16] Trinh is quoting Deloria, 86. Compare Dollimore's idea of resistance through subversion of authenticity itself (190). In a similar vein, Murray analyzes the tendency of the dominant culture to claim the ability to recognize and define "what is essential and authentic" in the Native North American, citing an example from an anonymous writer on "Indian Eloquence" in *The Knickerbocker*, 1836: "'The iron encasement of apparent apathy in which the savage had fortified himself, impenetrable at ordinary moments, is laid aside in the council-room. The genius of eloquence bursts the swathing bands of custom, and the Indian stands forth accessible, natural, and legible'" (41).

[17] See *The Empire Writes Back*, 52-53, for a discussion of linguistic variation as metonym.

[18] Highway received a degree in music (as well as a B.A.) from the University of Western Ontario, and studied in Europe in preparation for a concert career.

Works Cited

Appiah, Kwame Anthony. *In My Father's House: Africa in the Philosophy of Culture.* New York: Oxford UP, 1992.

Armstrong, Jeannette C. "The Disempowerment of First North American Native Peoples and Empowerment Through Their Writings." *Gatherings: The En'owkin Journal of First North American Peoples.* 1.1 (Fall 1990). 141-46.

Ashcroft, Bill, Gareth Griffiths, and Helen Tiffin. *The Empire Writes Back. Theory and Practice in Post-Colonial Literatures.* New Accents. London: Routledge, 1989.

Bennett, Susan. "Subject to the Tourist Gaze: A Response to 'Weesageechak Begins to Dance.'" Responses by Jennifer Preston, Doris Linklater, Bill Henderson, and Richard Schechner. *The Drama Review* 37.1 (Spring 1993): 9-17.

Bentley, D. M. R. "Calibanned." *The Gay / Grey Moose.* Ottawa: U of Ottawa P, 1992. 143-62.

———. "Savage, Degenerate, and Dispossessed: Some Sociological, Anthropological, and Legal Backgrounds to the Depiction of Native Peoples in Early Long Poems on Canada." *Canadian Literature* 124/125 (Spring-Summer 1990): 76-90.

Berkhofer, Robert F., Jr. *The White Man's Indian: Images of the American Indian from Columbus to the Present.* New York: Knopf, 1978.

Bhabha, Homi K. "Of Mimicry and Man: The Ambivalence of Colonial Discourse." *October* 28 (Spring 1984): 125-33.

———. "The Other Question: Difference, Discrimination and the Discourse of Colonialism." *Out There: Marginalization and Contemporary Cultures.* Ed. Russell Ferguson, Martha Gever, Trinh T. Minh-ha, and Cornell West. Cambridge: MIT P, 1990. 71-88.

———. "The Other Question: Homi K. Bhabha Reconsiders The Stereotype and Colonial Discourse." *Screen* 24 (November/December 1983): 18-36.

———. "Representation and the Colonial Text: A Critical Exploration of Some Forms of Mimeticism." *The Theory of Reading.* Ed. Frank Gloversmith. Brighton: Harvester, 1984. 93-122.

———. "Signs Taken for Wonders: Questions of Ambivalence and Authority under a Tree Outside Delhi, May 1817." *Europe and Its Others: Proceedings of the Essex Conference on the Sociology of Literature, July 1984.* Ed. Francis Barker, Peter Hulme, Margaret Iverson, and Diana Loxley. Vol. 1. Colchester: U of Essex P, 1985. 89-106.

———. "Sly Civility." *October* 34 (Fall 1985): 71-80.

Charnley, Kerrie. "Concepts of Anger, Identity and Power and the Vision in the Writings and Voices of First Nation Women." *Gatherings: The En'owkin Journal of First North American Peoples* 1.1 (Fall 1990). 19-20.

Deloria, Vine, Jr. *Custer Died for Your Sins: An Indian Manifesto.* New York: Macmillan, 1969.

Dimanno, Rosie. "René Dances to Brother's Tune in Cree Tale." *Toronto Star* 18 March 1988: E10.

Dollimore, Jonathan. "The Dominant and the Deviant: A Violent Dialectic." *Critical Quarterly* 28.1/2 (Spring-Summer 1986): 179-92.

Goldie, Terry. *Fear and Temptation: The Image of the Indigene in Canadian, Australian, and New Zealand Literatures.* Kingston: McGill/Queen's UP, 1989.

Greenblatt, Stephen. "Learning to Curse: Aspects of Linguistic Colonialism in the Sixteenth Century." *First Images of America: The Impact of the New World on the Old.* Ed. Fredi Chiappelli. Vol. 2. Berkeley: U of California P, 1976. 561-80.

Highway, Tomson. *Dry Lips Oughta Move to Kapuskasing.* Saskatoon: Fifth House, 1989.

———. "Another Glimpse: Excerpts from a Conversation with Tomson Highway." Interview by Bryan Loucks. *Canadian Theatre Review* 68 (Fall 1991): 9-11.

———. "On Native Mythology." *Theatrum* 6 (Spring 1987): 29-30.

———. *The Rez Sisters.* Saskatoon: Fifth House, 1988.

———. Talk. University of Victoria, 20 October 1992.

———. Talk. University of Western Ontario, Fall 1990.

Hill, Richard. "One Part per Million: White Appropriation and Native Voices." *Fuse* 15.3 (Winter 1992): 12-22.

———. "Savage Splendor: Sex, Lies and Stereotypes." *Turtle Quarterly* 4.1 (Spring-Summer 1991): 14-23.

Honegger, Gitta. "Native Playwright: Tomson Highway." *Theater* 23.1 (Winter 1992): 88-92.

JanMohamed, Abdul R. "The Function of Manichean Allegory: The Function of Racial Difference in Colonialist Literature." *Critical Inquiry* 12 (1985): 59-87.

Keeshig-Tobias, Lenore. "The Magic of Others." *Language in Her Eye: Views on Writing and Gender by Canadian Women Writing in English.* Ed. Libby Scheier, Sarah Sheard, and Eleanor Wachtel. Toronto: Coach House, 1990. 173-77.

Kincaid, James R. "Who Gets to Tell Their Stories?" *New York Times Book Review* 3 May 1992: 1, 24-29.

Lloyd, David. "Race Under Representation." *Oxford Literary Review* 13.1-2 (1991): 62-94.

Maracle, Lee. "Native Myths: Trickster Alive and Crowing." *Language in Her Eye: Views on Writing and Gender by Canadian Women Writing in English.* Ed. Libby Scheier, Sarah Sheard, and Eleanor Wachtel. Toronto: Coach House, 1990. 182-87.

Monkman, Leslie. "A Native Heritage." *The Native in Literature.* Ed. Thomas King, Cheryl Calver, and Helen Hoy. Toronto: ECW, 1987. 80-98.

Moses, Daniel David. "The Trickster Theatre of Tomson Highway." *Canadian Fiction Magazine* 60 (1987): 83-88.

Murray, David. *Forked Tongues: Speech, Writing and Representation in North American Indian Texts.* Bloomington: Indiana UP, 1991.

Nunn, Robert. "Marginality and English-Canadian Theatre." *Theatre Research International* 17 (1992): 217-25.

Parry, Benita. "Problems in Current Theories of Colonial Discourse." *Oxford Literary Review* 9:1/2 (1987): 27-58.

Preston, Jennifer. "Weesageechak Begins to Dance: Native Earth Performing Arts Inc." *The Drama Review* 36.1 (Spring 1992): 133-59.

Radin, Paul. *The Trickster: A Study in American Indian Mythology.* London: Routledge, 1956.

Said, Edward. *Orientalism.* New York: Random, 1978.

———. "Orientalism Reconsidered." *Europe and Its Others: Proceedings of the Essex Conference on the Sociology of Literature, July 1984.* Ed. Francis Barker, Peter Hulme, Margaret Iverson, and Diana Loxley. Vol. 1. Colchester: U of Essex P, 1985. 14-27.

Scott, Duncan Campbell. *The Poems of Duncan Campbell Scott.* Toronto: McClelland, 1926.

Spivak, Gayatri. "Neocolonialism and the Secret Agent of Knowledge." Interview by Robert Young. *Oxford Literary Review* 13.1/2 (1991): 220-51.

Torgovnick, Marianna. *Gone Primitive: Savage Intellects, Modern Lives.* Chicago: U of Chicago P, 1990.

Trinh, T. Minh-ha. *Woman, Native, Other: Writing Postcoloniality and Feminism.* Bloomington: Indiana UP, 1989.

The theatre of orphans/
Native languages on stage [1]

by Floyd Favel Starr

First of all I have to say that I am not a linguist, or a traditional theatre writing specialist of any sort. I am just someone who went to theatre school for a while, wrote and directed some plays, and acted a bit (albeit not very well), but just enough to count myself among those who have felt the terror, exhilaration and humiliation of that first light cue, not that this gives me any credentials to write selfishly the following pages. I am not a noble savage who learned the basics of theatre at the foot of his wise grandmother or grandfather, sorry to disappoint you. One time I was acting in a film and we were on one of those frequent coffee breaks and one of the assistant directors deigned to converse with me, oh where did you learn about films? I had to disappoint her when I said, "oh, I went to theatre school." Then she realized her tone of voice and left in an uncomfortable manner. She probably never realized that my working vocabulary combined with Cree was more than hers.

I have been given the opportunity and pages to scribble a few words and try to put in a form some thoughts and I feel an immense satisfaction in that simple ability of movement. The movement of my brain, my eyes, my hands, my heart. Movement is life, a life without movement is biological death. I discovered this, not comparing myself to a Louis Pasteur or any one of our unnamed scientists, but when I meditated upon the words "waskowee yowin" meaning movement, and "poon waskowee yowin" meaning death, defined by the cessation of biological movement. I put these two ideas together and came to a minor realization of the concepts indicated in my language. A word is never one-dimensional.

When a native language is not spoken, an understanding of the worldview of that nation is purely theoretical. I am sad to feel this way but I do not see how it can be otherwise. If I wanted to get into the Oriental mind I would need to know a dialect of Chinese, right? This is a minimum requirement. Direct perception and experience is what I would define as an understanding of anything, and this is what you have when you have a working vocabulary of your mother tongue.

There is a lot of difficulty in the pronunciation of a lot of English words even though that is my main language of commerce, transaction, art, love and betrayal. I curse that dratted language which makes it necessary to have a lawyer present at all times, and which has caused me to curse my Creator and my mother, concepts which do not exist in my language. I still giggle at some words because they sound funny to my ears, and it surprises me to know that there are lots of words in English that have no meaning, root. In short a lot of words have no mother. The tongue of the orphans whose mother lives some place across the big water in the olive groves and oaken forests, Alpine heights and Bavarian brooks. She cries for her children. Like most human beings, I have compassion for orphans.

Language is related to place; it is our umbilical cord to our place of origin, literally and symbolically. When I was just a baby, my mother buried my umbilical cord in the bush near my house. She wrapped it in paper that had writing in English. She did this in order to influence my future. She wanted me to understand English and work in the field of words. As I sit and write this I feel gratitude to my mother and my place and wonder at the idea of how this moment is the result of an action that took place on a lonely prairie Indian reserve 28 years ago, presumably on a hot summer day.

When I dream and am weak, my thoughts and spirit go back to the poplar trees and clear stream of my birthplace. The soothing sounds of my language give me strength as I walk thru the dark valleys of modern existential angst caused by and the result of a fractured tongue. Like the hands, feelings, thoughts which become separate from each other, operating as disparate mechanical units, the tongue becomes just an appendage.

When I have been far from home and sick with loneliness I have tasted the taste of the berries and water, and whispered their names to myself, "meensa," "neepee," like you whisper the name of your beloved.

One goes for days by circumstance, and sometimes by choice, not speaking the mother tongue. It is painful to open and stir the memories and feelings which lie bereaved so close to the surface. One knows that it will never be like it was once before in the not so long ago past, therefore sometimes it is better to clamp one's jaws tight as the remembered language intrudes in the present life.

For native people the theatre is where a lot of our dreams, fears and visions live and dance in the living present. Language is just one of the elements of a total production. I feel that we are at a turning point towards a something. The theatre is a puzzle and riddle for us; how do we incorporate our concept of time, space, architecture, language, colours, rhythms, sounds and movements into a contemporary performance? My dream is to work with an architect to design a performance space that is informed by our needs.

An orphan on stage is pitiful to see. The words drift from an exile and loneliness. Where is your mother? Where is your father? They do not live in your words and eyes. I want to see the face of your mother in your eyes.

My mother taught me her language. Therefore when I speak to people it is not only me who speaks, my mother lives in my words, as it was she who gave me my speech. My mother lives in me, my mother lives in my words. The sound of our native languages on stage is a totally different experience of theatrical sound from English. The voice immediately gets more rooted in the body, it is richer and more musical, and a whole different mood is evoked. Present in the immediate words are the ancestors, which go back generation by generation, right back to the day our language bubbled up from the springs and whispers of the trees and grass. It is a doorway, and a window.

The use of words is dangerous, risky. The language evokes all manner of entities and memories, and spirits. The word conjures. For instance we were taught never to say the name of a departed person because if you say their name you have called out to them, and they just might come back. Or one never talked openly and freely about religious or spiritual ceremonies under the understanding that the eyes and ears of the spirit world would listen to you, wondering if you were being sincere or just "pretending to know".

A friend once said that the spirits don't understand English, you can't conjure, evoke, dialogue, ask in that spiritless language of English, and besides English does not belong on this part of the world, it does not know the trees and rocks, brooks and gnomes, and all manner of sentient beings. I don't know if this is so, this is just what I was told. Is it possible then that this part of the world is not yet bilingual? That if you do not speak a language then a bridge between you and the earth is missing? Perhaps it's so, because I use as an example my grandmother who does not understand or speak English. The reason I use my grandmother is this world, here, is a reflection on how spiritual laws work. Talk to my grandmother in English and she won't understand a thing, and she won't answer you, maybe she'll just give a chuckle. What is open to her though is she can feel your thoughts and feelings and hence sympathize or not. I imagine that this is how all the spirits are, they can sympathize but they can't dialogue. Maybe what is more important is the language of the heart and spirit.

All this is pure speculation, we can't really know unless we find out directly, I guess.

To hear English on stage in the mouths of native people, the voice is higher, less in the body, and resonates less with the total life of the performer. A whole spiritual dimension is lost. We have faint traces of the mystery and magic, but mostly the soul is burdened by the mechanicity of a foreign language which has colonized the soul's expression. Maybe it's better not to speak in words at all, just make a sound, or sing a song in a language which is neither English, and neither a mother tongue. Or invent a language of one's own that touches more truly the feelings trapped in blood, muscle and genes (not to be confused with jeans).

I guess this is the difficulty with working in English. Mind you, the whole heart and spirit of a people's soul can be filtered thru the form of a foreign language. It's been done before, and will be done again. This refers mostly to the individuals with knowledge of their mother tongue whose access to their riches is more accessible and direct, whereas those with no knowledge of their mother tongue I imagine would have difficulty as their interior world is unnamed and uncharted and therefore what happens is like the "discovery of North America." The terrains which are traversed are named in English, and hence colonized. They Columbus and Cortez themselves unconsciously. We can then speak of the colonized territory called the mind and the process of decolonization is what theatre training is all about. In that training the hidden life beneath the words is often touched, leading to inner freedom from strictures imposed by the foreign language. The unsubtle message in the European languages is human superiority over nature, man over woman, man over the birds and bees and the beast, and all brown, black and yellow folks. Sometimes when I talk to native people who do not speak their language, I am aware that I feel I am speaking with a foreigner. They understand words—my words—and I understand theirs from different reference points. But I feel on an intuitive level that some place in those eyes peers out my sister or brother and all that is blocking us from a simple collaboration is English, the *lingua franca* among the native people of the Americas. Two different minds meet, but we have a common denominator.

I guess that is what theatre training is all about. To get to the language of the heart and spirit as that is all that is now open to us, and whatever words, sounds, music and movement we have come up with is our language, the language of theatre, which is the language of the trees and birds.

I work in the theatre, so most of the time I find myself on an island and the only inhabitant on that island. Like a Robinson Crusoe without the beard and without a Friday to subjugate. I find myself mumbling to myself in my own language like some senile young man, and I still run into the problem of trying to work in this English. But, that's life and there is not a hell of a lot I can do about that now.

Sometimes I get political, a decision or theory forms of using the theatre to develop and rejuvenate our culture, so once in a while I toss in a few words of Cree here and there. I cringe when I hear it being butchered, then make a typical Cree reaction which is to laugh. This is a start, I reason, and where it can lead is to a play written totally in Cree. In that case my audience would be severely limited as my dialect of Cree is from a very specific geographical area of Canada. My box office would suffer and I would wind up with a deficit, probably get my funding cut, then where would I be, probably just mumbling to myself in my own language, cussing at my business practice.

Then I think what is the point, my own people don't even care. Our native government must be the only government in the whole wide world without any cultural or artistic mandate. I burn when I think of all the money they spend on one conference, we could have created and staged one or two productions that would live in the hearts of the audience forever. I guess that is why I am quite cynical at times about the marriage of theatre and my people, language and my people.

We are bad daughters and sons, we neglect our mothers and fathers. For most of us we are orphans by choice so what is left to us is to form an orphanage. I know this sounds silly, but a theatre group with common goals and vision where a family and community is created is in a sense an orphanage. Our art, idiosyncrasies, makes it impossible for us to live elsewhere, we search for our own kind and sooner or later we succeed and set up fruitful working relationships.

A bad dancer is someone who is separate from his mother, a tight singing voice is also that. The body needs to relax, the feet need to give in to the earth and the drum has to enter the spine and heart, and the voice is finally home, has a mother. This is my hope in any theatrical training that I am involved in. Finding a home where sit our mothers and fathers so that we realize we are the daughters and sons of someone.

(1993)

Note

[1]   Editor's note: The author wished to include the following proviso with the republication of this essay: "I also want to stress that there [are] many ways of working, and all are valid, and my essays [included in this volume] are just one aspect of one phase of my career" (personal correspondence, 28 October 2004).

Receiving Aboriginality: Tomson Highway
and the Crisis of Cultural Authenticity

by Alan Filewod

Recent developments in aboriginal playwriting and performance in the cultures of the so-called settler colonies (particularly Australia, Canada, New Zealand and the United States) challenge critical strategies by which mainly white scholars synthesize cultural histories.[1] In particular we are faced with the challenge of understanding our complicity in the historical processes of colonization which have suppressed aboriginal responses—both by repression and under the guise of encouragement. An exploration of some of the problems of that process of explication may determine how they shaped the terms of the controversy that followed in the wake of the 1991 revival of the Canadian Cree dramatist Tomson Highway's play *Dry Lips Oughta Move to Kapuskasing.*

Highway is the most celebrated Native Indian writer in Canada today, and one of the most prominent of Canadian playwrights. Born in 1951 on a trapline on a Native Indian reserve in Northern Manitoba, he grew up speaking Cree, and learned English in the residential schools to which many of the children of his generation were taken, often against the wishes of their communities. After studies at the University of Western Ontario and advanced training as a concert pianist, Highway turned to the theatre as a forum for cultural recuperation, and established his reputation quickly with two comedies set on a Native reserve in northern Ontario: *The Rez Sisters* (originally produced by Native Earth Performing Arts Toronto in 1986) and its sequel and "flip side," *Dry Lips Oughta Move to Kapuskasing,* produced at Theatre Passe Muraille in Toronto in 1989). In *The Rez Sisters,* a group of women put aside their differences and travel to Toronto to the world's biggest bingo; in *Dry Lips* the men of the reserve confront their political impotence as first the women of the reserve, then all the aboriginal women of the world invade the men's domain and form a hockey league. In both plays the surface comedy is disrupted by images and memories of horrifying abuse of women, but whereas in *The Rez Sisters* past abuse forms the structure of the present, in *Dry Lips* the past abuse is reenacted in the present. The context of that re-enactment gives the play its causal structure.

With these two plays (and several others that have received less attention), Highway became the first Native playwright to break through into the theatrical "mainstream" and win as much celebrity as Canadian theatre accords. When the Mirvishes (the Canadian producers of *Miss Saigon)* contracted to revive *Dry Lips* at Toronto's Royal Alexandra Theatre (which had previously been home to the Mirvish franchise of *Les Misérables)* in 1991, Highway joined the very small and select group of Canadian playwrights to be offered a major commercial production in Toronto.

Mindful of Gary Boire's warning that apparent parallels in aboriginal experience in different countries also conceal very different historical and cultural experiences, this analysis of the controversial reception of the *Dry Lips* revival draws upon some recent Australian examples to support the Canadian experience I describe. Reviewing Terry Goldie's study of the literary image of the indigene in Australia, Canada and New Zealand, *Fear and Temptation,* Boire cautions that,

> The superficial crime of superimposition may have been the same in all colonies, but given the specificities of history, ethnicity, gender, culture and geography, there are significant and subtle variations between each repetition and amongst the multiple reactions to it. (306)

The historical experiences of colonization and displacement were indeed significantly different in Canada and Australia. But in respect to the reception of aboriginality in the theatre, the two countries offer useful comparisons. While the Canadian experience of displacement has obvious parallels and intersections with the American experience (given that the national border cuts through traditional Native cultures and territories), Australia offers the closest parallel when aboriginality is considered in terms of the postcolonial crisis of nationhood. The affinities of the British imperial experience have resulted in structural similarities in the cultures of the two countries. In Canada and Australia the emergence of a professional public theatre industry devoted to producing local playwrights has followed a remarkably similar path, marked by issues of cultural nationalism and decolonization. Because of their similar historical patterns (notwithstanding their complex differences), aboriginal writing has likewise encountered similar problems of reception in the two countries.

The problem of white reception of aboriginal theatre is a problem in the dialectics of decolonization and reinscribed colonization, in which voices of cultural affirmation and resistance are received by white critics as a testament of authentic and unmediated reality, which, in critical response, disallows the agency of resistance itself. These critics propose mediation (most commonly by urbanization and postcolonial deracination) as the condition that diminishes the authenticity of a culture. In this essentialist and humanist view (which owes much to Rousseau), the more authentic the culture, the less mediated it is. The contradiction develops when critics who accept western realist dramaturgy as the least mediated, most natural theatrical form find these two essentialisms, aboriginal and dramaturgical, in conflict. The difficulties of reconciling them results in an analysis which effectively replicates the process of European colonization.

The reconfiguring of the notion of authenticity into its own negation is similar to recent developments in Australia, where according to Annette Hamilton,

> whereas up until the 1960s, Aboriginality was construed as an ineluctable "Otherness" (providing it was 'real' and 'authentic'), changes in con-

> temporary cultural consciousness have made it possible to absorb…
> and re-negotiate it in terms of 'Australianess.' (qtd. in Mitchell 21)

When speaking of ethnic culture, the notion of authenticity poses different problems than it does in gender studies, no matter how closely the term seems to accord, because although it can be argued in terms of gender that there is no essential self, the proposition by a white writer that there is no essential aboriginal culture is unacceptable; even if we reject essentialist notions of ethnicity, we cannot deny claims to authenticity by cultures that we—as products and agents of ethnically divided societies—have been complicit in suppressing. It is possible to identify the critical/scholarly establishment as "white" while repudiating racialist constructions of ethnicity based solely on colour. The notion of a "white race" is seriously proposed only by those groups which have been forced to ethnic binarism by the experience of oppression, or by those (such as white supremacists) who employ it as a epistemological strategy to eradicate the corollary of "non-white." By "white" therefore I do not refer to an ethnicity but to a cultural formation that cannot escape the ethnic binarism resulting from the historical experience of racism. "White" therefore defines the social formation that constructs and suppresses aboriginality. The essentialism found in the works of aboriginal writers can in these terms be seen as a defensive strategy which implies that ethnicity is a category of power, not of biology.

The idea of authenticity, of authentic voice, is the idea of culture ratified by historical experience, and to a large extent is a reinscribed reaction to oppression—reinscribed in that the very notion of aboriginality which is itself a category of understanding introduced by colonialism. The terms of repression are integrated and reinscribed as terms of transgression. My argument is that in the critical reception of aboriginal playwriting we can trace a process of reordered inscription, in which the terms of transgression, defined as they are by the order they transgress, are subverted to reinforce the colonial framework. In this, I suggest, the material mechanisms of institutional production in the theatre and critical reception may function as a containment field of the kind that Dollimore, for example, critiques (85).

This response in the writings of white critics is symptomatic of a wider cultural response. In its simplest form, it can be seen in the comment of a student of mine in an undergraduate seminar, who read The Rez Sisters and then told me that she wished she were Native because "their lives seem so real." Reviewing a production of The Rez Sisters in 1987, David Prosser, of the Kingston (Ont.) Whig Standard, made a similar point when he wrote that the play,

> articulates the voice of a people, admitting of one reality but cognisant
> of others, secure in the truth, the worth and the interest of what it has to
> say. We might wish that more of our country's non-native culture shared
> the same, quiet, exuberant assurance. (10-11)

Prosser's envy of Native cultural affirmation and the student's sentimental wish she were Native on the basis of the community expressed by The Rez Sisters are expressions of nostalgia for an essentialist cultural identity derived from cultural formation in humanist traditions at a time when theoretical and political experience suggests that identity is a product of social and cultural formation. Critic and student alike are unable to perceive this process of recuperation as discursive; they assume that they are responding to authenticity rather than icons of resistance. This tends to support the Australian Aboriginal critic Cliff Watego who has argued that

> If... the white Australian conscience must be appeased before any serious consideration about Blacks can be broached, then it bespeaks a fickle imagination in which the development of white cultural constructs remains at odds with itself.... (41)

The representation of authentic voice is a common element in aboriginal drama, although some Native writers have cautioned that representation does not in itself construct authentic aboriginality. Daniel David Moses, a Canadian playwright of the Delaware Nation, has commented that

> The idea of presenting something that someone will decide is authentically "Native" seems absurd to me.... Does that mean that Margaret Atwood is authentically Caucasian? (qtd. in Appleford 21)

The representation of displaced cultural traditions frequently entails the recuperation of traditional characters and performative modes, commonly perceived in terms of "spirituality." These elements when introduced in the frame of European derived dramaturgy function as transgressive devices which by their inclusion contest the causality of western dramatic convention. In Jack Davis's *The Dreamers*, for example, Australian Aboriginal consciousness is materialized by the inclusion of a traditional dancer invoked by an elder, played by the author in the original production, who functions as a choral touchstone to the past:

> Didgeridoo crashes in, the lights change. The DANCER appears at front of stage and in stylized rhythmic steps searches for a straight stick, finds it, straightens it, pares and tips it before sprinting up the ramp onto the escarpment and striking the *mirrolgah* stance against a dramatic sunset as the music climaxes and cuts. (Davis 31)

The piling up of artifice in this scene exposes the Dancer as a performative representation which transgresses the realist frame of the play's main action. The elder whose dreams of the past come to life in representation is both metaphorically and, in the original production literally, the playwright who creates the images he invokes as a character.

In Native Canadian playwriting, the representation of identity is frequently enacted through a similarly locational figure in the character of the Trickster, whose transformative function defies simple readings. The Trickster is not presented as a touchstone to a lost past but as an element of aboriginal life mediated by colonialism. In effect, the Trickster functions as a transformative principle of expressing *difference* by upsetting cartesian causality in drama. Daniel David Moses, whose plays such as *Coyote City* and *Big Buck City* resituate the Trickster in a modern urban context (such as a love returned from the dead, or a young man obsessed with Bugs Bunny), states that

> The trickster figure shows the difference between native and Western cultures.... Mainstream culture creates heroes to emulate; native cultures have the trickster figure, who more often than not you don't want to emulate. (qtd. in Kaplan 19)

In Tomson Highway's plays, the Trickster Nanabush personifies this notion of difference. In *The Rez Sisters*, Nanabush is performed by a dancer (the only male in the cast), who appears first as a seagull, and later as a surreal bingo caller; in *Dry Lips*, with an otherwise all-male cast, Nanabush is gendered as female; her exaggerated representation of male images of women is one of the major sources of the controversy that attended the play in 1991. In both plays, Nanabush is a transformative agent whose presence enables the development of plot. Highway's declared purpose in both plays is to show the still active role of the Trickster, as a metonym for suppressed spirituality, in the material lives of Native people.

The presence of the Trickster figure is one of the main elements that have led white critics to accept such plays as unmediated testaments of authenticity, overlooking the fact that by making the inexplicable coherent, the playwright is offering a mediated representation. Marie Annharte Baker has argued that because the Trickster is transformative, we are "forced to be particular to understand" and that "Because it is so difficult to define the Trickster we always need to define the moment of the Trickster" (48).

White critics have tended to the opposite, to see the Trickster as proof of a shamanistic authenticity that excuses transgression. Reviews of Highway's plays frequently describe them as "magic" while at the same time finding fault with dramatic structure. In *Dry Lips*, for example, the "overlong presentation" is justified by "cleansing magic" (Chapman C1); in a review of another production of that same play, we read that despite being "overlong, loosely structured... and... hurt by lack of clarity... it's still a stunning evening of theatre filled with ritual, magic, grim realism and the spirit of life" (Crew C1). Highway himself has encouraged this reading with public statements that stress cultural reconciliation, referring at one point to the possibility of interculturalism as "this magical transformation that is potentially quite magnificent" (qtd. in Wilson 354).

In his analysis of the critical strategies white critics have brought to bear on Aboriginal drama in Australia, Tony Mitchell has observed that critics "willingly overlooked any 'lapses' which transgressed the European rules and regulations of imaginary dramatic worlds by providing unmediated real-life experience" but "seek refuge in formal and stylistic criteria, thus avoiding any engagement with the critical glance at white Australia" (20). This seems to apply as well to the Canadian responses. Newspaper reviewers commonly assert authority by finding fault while claiming privileged understanding, as in Ray Conlogue's review of the 1989 premiere of *Dry Lips*. His review begins with a claim to understanding of the Native cultural experience.

Departing from a program note that states "Before the healing can take place, the poison must be exposed," Conlogue writes,

> The 'poison' is the rage and humiliation locked up inside the native people.... The "healing" is the power of laughter and the power of dreams. Both these medicines are part of native thought, but it is Highway's particular talent to ransack the conventions of Western theatre and find forms appropriate for them that make sense for non-natives as well. (A17)

Conlogue's claim to authority here rests on a rhetorical tripod: firstly by taking his cue from a quotation of Native source; secondly by asserting familiarity with Native vocabulary and experience ("Both these medicines are part of native thought") and finally by placing himself in the shadow of Highway's ability "to find forms that make sense for non-natives." It is this assertion of authority that enables the reviewer to conclude by saying that "the play transcends its confusions and creates moments that are among the most emotionally riveting that I have seen this theatre season. What it could be with an energetic rewrite is intriguing to contemplate." Mitchell has referred to similar strategies in Australia as "cultural apartheid"—which enforces a distinction between aboriginal experience and the standards of the theatrical profession. Scholarly criticism resorts to this same strategy, although in more subtle ways, as is the case with Denis Johnston's comparative analysis of *The Rez Sisters* and *Dry Lips* which explicates the plays in terms of aristotlean structuralism; this enables him to state that in *Dry Lips,* "more of the action is imposed on the characters and less arises organically from their own needs" (260).

Such responses reveal the paralysis of humanist discourse, which stipulates that since all human experiences are understandable, if they are not presented understandably then they are presented badly, that is inartistically. Transgressive markers of authenticity are thus perceived as justifiable to the extent that the "magic" they are seen to embody excuses dramaturgical lapses; or, stated inversely, to the extent that they are invalidated by the terms of reception. The Trickster figure is perceived as authentic because it is transgressive but by the same token perceived as problematic, inaccessible and possibly disruptive. Highway is celebrated because of his magic and his lyrical use of language; conversely, Moses has been criticized as "incredibly inept" because the transgressive elements in his plays are not as "authentic" according to the standards of "professionalism." The logical conclusion of this strategy is to suggest therefore that when a Native play is perceived as inept it is because it more completely transgressive, less understandable to white aesthetic systems, and therefore perhaps more truly aboriginal, different, indigenous. The Canadian example suggests that this may in fact be the case; some of the most transgressive Native performances, such as Monique Mojica's *Princess Pocahontas and the Blue Spots,* a transformative performance that articulates a feminist critique of male sexual and racial colonialism, are scarcely noticed by the fraternity of white reviewers (Mojica).

This analysis leads to the suggestion that the elements of apparent authenticity in Highway's plays are received as exoticized invitations to appropriate aboriginality.

This reception may explain, in part, the singular respect accorded to Highway over other Native playwrights in Canada, and it casts light on the intense controversy that followed the 1991 commercial revival of *Dry Lips*.

When first produced at Theatre Passe Muraille in Toronto in 1989, *Dry Lips* was received as confirmation of Highway's talent; critics invariably compared it to *The Rez Sisters* and found it more complex, less celebratory, or as Johnston asserts, "a litany of disturbing and violent events, set within a thin frame of hopefulness which is ultimately unconvincing" (260). The violent event which drew the strongest response is a scene in which a disturbed young man, born with foetal alcohol syndrome, brutally rapes Nanabush, who is personified as a young woman, with a crucifix. Critics invariably responded that the rape was horrifying but justifiable, dramatically and metaphorically, and spoke of *Dry Lips* as the masculine "flip side" in a dialectic of gender initiated in the "feminine" *The Rez Sisters*. Following *The Rez Sisters*, Highway was widely praised for what one (male) critic called "his extraordinary empathy with women." Responding to this point, Highway said that

> I am sensitive to women because of the matrilineal principle in our culture, which has gone on for thousands of years. Women have such an ability to express themselves emotionally.... People often tell me when they see the play, even if it is in English, that these are not French women or English women, but Indian women who are speaking. (Conlogue, "Mixing" C5)

Although Susan Bennett has observed that these women are in fact male constructs, no attention whatsoever has been placed on Highway's occasional public comments about his homosexuality, nor have critics addressed the complexities of the gay male claiming insight into female experience (10). Highway implies that this insight derives from aboriginality rather than sexuality, but the problems of that position emerged in force with the 1991 revival of *Dry Lips*.

When the entrepreneurial Mirvish Productions, owners of the Royal Alexandra Theatre in Toronto and the Old Vic in London announced plans for a commercial revival of *Dry Lips* for 1991, they were greeted with enthusiasm from the press. This would be one of the first commercial transfers of a Canadian play to the Royal Alex, and it was seen as a breakthrough for Native writing. The Mirvishes restaged the play, with the original cast and director, but added more lavish production values. The controversy reflects the shifting expectations generated by the rearranged structures of power in the commercial theatre, which recontextualized the play, separated it from its former intertextual relationship with *The Rez Sisters* and created a new field of potential readings.

The controversy reached the white public in the pages of the *The Globe and Mail* in a column by a white feminist who argued that *Dry Lips* was profoundly misogynist. Acknowledging the play to be "great drama," Marion Botsford Fraser wrote

> The two central events in the play are horrible abuses of women, unmitigated by compassion... our attention is drawn not to the women

who are suffering but to the men who are watching.... *Dry Lips* is not only about misogyny but is a drama studded with misogyny.... But I wonder how a native woman dramatist would tell this tale. (C1)

She needn't have wondered, because some Native women had already expressed similar anger. Two weeks prior to Fraser's column, Anita Tuharsky, a Métis woman who had seen the play during its pre-Toronto shakedown at the National Arts Centre in Ottawa, wrote in a letter to the editor of the aboriginal newspaper *Windspeaker*:

> This play sadly disappointed me and tore at my heart because it so terribly misrepresented aboriginal peoples.... He did not balance the negativity being presented about life on the reserves and the prevailing attitudes. He also failed to make the public aware that many aboriginal communities are going through a healing process, working desperately with dedication to rebuild their nations. Highway abused his writing abilities and chose to disregard respect to create pleasures for the public which enjoys these stereotypes and images. It justifies their reluctance to see aboriginal peoples as equals. (5)

Although it could be argued that this response placed unfair expectations on the playwright, perceiving him as an exemplar of aboriginality, such expectations were inevitable consequences of the critical reception and commercial marketing that presented the play in those terms. Some months later, the poet and playwright Marie Annharte Baker expressed her reactions in the quarterly *Canadian Theatre Review*:

> I have heard of Native women having nightmares for a week or feeling depressed after seeing *Dry Lips*; myself, I had to fight the downer I experienced.... Although the victim merry-go-round is well depicted, the men's passivity does nothing to change their helpless life-styles. The women in the audience must again feel that it is the men who suffer more... it is hard to resist the mesmerizing male dogma that is the backbone or wishbone of the play. But when the seduction wears off, you realize you've been had. (89)

Of these three responses by women, unanimous in their perception of misogyny, two are from Native women. That fact was sadly absent from later discussions, in all likelihood because the white woman wrote in the pages of a national newspaper and the Native women in small-circulation periodicals. In the conversation between Terry Goldie and Daniel David Moses that comprises the preface to their *Anthology of Canadian Native Literature in English*, Goldie remarks that

> ...Native writers are writing first for their own. That is one reason some people reject certain Native texts. When people said Tomson Highway's *Dry Lips Oughta Move To Kapuskasing* was misogynist it seemed to be because they weren't trained by the culture to understand it. (xxi)

His erasure of the Native women's response is unchallenged by his male Native co-editor. An echo of this same erasure can be found in the pages of *The Drama*

Review, following Susan Bennett's letter to the editor (9-12) in which she challeng-es the totalizing and positivist "tourist gaze" of Jennifer Preston's prior article on Native Earth Performing Arts, the company that originated Highway's plays (136-59). Bennett had cited Marie Annharte Baker's response to *Dry Lips* as evidence of native women's discontent with Highway, to which Preston countered that

> Her quote from Marie Baker is emotional but poorly chosen. For every piece of negative criticism Tomson's work has received—and every great artist has critics—there has been volumes of overwhelmingly positive responses. (14)

Certainly Highway has many women supporters, including the women who act in his plays. But the silencing of Native women's criticism of *Dry Lips* redefined the controversy by configuring it as a debate between middle-class white feminists and marginalized Native artists. In an attempt to reconcile these two positions, the respected film critic Jay Scott argued in *The Globe and Mail* that the revival of *Dry Lips* was misunderstood because the Royal Alexandra production robbed it of intimacy, and that the original audiences at Passe Muraille had received the play as a

> complex but unambiguous examination explanation [sic] of misogyny on an Indian reserve, never as a simplistic but ambiguous celebration/ rationalization of it. (C1)

The debate has since subsided but will affect readings of *Dry Lips* for some time to come. There are, I suggest, two main conditions that transformed this production into the site of intercultural, cross-gender contention. The first has to do with the developments of Native politics in Canada in the two years since the play had first appeared. In that period, the events surrounding the 1992 Referendum over the Charlottetown Constitutional Accord introduced Native groups as major players on the political stage, and advanced the notion of aboriginal self-government as a feasi-ble proposal in a constitutional restructuring. But at the same time, the referendum debate split the Native communities, with the newly formed Native women's lobby at odds with the male-dominated Assembly of First Nations. The totalizing concept of a "Native identity" was increasingly revealed to be discursive and indeed divisive. In these terms, the response of native feminists to *Dry Lips* was reflective of the differences in Native political groups around the referendum debate.

The second reason has to do with the reconfigured fields of expectations when *Dry Lips* transferred to the commercial stage. In the vast house of the Royal Alexandra, critics and audiences could not position themselves as privileged witnesses to a Native community speaking to itself, nor could they justify transgression in terms of constructed authenticity. Instead they were placed in a humanist field where they were invited to empathize with the folksy character. When that empathic bridge was broken, many members of the audience walked out; they could not reconcile their expectations of structure and causality with the transgressions of the text. Had they stayed they would have seen those transgressions reconciled in the idealized family scene that closes the play. This humanism, I suspect, invited the audience to see this community as an extension of their own. As in the original production the unknowable was presented as knowable and thus re-inscribed the colonialism from which the play emerged. The restructured class context of this production brought this contradiction into the foreground. Not only did the play assume the possibility of reinforcing overt racism, as Tuharsky claims, it also enabled the (mainly) white establishment audience to identify with the oppressed and therefore deny the racism in which they were complicit.

The revival of *Dry Lips* and the debate that attended it reproduced in a larger scale the dynamics of reinscribed colonialism found in the critical reception to Native plays in general. The fact of the commercial revival was a self-testament to the liberality of the producers, who gained considerable esteem for their risk-taking commitment to Canadian Native drama. In fact there was little risk, as the play was presented as part of a subscription season and made a small profit for the Mirvishes—although in the sense that the project of commercial theatre is to reproduce the process of making profit by expanding the market through replication (as is the case with Andrew Lloyd Webber), the *Dry Lips* revival might be considered unsuccessful.

The singularity of *Dry Lips*'s revival isolated the play from the inter-productive field of Native theatre in Canada, a field in which a matrix of texts, performers and audiences constitutes a discourse of material practice, and which therefore can absorb and synthesize contradictions. That field overlaps into the small public theatres in Toronto which have entered into co-productions with Native artists, as was the case when Factory Theatre picked up *The Rez Sisters* and Theatre Passe Muraille produced the original *Dry Lips*. In that field of intercultural audiences and intertextual knowledge, the misogyny of *Dry Lips* was more easily perceived as ironic and perhaps metaphorical. When the Mirvish revival resituated the play, the cultural discourse that framed that misogyny was negated. This was not simply a case therefore of the Royal Alexandra audience misunderstanding the play, as Jay Scott suggests, but rather an example of how a new context reorders and transforms the generation of meaning in performance. If in the original production the intertextual relationship with *The Rez Sisters* and the community of Native theatre enabled audiences to receive the rape scene as a metaphor (the crucifix raping the Trickster), the isolation of the Mirvish production made a more literal reading—Bennett's "tourist gaze"—inevitable. *Dry Lips* was revived because critics originally saw it as an expression of unmediated authenticity; like all revivals it was marketed as a proof of the success it announced. Consequently it reproduced the process of appropriation and disallowance, in which the terms of critical reception of the first production became the predicate of the revival.

(1994)

Note

1 The terminology of race is always reflective of changing political contexts which demand reconfigurations of language. There is no one universally accepted term used in Canada to replace the now discredited "Indian." "Native" and "Native Indian" are the most common constructions in public discourse, and "tribe" has been superseded by "nation" (as in the Assembly of First Nations, the national political organization of Native peoples in Canada). The term "aboriginal" is also used, but more frequently in the adjectival than the proper sense. My usage follows general convention in Canada, where aboriginal refers to not only Native Indian but Inuit and Métis cultures as well. It should be noted that in Canada, such usages increasingly defer to the preferences of the aboriginal communities.

In Australia, "Aboriginal" refers specifically to the indigenous Australians, and is therefore capitalized. Australian usage thus reverses the Canadian convention, reflecting different historical applications of language as an instrument of colonization and resistance.

Works Cited

Appleford, Rob. "The Desire to Crunch Bone: Daniel David Moses and the 'True-Real Indian'." *Canadian Theatre Review* 77 (Winter 1993): 21-26.

Baker, Marie Annharte. "Angry Enough to Spit, but with Dry Lips it Hurts More than You Know." *Canadian Theatre Review* 68 (Fall 1991): 88-90.

———. "An Old Indian Trick is to Laugh." *Canadian Theatre Review* 68 (Fall 1991): 48-49.

Bennett, Susan. "Subject to the Tourist Gaze: A Response to 'Weesageechak Begins to Dance'." *The Drama Review* 37 (Spring 1993): 10-11.

Boire, Gary. "Sucking Kumaras." *Canadian Literature* 124/125 (Spring/Summer 1990): 301-06.

Chapman, Geoff. "Royal Treatment for Dry Lips." *Toronto Star* 14 April 1991: C1.

Conlogue, Ray. "An emotionally riveting Dry Lips." *The Globe and Mail* 24 April 1989: A17.

———. "Mixing stories, bingo and genius." *The Globe and Mail* 21 November 1987: C5.

Crew, Robert. "Hope Flickers in Disturbing Probe of Native Spirit." *Toronto Star* 23 April 1989: C1.

Davis, Jack. *The Dreamers. Plays From Black Australia.* Ed. Justine Saunders. Sydney: Currency Press, 1989.

Dollimore, Jonathan. *Sexual Dissidence.* Oxford: Clarendon Press, 1991.

Fraser, Marion Botsford. "Contempt for women overshadows powerful play." *The Globe and Mail* 17 April 1991: C1.

Goldie, Terry and Daniel David Moses, ed. *An Anthology of Canadian Native Literature in English.* Toronto: Oxford University Press, 1992.

Highway, Tomson. *Dry Lips Oughta Move To Kapuskasing.* Saskatoon: Fifth House, 1991.

———. *The Rez Sisters.* Saskatoon: Fifth House, 1988.

Johnston, Denis W. "Lines and Circles: The 'Rez' Plays of Tomson Highway." *Canadian Literature* 124-125 (Spring-Summer 1990): 254-64.

Kaplan, Jon. "Playwright Moses awakens the dead." *Now* 15-25 (May 2, 1988).

Mitchell, Tony. "Colonial Discourse and the National Imaginary." *Canadian Theatre Review* 74 (Spring 1993): 18-21.

Mojica, Monique. *Princess Pocahontas and the Blue Spots. Canadian Theatre Review* 64 (Fall 1990): 66-77.

Preston, Jennifer. "Preston responds." Letter to the editor. *The Drama Review* 37 (Spring 1993): 13-15.

———. "Weesageechak Begins to Dance: Native Earth Performing Arts Inc." *The Drama Review* 36.1 (Spring 1992): 135-59.

Prosser, David. "Other truths, other realities." *The Whig Standard Magazine,* Kingston *Whig Standard* 5 December 1987: 10-11.

Scott, Jay. "Dry Lips' Loss of Intimacy Transforms Visceral Images into Picturesque Tableaux." *The Globe and Mail* 21 April 1991: C1.

Tuharsky, Anita. "Play promotes racism, sexism and oppression." Letter to the editor. *Windspeaker* 12 March 1991: 5.

Watego, Cliff. "'Extremely Funny... utterly tragic': an interview with Richard Walley with notes on Black interviews / Black discourse." *Australasian Drama Studies* 17 (October 1990): 40-50.

Wilson, Ann. "Tomson Highway, Interview." *Other Solitudes: Canadian Multicultural Fictions.* Ed. Linda Hutcheon and Marion Richmond. Toronto: Oxford U P, 1990. 350-55.

"Shine on us, Grandmother Moon": Coding in Canadian First Nations Drama

by Reid Gilbert

Current productions written, directed, and/or performed by First Nations Canadians are often characterized by a complex layering of myth and iconography operating simultaneously in more than one cultural system. The effect is richly visual and auditory theatre, but, more important, such performances highlight the essentially indexical and iconographic nature of theatre itself by writing text at the intersection of discourses with quite different political and historical markers and, in the process, bringing those discourses together to form a new typology of signs. What is problematic is the effect of such signs.

These new signs add to earlier sign-vehicles. They are often quite translucent overlays which urge us to read down through the layers of the composite, multidimensional icon. They are a recent development in Canadian (and Aboriginal) theatre. They are strongly political in intent. They reposition the spectator as subject. They resist suture. Given these characteristics, an important question emerges: do such signs signal a move toward a post-colonial (and postmodern) iconography, or do they simply attest to a state of cultural colonization which First Nations Canadians now share with non-Native Canadians who still, in the 1990s, trail their ancestral mythologies?

That Canadian theatre has until recently—and particularly in its early attempts to create a "national theatre"—accepted a Eurocentric and colonial posture is evident. Theatre historians like Denis Salter point out the assumptions implicit in important Canadian movements to define a national theatre, like the establishment of Hart House Theatre in the University of Toronto in 1919, the Dominion Drama Festival of 1932-78, and the creation of the Stratford Shakespearian Festival in 1953. Salter asserts that conservatism—"representative" of those in political and cultural power in Canada between the Wars—coloured expectations for a national theatre (82). While a regional system did come into being in the 1960s, it has generally presented standard plays from the American, and European repertoire, mixed with those Canadian plays which have entered the canon by expressing the attitudes and images covertly instilled by the early arbiters of taste in central Canada and the influence of the educational system. Robert Wallace warns that the "notions of 'quality', 'merit', and 'excellence'... valorized [by anthologizing plays and building a national canon] are not just socially produced variables: they are systemic strategies by which critics, editors and teachers confirm their power both to arbitrate and to inculcate cultural values... [leading to] intellectual control" (222). Valuing Shakespeare as the model of excellence, and always rather embarrassed at Canada's colonial face (while subtly prolonging it), these institutions promoted a national theatre in English Canada in the face of the scholarly argument that it was inappropriate and without reference to indigenous idiom, human geography, or local iconography. In this, proponents of an "official" theatre failed to incorporate images from the vigorous alternative theatre movement of the 1970s, or the much more regional issues and deixis of older amateur companies across the country (Filewod 200-06), despite the recognized position of an amateur tradition within the history of Canadian theatre. Indeed, the Dominion Drama Festival discouraged plays whose subject matter or style deviated from European good taste (Salter 86), and George Woodcock, Ann Wilson, and Robert Wallace contend that peer juries of funding agencies still promote safe, conformist performance (Woodcock; Wallace; Wilson 11-16). Outside these institutions, standards of commercial viability frequently determine playbills, an attitude which has internalized rather than removed the colonial focus: if it can sell to the urban Toronto or Vancouver audience, this attitude suggests, it should be seen in other regional centres in English Canada.

Plays such as Floyd Favel's *Requiem,* Tomson Highway's *The Rez Sisters* and *Dry Lips Oughta Move to Kapuskasing,* Tina Mason's opera *Diva Ojibway* and Marie Humber Clements's re-staging of the Troy myth, *Age of Iron,* present important reactions to this theatrical history and to the history of oppression of Aboriginal people. Beyond their common thematic statements, however, some of these plays create new images—indeed, propose new icons—which ask for evaluation. Do such plays merely add to the store of Canadian imagery by redressing the absence of indigenous markers, or by providing some new signs which contemporary Canadians are eager to include in changing attitudes to the ecology or maternalistic spirituality? Or do they posit alternate or resistant symbols which seek to replace the earlier and familiar European images? In doing either, do they somehow reform the national consciousness?

Postmodern criticism cautions against any quick assumption that new pictures can replace anything, that the images of any moment in (Canadian) history are unified, static or essential. To position Canadian (theatrical) icons within the history of Canada in order to evaluate their importance in the development of a national consciousness is, of course, to subscribe to the notion—now suspect—that one national history exists, or that the process of history making is somehow apart from the notion of creating theatre, the mimetic one to be weighed in terms of the absolute other. In C. S. Peirce's terminology, signs are themselves representations of earlier signs, each imbricating the earlier discourse, creating what Pécheux calls an "interdiscourse" with complex semiological coding and undercoding prompting positive and negative, patriotic and ironic responses (113). In such a reading of history—or historically driven national subjectivity—what appear as "new" signs are part of an unfolding metanarrative. In a play like *Requiem,* the power of this larger narrative is clear; in plays like *Age of Iron,* however, a new order of sign appears to be emerging which may, indeed, reform the Canadian narrative, rather than simply allowing Native images into the national memory bank or appropriating them into the evolving central narrative. Even more important, these plays raise the question of identity of a personal, psychological nature as well as of a national nature. This is particularly true of plays such as Marie Clements's *Age of Iron* where local semiosis, a personal engagement with the text by its writer-actor, the fact that the writer is a woman, the appearance on stage of important, complex characters which combine Native and western mythologies, and the venue of its first production all contribute to an intense discussion of identity for actor(s) and audience.

The Tempest directed by Baumander

The 1987 direction of Shakespeare's *The Tempest* by Louis Baumander has been the subject of considerable critical discussion in Canada.[1] Its repositioning of iconography, as Helen Peters argues ("Towards" 14, 15, 17), demonstrates the "dramaturgy of the perverse," employing the term which Richard Paul Knowles believes defines Canadian postmodern theatre (226-35). In a review of the production, Paul Leonard raises the notion that the "making" of a play is, itself, an act of situating the "here." He questions how the Canadian "here" "differs from elsewhere," wondering whether the "Making [of] a Canadian play asserts the priority of indigenous experience." "Ultimately," he says, "the act of producing our own theatre argues that non-Canadian plays are not relevant here." Leonard attempts to discover what in Baumander's *Tempest* "transcend[s] the specific cultural context of [Shakespeare's] original creation [and exhibits] a kernel of meaning... that applies to Canada" (11). Looking at the national rather than the personal, he does not extend his argument to the larger Lacanian notion that the making of the "here" also establishes the space occupied by the subject and, therefore, at least partly defines that subject. By so defining the subject, theatrical space also limits what may constitute the Self-observing-the-Other and, by extension, what can constitute the Other. Such a theoretical construct is at the heart of the iconography of identity. Christian Metz observes in *The Imaginary Signifier* that:

> The perceptions that theatre and other spectacles offer to the eye and ear are inscribed in a true space... the same one as that occupied by the public during the performance; everything the audience hear[s] and see[s] is actively produced in [its] presence, by human beings or props which are themselves present. ...whether or not the theatrical play mimes a fable, its action, if need be mimetic, is still managed by real persons evolving in real time and space *on the same stage or "scene" as the public.* (qtd. in Carlson 79, emphasis in original)

For the audiences of the Skylight production in Toronto reading *The Tempest* as condemnation of imperialism, the Haida images established an indexical position as subject which not only allowed for a collective non-Native catharsis (or, conversely, a refusal to accept responsibility for historical wrongdoing) but a complex layering of Self. The fact that the setting was a British Columbia coast Haida village invited self--recognition as Canadian, but a reassuring distance for those reading the imperialist history of some other Canadian colonists two thousand miles away. It allowed Self identification as that which "is not" Native (particularly by depicting Caliban as the "drunk Indian" of Canadian racism) but congruently demanded recognition as that which "is" (or is heir to) Prospero or his troops. To refuse to "be" either Prospero or Caliban would position the spectator outside the signifying chain as an empty subject, but Lacan proposes that no such thing can exist once language has been accepted: the spectator here exists in the future anterior tense; the Self is always in "the process of becoming" (304). The fear of loss, or the desire for Self, or the confusion of identification "prompts him or her to seek compensation in an idealised image... which will fend off the lack. Such a specular image, whose prototype is the image in the mirror, produces a misrecognition of the self... effecting the junction of the imaginary and the symbolic, otherwise known as suture" (Lapsley and Westlake 76).

For the contemporary Canadian, such suture develops from the attempt to avoid an uncomfortable self-recognition made doubly difficult by its expression in a "lexicon" of images and through a "grammar" that is unfamiliar. No wonder mainstream Canadians have preferred to read *with* the text, using a Eurocentric vocabulary, rather than to learn a new, polysemic language. In the work of new Aboriginal playwrights, however, a reading "across the text" sometimes asserts itself as it does in feminist and other resistance theatre (Case). Such a reading requires a new language which, if Lacan is correct, will generate a new sense of Self.

"Raven" and Clements, *Age of Iron*

One of the key figures in this new language is Raven or Trickster, a figure who inscribes himself under a variety of signs and, as a result, avoids ultimate signification. Trickster becomes, in this context, a figure very alien to a non-Native sense of Self, denying the very system of language in which this Self is established. He is, however, a "pivotal... figure in North American Indian mythology", as Tomson Highway remarks in notes to *Dry Lips Oughta Move to Kapuskasing* (12).

Despite the almost successful attempt to erase him from First Nations Canadian minds as part of governmental and religious hegemony, "he/she did not leave the continent when the White man came," Highway quips, "[but] is still here among us— albeit a little the worse for wear—...having assumed other guises" (13). Nanabush is now (re)appearing on many Canadian stages. The figure has been the subject of considerable critical comment and has, even, generated her/his own eponymous little magazine. Yet he/she is not easy to capture, existing more as a "cultural activity [which] indexes the ambiguities" (Godard 184) which confront attempts to bring Indian story telling to non-Native audiences than as a *persona*. The various versions of Raven which have lately appeared elude inscription under any particular politic, including any gender politic, or even Native identity politics. In Highway's *The Rez Sisters*, a male Nanabush appears as a figure of encouragement; in Highway's *Dry Lips Oughta Move to Kapuskasing*, a female Nanabush suffers male aggression; in the Tamanhous Theatre production of Dancoes' *Paradise and the Wasteland*, a male punk Groucho Marx Trickster inhabits the body of Merlin. In *Age of Iron*, Raven becomes a young Native drug addict deploring the lack of "any place to land". He is fully described in the cast list: "Trojan Warrior/Half-bird, Half Boy, Half Man in Flight. Trickster" (Clements i). As Barbara Godard notes, "Such intersemiotic 'translation' will inevitably... dis/place... and hybridize... conventions, [posing] a challenge to the Canadian literary institution... [by positing] the word as a process of knowing, provisional and partial, rather than as revealed knowledge itself, and aiming to produce texts in performance that would create truth as interpretation" (184). The question, again, is whether Raven can effectively "dis/place" convention before he is appropriated into an enlarged, but still totalizing signifying practice within the nation's political, social and literary establishments. His appearance in *Age of Iron* seems to suggest that he may be able to withstand the pressures of a traditional western audience to reduce him to easy signification. On the surface in this play he is such a strong cultural icon of the self-destructive Native youth that this inscription threatens to overshadow his other identities. Clements, however, resists the immediate attempt of the audience to assign meaning (and, thereby, to secure its own subject position).

Clements has Raven come into life after he is knocked down from a wall of inner city debris of which he has actually been part. As Hecuba (here seen as a derelict bag lady) strikes him with her stick, his "Sqwack" as bird precedes his physical manifestation as man and his first speech establishes his mythological being before the action announces his narrative being: "Squaaack. Not only did you wake me up, you made me drop all my possessions" (Clements 11), which he "indignantly" picks up, dusts off and places "back inside his wings." Hecuba speaks from within her character as a member of the Troy myth (the *fabula*) and as a dispossessed Native, now denizen of the inner city (the *sjuzet*). Raven speaks only from his position as Trickster, outside the *fabula*, as, indeed, outside any narratological system. Hecuba rails against her fate in losing her throne in language which clearly connotes the loss by the Native woman/ mother of her ownership of North America and of a system of governance, "I'll tell you who I was and then you'll pity me. I ruled a country once.... Now I must be a slave. My dress is torn and ragged and filthy, my whole body's filthy." Raven replies in a wisecracking aside, "You're not kiddin' me. And stinky." As Hecuba escalates her grief and shame, Raven picks up the tone, sliding into bird sounds and ushering in a "frenzy of cane hitting and stamping" by both actors which suggests "a loud drum-like beat" (11).

This mad behaviour dislodges viewer expectation. This Hecuba cannot be seen only as bag lady; prompted by raven she exhibits much more dangerous behaviour. She has been carrying a doll—part of her indexing as pathetic and mad—which she now "throws down." She and Raven "stamp on it viciously, pieces of it scattering and crunching under them" as she screams:

> HECUBA. I shall sing as I never did when our people sang, when the
> drums beat.
> RAVEN. Swaak
> HECUBA. ...and I was Queen of the Land
> RAVEN. Swakkk. (12)

The rhythm alters, as Cassandra speaks (also from the wall), and Hecuba responds to the voice as though from her broken doll-child. Desperately trying to reassemble the doll, she croons to it in response to Cassandra's speech, "Don't worry… mama will make it okay. Everything will be fine… in a few weeks you can come back and live with me and we will be together again" (12). Suddenly, Hecuba is the Artemis figure which western mythology has sought to deny, the woman as both nurturer and destroyer; she is an entirely unromanticized Mother. She is also the First Nations mother who has failed to protect her child from her own self-destructive behaviour and from the authorities (in this instance, residential Christian schools which took Native children away to reculturalize them).

The semiosis of this scene is complex and illustrative of the layering throughout the play. Raven avoids situation; Hecuba operates in both plots; Cassandra transcends the plots to exist as pure symbol of the raped and colonized Native girl and, simultaneously, of women generally within the patriarchy. On stage, the action divides. Wiseguy (the figure of the male elder) attempts to put the doll together again with the enforced help of Raven. Cassandra attempts to comfort Hecuba by becoming her daughter. At no time, however, is the audience allowed to homogenize these images into a picture of recuperation: Raven's remarks and swearing prevent the sentimentality with which the audience would like to respond to the spectacle of street people trying to mend one another while everything about them denotes their desperate hopelessness.

> HECUBA. O dear mouth, you are gone with all your pretty prattle…
> CASSANDRA. You can brush my hair, Mother. Here just like you like to… a hundred times.
> RAVEN. That's the piece there. If you don't put the spring in properly it will look like it has bug eyes, not that it was a pretty sight anyway, but it will look really creepy with bulging eyes…
> WISEGUY. Yeah, well it's not going to look any too good with no arms or legs either is it…?
> RAVEN. Fuck it!
> WISEGUY. She's a goner, Hecuba. (14-15)

Denied by Raven the subject position of caring (but helpless) observer of the tribulations of the poor, the audience is forced to respond to the various images and symbols and to occupy a place within the semiosis. In this way, *Age of Iron* avoids the trap into which Floyd Favel's *Requiem* falls.

Favel, *Requiem*

Requiem is a highly stylized document of the coming of Europeans to North America (of the coming of the "age of iron," indeed) presented as a masque. Despite the beauty of the piece and its aim, the play ultimately becomes a false depiction of a Golden Age before colonization. A White audience may accept blame for the social and moral ills suffered by those for whom the masque is a requiem, but such recognition, especially if it leads to catharsis, reinforces a Self as different from and politically stronger (if morally weaker) than the dying Aboriginals. More: the histrionics and costumes of the play submit, themselves, to the proposition that the First Nations are dead by clothing their protest in the forms of the dominant race. In a play like *Requiem* the iconography is not, in fact, polyvalent: the thesis of the play may be a statement of Aboriginal anger, but the appearances, styles and attitudes of the piece conform to western theatrical practice. If the thesis of the play is that First Canadians have been raped, the vehicle states it more eloquently than the dialogue. It seems, however, that the play means to argue that the ill done to First Nations people must be recognized and redressed; if this is Favel's intention, the play sends confusing messages. Is the audience simply to agree that historic wrong has been committed? If so, what good will come of a political statement which merely makes a few decent, middle-class White spectators uncomfortable for ninety minutes? Is the audience supposed to notice that a new generation of Indians is highly educated in theatrical tradition and uses the English language very well? If so, it seems to validate the hegemonic system of residential schools and the insistence on education in English, a historical fact deplored in many other First Nations productions. Is the audience meant to learn Native ways of seeing? None are presented within the iconography of the piece though some are suggested on an intellectual level within its dialogue. Here, the icons are not multilayered nor translucent; instead, a conventional set of images is imposed onto an abstract (and clichéd) theme.

C. S. Peirce defined the icon as having "similitude" to its "object," and being an icon "in so far as it is like that thing and used as a sign of it." Further, Peirce suggests a figurative painting can be an icon in that while viewing it "we lose the consciousness that it is not the thing" (qtd. in Elam 20). Even given the elasticity of Peirce's definitions, it is obvious that there is no similitude between the thesis of *Requiem* and the sign-vehicles which carry it on stage. The audience never loses consciousness that it is viewing a seventeenth-century masque of European origin and it also never loses consciousness that this vehicle, whose space the spectator occupies, is an icon of the *spectator*, himself, not of the object of his gaze. In this, *Requiem* differs radically from *Age of Iron* where Raven's movement into the *fabula* as a junkie carries with it all the iconographic resonance of his earlier distance from the plot. His bird movements and voice inflections continue through the events of his incarnation as Trojan warrior in the *fabula* and pawn of the police in the *sjuzet*, endlessly reminding that he is also, and at bottom, neither of these things. This icon is translucent, with semantic meaning on both plot levels but power at the level of its mythological referent. It forces the "co-operation of sign, object and interpretant" which Peirce suggested is the basis of semiosis, and excites the viewer to form an image similar to that "in the mind of the deliverer" (25). When a First Nations writer (and, one might add, a female First Nations writer) can excite an icon with Peircean similitude in the mind of a White, bourgeois spectator (and, one might add, a male spectator) it seems possible that a new order of Canadian iconography can be born. If this is true, *Requiem* underlines the degree of submission of all Canadians (First and subsequent) to imperialism, while *Age of Iron* points to a new, postmodern Canadian iconography born of overlapping signification and forced recognition.

Age of Iron and Canadian iconography

In *Age of Iron* this forced involvement is intensified by the highly theatrical presence on stage of yet another mother, Earth Mother herself. Together with Raven and the figures of Grandmother Moon and her Seven (star) Sisters, Earth Mother completes a pantheon of Aboriginal divinities which grows from a belief in the power of Fire, Water, Wind, and the Earth/Body as part of a great Hoop or Circle of Life. These Forces echo the Greek elements and the Earthbound divinities of pre-Olympian Greece. It is in the figure of Earth Mother that *Age of Iron* establishes another of the key figures in a new language and forces the non-Native spectator to reinvent her/himself within performance.

Earth Mother is both character and set. This set is of key importance in *Age of Iron*, as it is in many postmodern productions where, as Arnold Aronson points out, "the *mise en scène* can become the dominant element of a production, establishing the whole tone and shaping the interpretation…" (5). In *Age of Iron*, the inner city cement not only functions to establish tone but (literally) concretizes the theme, by forming the bridge between the two plots. It also forms the characterization of Mother Earth. At the outset, the dominant image on stage, the (male) red sun of Mars, "looks to be made of exposed muscles and arteries. It… grows redder and more exposed" (Clements Stage Direction 1).

As the action commences, Wiseguy and the Chorus come to life (in sounds before movement) out of the debris and rubble of the street and concrete walls upstage. Masked as Trojan warriors, they are also metonymic of the decay of the inner city, dressed in armour made of street rubble—costumes that "individualize the warrior and characterize Darkness" (S.D. 1). To drum sounds, they chant about the discovery of metals and "the first attempts at civilization." As they speak, "layers of earth light up with different hues of red and a glowing fire in her bowels" (S.D. 2). The sound of rain accompanies Wiseguy's lament about the history of his (Trojan and Native) people: "Water from her terror, air from the consolidation of her grief… our ignorance lay concealed in these three sufferings of the contemporary age, our Age, the Age of Iron" (2). The Chorus universalizes the elements, "If I do not understand how the fire came to be, I will burn in it because I will not know my root", and later, "If I do not first understand the water, I will not know anything", and "If I do not understand how the wind that blows came to be, I will run with it" (2). Finally, as the Chorus chants, "If I do understand how the body that I wear came to be, I will perish with it" (3), genesis occurs, the sky clears, the water effect stops and the clear night sky with Sister Stars and Grandmother Moon emerges. Wiseguy greets the celestial women but notes the absence of the Seventh Star Sister, the star Cassandra will become in constellation at the conclusion of the play. Wiseguy "stares at the cement beneath his feet," and observes, "Earth beneath my feet. Poor ol' Mother. Suffocating with this heavy load"

(5). As he comforts the Earth, he tears up slabs of cement. As Cassandra enters the scene, Earth Mother begins to rise from the cement, pushing concrete off her body; Wiseguy "runs to earth and digs his hands in the dirt" (S.D. 7). Earth Mother emerges, a masked and extravagantly costumed figure, who "rubs her earth hands on [Wiseguy's] face as a caress" (7). He announces her fundamental presence:

> You have only seen this land of Troy
> from the outside.
> The walls and floors are thick with
> grime with the wars and plagues and
> how hardened.
> But inside is a beautiful woman.
> Alive with happiness and living.
> The ancient ones talk to us. (7)

He addresses the spectators, declaring their position as those who do not understand (or value) this chthonic Mother, "You envy that. You have no such land because you have covered it with an ungiving surface. You call us barbarians. But that is what we call you" (7). Earth Mother finally speaks, "Shhhh… now. Come inside and try to get some rest. I'll make your bed in my safe corner" (9) as she cradles Wiseguy. Cassandra covers them both with cement slabs.

Again, the icons are translucent and quite complex. Within the Trojan *fabula*, the Bronze Age warrior shelters from the Iron Age invaders in the rubble of his once proud city. Within the surface narrative of the *sjuzet*, the street person—and the "drunken Indian"—shelters in a mound of broken concrete, warmed by "the gleaming wine" (8) he has been drinking throughout the scene. Deeper within the *sjuzet*, the Aboriginal warrior shelters from the Iron Age of the imperialist invaders within the Earth which dominates his cosmology. As the blanket of the Earth becomes all three scapes, the image multiplies and splits, denying easy closure,[2] juxtaposing historical and contemporary emblems, creating a new icon that cannot be simply named. The cliché comment of social injustice is made more profound by these multiple significations. Most important, the audience is forced to recognize itself within a number of narratives of war, nurture and decay—all narratives which form the history of humankind and bind the other (street person, Indian) to the bourgeois spectator as Subject. If one's roots somehow grow in the myths of Greece—as the educational system, Christianity and traditional theatre aetiology have told Canadians they do—then the viewer must see her/himself somewhere among the available character icons on stage. Like the Baumander *Tempest*, the play prevents the eluding of recognition. It is "perverse" rather than "subversive," in Knowles's terminology. The verbal language of the play enunciates both a "classical diction" (albeit a rather awkward one) in the speeches of the Trojans and an authentic contemporary street diction. It also captures the cadence of First Nations Canadian speech and the ironic humour which characterizes Native story telling (the same humour of mothers and grandmothers which forms the subtext of Mason's opera in the Cree-Ojibway language, *Diva Ojibway*).

The visual language captures the same set of markers, inviting the audience to read through the easy street scene to the less accessible memory narrative of Troy and back through an expanded semiosis to the First Nations thesis inscribed in Raven and Earth Mother and ultimately carried by the most fundamental of icons—the bodies of Native actors. By this process *Age of Iron* situates the viewer within the theatrical space, forcing identification and suggesting a vocabulary in which a Canadian *je* might describe itself apart from the various "official" versions of the *moi* (Lacan *The Seminar* 141), which have been offered as Canadian identities. The non-Native spectator attending *Age of Iron* recognizes one or more of the discourses in which the play speaks—the classical allusions, the contemporary social comment, the ideological comment of racial politics, the feminist intertext. Such a spectator attempts suture—to "sew together" a subject who will bear the guilt or inherit the history, who will allow such a spectator to retain an earlier sense of the *moi*, and to observe with quiescence the response of the "Absent One" to the multiple iconographies which include this, as all, spectators. In this way, the non-Native spectator attempts what Lacan argues is desire in all discourse, a "pseudo-identification" aimed at creating an imaginary unity (*Écrits* 304; Lapsley and Westlake 86). But the psychoanalytic construct is too overloaded to support this illusion. No urban spectator can escape identification within the semiotic field because the character, Earth Mother, simultaneously signifies the body of the earth, the crushed body of the Native woman and the broken body of the contemporary city. Hecuba is the imaginary image of this Queen/ Gaea/Native Grandmother/Bag Lady, but Earth Mother is the symbolic image of the same concepts, and in this moment of juncture, real understanding of the audience's position occurs. The attempt to suture a surrogate subject fails and the non-Native spectator is forced to confront a primitive and non-idealized Self.

The spectator watches Earth Mother on stage, Hecuba further inside the frame, and Cassandra yet further inside the multiple narratives. But the fact that Earth Mother is the broken city pavement, itself, also means that she exists outside the theatre, behind the audience (especially in the venue of the first production),[3] clearly placing the spectator—like Wiseguy—inside her "red bowels," in her arms. By exposing the fluidity of the signs and their multiple inscriptions, *Age of Iron* demands that the viewer accept that his/her subject position is "at once production and product... just as there is 'permanent performance of the subject in language itself'" (Stephen Heath qtd. in Lapsley and Westlake 90). In this way, it forms a new order of iconography which may allow First Canadian writers, as Barbara Godard so succinctly put it, to "write the other, otherwise" (222). Plays such as Marie Humber Clements's *Age of Iron* suggest that, very possibly, new Aboriginal drama is, in fact, creating a post-colonial, postmodern iconography, one which may free both its people and members of the non-Native Canadian audience from the patriarchal metanarrative in which Canada has, till recently, sought to form itself.

(1996)

Notes

1 Baumander repeated the production in 1989. See Peters, "The Aboriginal Presence", 197-205.

2 In Lacanian terms, denying the slide into the idealized in the field of the other, the *i (a)* of the *Graphe Complet.* See Lacan *Écrits* 304.

3 The Firehall Theatre in Vancouver, Canada is in an impoverished section of town, where Native Canadians and the homeless are often seen living on the streets.

Works Cited

Aronson, Arnold. "Postmodern Design." *Theatre Journal* 43.1 (March 1991): 1-13.

Carlson, Marvin. *Theatre Semiotics: Signs of Life.* Bloomington: Indiana University Press, 1990.

Case, Sue-Ellen. "Classic Drag: The Greek Creation of Female Parts." *Theatre Journal* 37.3 (1985): 317-27.

Clements, Marie Humber. *Age of Iron.* Ms. First production. Firehall Theatre, Vancouver, BC, November 1993.

Elam, Keir. *The Semiotics of Theatre and Drama.* London: Methuen, 1980.

Filewod, Alan. "The Marginalization of the Canadian Popular Theatre Alliance in the Discourse of Canadian Theatre History." *Theatre History in Canada* 10 (1989): 200-06.

Favel, Floyd. *Requiem.* Touring production. Museum of Anthropology, Vancouver, BC, 1992.

Godard, Barbara. "The Politics of Representation: Some Native Canadian Women Writers." *Canadian Literature* 124-125 (1990): 183-225.

Highway, Tomson. "A Note On Nanabush." *Dry Lips Oughta Move to Kapuskasing.* Saskatoon, SK: Fifth House, 1989. 12-13.

Knowles, Richard Paul. "The Dramaturgy of the Perverse." *Theatre Research International* 17.3 (1992): 226-35.

Lacan, Jacques. *Écrits, A Selection.* Trans. Alan Sheridan. London: Tavistock, 1977.

———. *The Seminar of Jacques Lacan, Book I: Freud's Papers on Technique, 1953-1954.* Trans. John Forrester. Cambridge: Cambridge University Press, 1988.

Lapsley, Robert and Michael Westlake. *Film Theory: An Introduction.* Manchester: Manchester UP, 1988.

Leonard, Paul. "*The Tempest* X 2 in Toronto." *Canadian Theatre Review* 54 (1988): 7-12.

Pécheux, Michel. *Language, Semantics and Ideology.* Trans. Harbans Nagpal. New York: St. Martin's, 1982.

Peters, Helen. "The Aboriginal Presence in Canadian Theatre and the Evolution of Being Canadian." *Theatre Research International* 18.3 (1993): 197-205.

———. "Towards Canadian Postmodernism." *Canadian Theatre Review* 76 (1993): 13-17.

Salter, Denis. "The Idea of a National Theatre." *Canadian Canons: Essays in Literary Value.* Ed. Robert Lecker. Toronto: U of Toronto P, 1991. 71-90.

Wallace, Robert. "Constructing a Canon: A Review Essay." *Theatre History in Canada* 10 (1989): 218-22.

———. *Producing Marginality: Theatre and Criticism in Canada.* Saskatoon, SK: Fifth House, 1990.

Wilson, Ann. "Deadpan: Ideology and Criticism." *Canadian Theatre Review* 57 (1988): 11-16.

Woodcock, George. *Strange Bedfellows: The State and the Arts in Canada.* Vancouver: Douglas, 1985.

Alive and well: Native theatre in Canada

by Drew Hayden Taylor

Native theatre is alive and well and living in Canada. Today Native theatre is strong, popular and practically everywhere in terms of the Canadian theatrical community. What once was barren is now bountiful. If in 1986 there was one working Native playwright in all of Canada, today at least two dozen playwrights of aboriginal descent are being produced. If the rate of increase continues, by the year 2020 it is conceivable that everybody in Canada will be a Native Playwright!

I have a theory as to why theatre seems to be the medium of choice amongst Native Canadians. We have novelists, we have short story writers, we have musicians, we have actors, etc., but in terms of artists per capita, theatre has become the predominant vehicle of expression. Theatre is a logical extension of the storytelling technique. Looking back at the roots and origins of traditional storytelling, not just Native storytelling but storytelling in general, it is the process of taking your audience on a journey, using your voice, your body and the spoken word. Moving that journey onto the stage is merely the next logical step. With their oral culture, Native people gravitate towards theatre, more so than towards the written word where you have to have perfect English or grammatically correct writing. The spotty education that has been granted Native people by the government and various societal institutions has not been great. This is one of the reasons I became a playwright: I write as people talk, and the way people talk is not always grammatically correct—therefore I can get away with less than "perfect" English.

At its origins, storytelling was a way of relating the history of the community. It was a way of explaining human nature. A single story could have metaphorical, philosophical, psychological implications. Unfortunately, in today's society, many Native legends of history have been relegated to the status of quaint children's stories. But, legends and stories were never meant to be quaint children stories. They were told to adults as well as for children, and as you got older, you could tap into a whole new understanding of the story. It was like an onion, you could always peel away more and more to get to the core of the story.

Let me give you an example—please forgive my delivery; I am many things but a traditional storyteller is not one of them. Telling a good story involves a special talent and years of practice, so please bear with me. There is a story about the creation of the earth. It starts with a woman on top of the back of a turtle. The woman has fallen through a hole in the sky, and discovers the whole world is flooded. She desperately wants to find land, so she sends animals, one after another, down to the bottom of the water to try to find some earth—a single speck of dirt. The animals keep going down, some returning empty handed, others dying and floating to the surface without any dirt in their paws. The beaver, the loon, all sorts of animals try but fail. Finally, the lowly muskrat approaches and says, "Please let me try." Now the muskrat is viewed with disdain; he is like a water rat. But he persists and says; "Let me try." So the muskrat goes down and he is gone for a long period of time. He goes down, down, down. Everybody thinks he's dead. But finally he surfaces. He is unconscious so he is pulled to shore on the back of the turtle. In his hand there is a tiny bit of dirt. That's all the woman needs to create an earth on the back of a turtle. And this is why North America is referred to by First Nations people as Turtle Island.

Now that is a very brief, rough summary of a creation myth, a small segment of that whole myth. How that legend is related for adult understanding was shown to me by the writer and storyteller Basil Johnston. The legend refers to the psychological process of reaching deep inside yourself to find that nugget that is your grounding, your earth, the essence of who you are. The story can be interpreted as the need to survive, as a dangerous journey with dangerous ramifications. The journey to find that nugget—that most important thing—is the story of creation from a different, more philosophical, psychological viewpoint: Taking that interpretation—the story as archetypal self exploration—and then putting it into theatre, seems like a natural progression. At the same time, the story has meaning for children. Take any story-teller, watch him work with kids, suspending their disbelief and taking them on a journey, using characters and an interesting plot line. This is the basis of any good theatrical presentation.

There have always been many different forms of theatre in our nations' history. During the onslaught of Christianity, of the government, the residential system etc., traditional Native beliefs were deemed offensive and unnecessary. There were numerous attempts to stamp them out and replace them with White North American/ European concepts. However, it is incredibly hard to eradicate the simple act of telling stories. Our culture persevered, and today we are getting our voice back.

Prior to World War II, it was illegal for Native people to leave the reserve without written permission from the Indian agent. With the advent of World War II, many Native people enlisted in the armed services. We were exempt from the draft because legally we were not considered citizens of Canada. However, because of our warrior traditions and some sort of bizarre loyalty to the King, many Native people enlisted and went to Europe. There they found there were different ways of doing things. They didn't have to just stay on the reserve and do what they were told. After the war, many Native people had a more worldly outlook. Also, in 1960, Native people finally got the right to vote in Canada. There was a progression of events; it was like a puzzle, each bit falling into place. Native people were beginning to understand that there were alternatives. We began to assert ourselves. In 1968 there was a demonstration in Kenora over a park that the local Native tribe wanted back. In 1973, there was Wounded Knee. And so on and so forth. Each event was a step towards getting our voice back. There were also little steps in between. In 1967, George Ryga wrote the play *The Ecstasy of Rita Joe* which became a milestone in terms of Canadian theatre and more accurate representations of the urban Indian experience. It was, however, written by a non-Native person and, though I believe Chief Dan George was in it, most of the original cast for the production in Vancouver was non-Native. It did start people talking however—about the power of theatre and about the plight of Native people. In 1974, an organization was created in Toronto called the Association for Native Development in the Performing and Visual Arts. One of the things it set up was the Native Theatre School, which was the first school of its kind to teach Native people how to act, to teach them theatrical production, and how to write their own stories. The Theatre School operates during the summer, for seven weeks; for four weeks the students train and for the other three they perform. In addition they also write their own play as a collective, direct it and then take it out on the road for a tour. It has been over 20 years since this school was created and many well-known Native actors have been a part of the school.

In 1979 the Association for Native Development in the Performing and Visual Arts was invited to perform a play at the International Theatre Festival in Monaco. They found themselves in the awkward position of having no play to take. So they decided to remedy the situation as best they could. They contacted a Native poet by the name of George Kenny who had written a book of poetry called *Indians Don't Cry*. One of the poems was called "October Stranger" and had good dramatic potential. With the help of an experienced Native actor, they adapted it into a play (also called *October Stranger*) and they took it to Monaco. It was pretty much a fiasco. Everybody in Europe seemed to be expecting buckskin, feathers and beads. Instead these contemporary Native youth came in to do a serious play about a person leaving the reserve to go and live in a city and becoming acculturated. This was not what people at the Monaco theatre festival wanted to see.

Another moment in the history of Native theatre was the 1984 creation of a drama company called the De-Ba-Jeh-Mu-Jig Theatre Group. De-Ba-Jeh-Mu-Jig is an Ojibway-Cree word meaning storytellers or tattler of tales. It was started by a woman named Shirley Cheechoo; an amazing painter, actress, model and playwright. Shirley Cheechoo is a person who does whatever intrigues her—if she wants to go write a play, she'll go write a play; if she wants to do a painting, she'll do a painting. She started De-Ba-Jeh-Mu-Jig as a summer theatre company on the West Bay Reserve on Manitoulin Island. It was created partly to showcase Native legends, both traditional and contemporary, and also to raise some money by performing for tourists in the summer. Every year the company produced a play. Although the professionalism of the work was rough to begin with, it gradually grew. The group performed plays such as *Nothing Personal, Nanabush of the 80s* and a whole series of others that toured communities in and around southern Ontario.

During the 1984-85 season, De-Ba-Jeh-Mu-Jig Theatre Group was catapulted into the theatrical limelight. The powers-that-be contacted a man whom they asked to be their artistic director; Shirley was busy and didn't have the time to devote fully to the company. The person they approached to go to Manitoulin Island and run the company was a Cree writer by the name of Tomson Highway.

Tomson Highway spent the winter on the island in a portable trailer. It was not the most enjoyable circumstances for him but he persevered. During his time on the island, he visited a nearby community, about 45 minutes away, called Wikwemikong or Wiki to the local people. It was there he first formulated the idea for a play that would become so important for Native Theatre. He noticed all these women rushing around, going to play a game called... bingo! He watched and saw people becoming really obsessed. They'd enter the bingo palace and there would be dead silence, there'd just be smoke floating through the room. That is where he first developed the idea for the play *The Rez Sisters*. He wrote the first draft there and workshopped it on the island too. After a year, he came back to Toronto with his script.

In Toronto there was another theatre company, slightly older than the one on Manitoulin. In 1982 the Native Earth Performing Arts was formed by a loose group of artistic friends, urban Indians who wanted to act. The company functioned as a collective. Basically people got together saying: "I have an idea for a show, let's go do it." There was no overall structure to the company, no artistic director, no administrator, no core funding, just a room at the Toronto Native Friendship Centre and an occasional show. Then Tomson came and became artistic director. He took his play *The Rez Sisters* to a dozen theatre companies in Toronto. Nobody was interested. They didn't want to do it for a very basic reason, in my opinion: the fundamental differences between Native theatre and European Western theatre or Canadian theatre. He took his play around, and every artistic director he showed it to said, "Nobody cares about a group of seven women wanting to play bingo" and "there's no drama in the story." I've had this experience, too, with one of my plays. What they were saying, by and large, is that European drama, is based on conflict. The story progresses through conflict, information is perceived through conflict. That is the Western dramatic structure, which is the opposite of Native theatre. To understand this you must remember Native theatre's origins in storytelling. Stories were told in small family groupings. For example, the Ojibway would be in family groupings during the winter because it was easier to feed a small group of people than a large one. People were living in close quarters. If somebody had a problem, or if somebody was angry and wanted to make a very aggressive point about something, it was frowned upon and discouraged because conflict would infringe upon the harmony of the community and therefore its survival. Overt or aggressive conflict was actively and urgently discouraged within the family group and this manifested itself within stories too. A lot of the traditional legends are more narrative than dramatic—the hero goes on a journey but he doesn't have to fight his way through, or slay dragons to get to the end. Again there are exceptions to that rule; I know of a lot of bloody legends within my Native community. But on the whole, conflict was discouraged within our community, and as a result our stories reflect that. *The Rez Sisters* is about a group of women going to Toronto to participate in the world's biggest bingo. They do that, then come back. There's no big fight, there's no big car chase, there's no big conflict *per se*. There's squabbling. But it's the squabbling of everyday life—not Shakespearean-style sword-fighting, which is a hell of a way to resolve conflict!

Most of the artistic directors didn't know how to handle this different way of telling a story. I have a play called *Someday* which is about the "scoop up" when Native children were taken away for adoption by the Children's Aid Society. It was produced last Christmas (1994) in Montreal. When I was first trying to interest Maurice Podbrey in producing my play, he said the structure went against everything he was taught about drama. All the information comes too easily, everybody gets along too well. He liked the story but felt it was missing something. Larry Lewis, who produced and directed both *Someday* and *The Rez Sisters* had a chat with Maurice, explained some things about Native theatre, and the play was produced.

Lack of conflict seems to be one of the fundamental differences between European and Native drama. For instance, one of the legends I know—again in rough because I'm not a storyteller—is Thunderbird children. Father thunderbird and thunderbird children fly around, doing the "thunderbird thing." The two children see a village of humans and watch what's going on. The male thunderbird sees the men out having these great epic battles and the female thunderbird sees the women giving birth and creating life. They become infatuated with human life. Back at thunderbird camp, the two children, after talking with each other, tell their father "We would like to become humans." One says, "I would like to become a great warrior" and the other one says "I would like to create life." Father thunderbird says, "Well, I wish you would remain here with me, but if that is your wish I will grant it under one condition. What you have to do is find me the cleanest lodge that exists. You have to go down to earth and find a house, a place to be born that is absolutely immaculate." The two thunderbird children go from village to village. They find some lodges that are very clean and some that are not very clean, but they can never find an absolutely immaculate and clean lodge.

One day they are travelling by a river and they see a woman heavy with child, washing herself in the river. They are curious and follow her back to her camp. They watch her enter her lodge and because they are invisible, they go in too. She has the cleanest lodge they've ever seen. So they say, "We've found it father. This is what you've asked and we've found it." As it happens, the woman gives birth to twins. The boy comes out of the birthing process covered in blood and immediately starts saying, "Oh no, I'm dying, I've been stabbed, I've been pierced, I'm never going to be a great warrior." The mother tells him, "No you're fine, you've just been born, you will grow up to be a great warrior." The same happens with the girl. The mother consoles the children who grow up to be a warrior and a great woman elder of the community. They live their lives, they die and they go back up to the great thunderbird father. Now that's a very rough telling of a legend, I'm not doing it justice. But in that legend there's no fight, there's no argument, there's no conflict really. They're given an objective, they achieve it, and they go on. This is the structure of a lot of traditional Native legends which, to reiterate, conflicts with the European dramatic process.

Because he couldn't get anybody to produce his play, Tomson Highway decided that he would have to produce it himself. It is a seven-character play and expensive to mount. Somehow Tomson managed to do it. He raised the money and he co-produced it with his friend Larry Lewis, who directed it. The first week it did abysmally. Part of the reason had to do with another common feature of Native theatre: the play had no major central character. *The Rez Sisters* has seven women, all of equal importance, all with an equally important story. No one person is more important than the other. Most people are not used to that. They are used to seeing a protagonist—Hamlet for example—at the centre of the story. Each of the Rez Sisters has her own story, and it is of equal weight and equal strength within the context of the play. The same can be said about *Dry Lips Oughta Move to Kapuskasing:* all seven men in the play have an equal and important story. This is why Tomson will never write for television, which requires protagonists and heroes.

So the first week *The Rez Sisters* almost died. Nobody came to watch it except for the reviewers. They had never seen anything like it before! It was like a breath of fresh air, something new, something interesting, something invigorating. So it had wonderful reviews. Many times in the first week or so, the director and stage manager had literally run out to the street, and handed free tickets to people passing by the Native Canadian Centre to come in and see the show. Then the word got out that it was fabulous. By the fourth week there was standing room only. They were turning people away. In the end, the play got such a great response that almost immediately there were offers from cities all across Canada to produce it. They ended up doing a production that toured from BC to Ontario, stopping in all the major capitals along the way, doing incredible business. Within the Native community, for the majority of us, *The Rez Sisters* marked the beginning of contemporary Native theatre because that's when people stood up and said, "Hey, what's this? People are telling their own story and they're telling it well."

Next came Highway's *Dry Lips*, which was a co-production between Theatre Passe-Muraille and Native Earth. Because of the success of *The Rez Sisters, Dry Lips* did amazing business. It did a three-city production—Winnipeg, Ottawa and Toronto (at the Royal Alex). It was the first Native play ever to be in any of those three places all at one time. From there, Native playwrights had their voice.

The second person to be produced was Daniel David Moses who is well known as a poet, and has also written short stories. Lately he has been getting more and more into theatre. Native Earth produced *Cloudy City*, his very first play, which did reasonably well. Around that time I was brought in as Artistic Director of Native Earth. Playwrights started to come out of the woodwork. We have a festival called "Weesageechak Begins to Dance." Chuck is another word for the Trickster, Nanabush, or the Raven. It is a festival or workshop of six new Native plays. They are given public readings. For the first festival, back in 1989, Tomson had to beat the bushes to find plays to workshop—Tomson and Dan were the only ones writing plays. He had to scramble to find six plays to workshop. Today I have a big stack of Native plays on my desk. I have to make tough decisions and weed out and pick six to produce. It's really quite striking, quite grand, to see how far Native theatre has come.

I was invited to be playwright-in-residence for Native Earth in the 1988-89 season. I'd been a journalist and I had written for television. I had done some documentaries and I was writing a drama series. The number of plays I had seen I could count on my fingers. I wasn't planning to get into theatre. Theatre was something done by dead White English people. But I was offered 20 weeks work—they had gotten a grant for playwright residency—20 weeks of salary just to come in and sit through rehearsals, so I accepted. I went in absolutely disinterested. But I was bitten by the bug and since 1989, I've had 22 productions of my eight plays. I feel so privileged to sit in the first row of Native theatre.

There are many interesting developments in Native theatre. We've been given back our voices to tell our stories. It is fascinating to see what stories are being told and what the voices are saying. I would say that a majority of plays produced in the past, and to a certain extent now, are very, very angry stories. They are talking about things that have happened that have prevented them from talking in the first place. Tomson likes to quote Lionel Longclaws from Saskatchewan who said that "before the healing can take place, the poison has to be exposed." This is the reasoning behind *Dry Lips Oughta Move to Kapuskasing*. I became a playwright in residence during the original rehearsal period of *Dry Lips*. This play was my introduction to Native theatre. I remember sitting through that rehearsal, seeing the play on stage. For anyone who has read or seen it, you know there's a horrific rape scene, where a young man with foetal alcohol syndrome rapes Nanabush, who is in the persona of Betsy Pegahmagahbow, and who is pregnant. He rapes her with a crucifix. The image of the young man with foetal alcohol syndrome raping Nanabush, who is at the centre of Native mythology, with a crucifix, just explodes with metaphoric intent. About the same time, there was a production of *The Ecstasy of Rita Joe*. Although it was written by a non-Native person, as I mentioned, it was an important step in the development of Native theatre, and I went to see it. In that play as well, there is a horrible rape.

And if we look at other plays, we find more rape scenes. There's mention of a rape in *The Rez Sisters*, there's a rape in *Moonlodge*, there's a homosexual rape in *Fireweed*, there are four or five rapes in *Night of the Trickster*, and I could name more. I'd say in 75 per cent of the Native plays written and produced, there is a rape. Why? One theory is that rape represents the horrific amount of sexual abuse that exists in Native communities because of the residential school system, because of alcoholism, because of the breakdown of the extended families, because of adoption. Sexual abuse is cyclical in that the abused becomes the abuser. The dramatic version of rape is also the perfect metaphor for what happened to Native culture. In many communities, culture was matrilinear or matriarchal. Another culture comes in, forcing itself on the community, basically eradicating everything there, subjugating that culture to its will.

I think that this (hi)story is still a large part of what Native playwrights and Native people in general are trying to work out through theatre, through art. This is important but sometimes the work can seem very fixated on that one point. I get a script on my desk and I wonder what the dysfunction *du jour* will be in *this* play. There are so many different aspects of Native culture waiting to be explored. I look at all the things that have happened to Native people that we're trying to document in our theatre, and I think what has gotten us through those periods is a sense of humour and a sense of storytelling. Those two things have kept us going. They have helped us grasp who we are. Native people have a very special sense of humour. Depending on where you are, it can be very sarcastic, biting and almost vicious, or it can be very laid-back. With a lot of my material I try to use humour. I have a series of plays that I refer to as "The Comedies" because I want to celebrate the Native sense of humour, a very important ingredient that has allowed us to survive the tragedies. I'm constantly urging people to explore different things about the Native community.

Because Native theatre is so young—it's barely 10 years old—we're still trying to find its parameters before cultural appropriation occurs—one way or another! People talk about taking our stories, but our stories are taking new forms too. Two years ago we produced a play called *Diva Ojibway*, a Native opera. I do Native comedies (I've been called the Neil Simon of the Native community). In two seasons, we are going to be presenting a show called *Shaman of Oz*, a Native version of the *Wizard of Oz*. The definition of Native theatre is continually expanding. It is still growing. In the 1970s, Native theatre was either a dramatization of a legend or about a rather didactic social issue that had to be explained, with no plot, or character. Now Native theatre can be practically anything. During the 1980s Native Earth was the only theatre company developing and producing Native theatre. I myself have six plays being produced across Canada this season (1995-96) and only one by a Native theatre company. Previously one play might be produced and then it would disappear. Now, people in other companies are saying, "I hear that's a good play, I'd like to see it, I'd like to produce it." Last Christmas (1994), there were two different productions of *The Rez Sisters*, one in Hamilton, one in London. Meanwhile my play *Someday* was running in Thunder Bay and Vancouver. The momentum is growing and growing and Native theatre, instead of being the exception, is now a dynamic component of contemporary Canadian theatre.

(1996)

The artificial tree:
native performance culture research 1991-1996 [1]

by Floyd Favel Starr

The concept, Native Performance Culture, could be described as developing practices of our ancestors. It came about not as a clearly formulated plan based on a clear vision, but as a feeling and intuition born out of personal, cultural and universal needs. There were no practical models to guide our diverse and contradictory Native Nations, save the visionary words and intuitions of certain Native artists of the past and present. So we began by trial and error, examining our own artistic training, our traditions, history, aspirations and ambitions, in light of the feeling and intuition which was taking us away from the known and familiar into the zone of incertitude and research. Who did we think we were?

The danger was to remain in an intellectual maze, in the sterile corridors of rhetoric and mystification, and political correctness.

"Developing a methodology based on the performance practices of our ancestors." What does this sentence mean? Is it a fusion/synthesis of the traditional and the contemporary? Or is it going beyond fusion and synthesis to the sources of the rivers of our cultures?

There was no choice but to begin, by making simple exercises that spoke for themselves. Exercises which can become enigmatic little puzzles which could allow us to mine the riches of our Soul. Exercises which fulfill the pretentious task of "developing a methodology."

I began to look to other cultures and world artists for inspiration. The words of Tadashai Suzuki, and of Butoh, were important in the formulation of the research. I could relate intellectually to Suzuki's work which rose out of a profound need for Japanese theatre artists to find their place within Western contemporary drama and thus articulate a method for actors based on Japanese performance principles. It is Butoh artists which have informed a spirit of research, poetic and vital, and an attitude of rebellion and individuality based on sound knowledge, necessary if we are to make our own unique paths.

After some years a process has become clear, a process that reduces Native songs and dances to bare essentials, a process that links us to, and leads us from, the sources of this country, our life, and the ancestors.

Through this process of reductionism we are able to isolate the basic building blocks of the song and dance, and these become the starting points for a creative and vital action. This does not differ in principle from other performance traditions; the main difference is that the reference points are from Native cultures and originate in this land. The artistic source is not transplanted and colonial, and from a Greco-Roman source.

This way of working with dances and songs through reducing them to their skeleton, is exemplified for me when one learns how to play the hand drum in a Plains Cree Round Dance style. The rhythm of the dancing and singing was explained to me in the image/action of "a duck bobbing in the lake water." This image, I understand now, is the basic DNA of the dance step, the voice, the drumming. This image is the technical and spiritual core of the dance and song.

Let's say we used the Round Dance spirit; we can also call it, the soul of the dance. This is revealed in the image of a duck bobbing in the lake water.

Through practice one searches for this rhythm, this Round Dance spirit. The spirit of the dance and singing is actually contained in the spaces between the waves of the water and the movement of the duck, between the drum beats and steps, between the dancers.

Through precision and firm precise guidelines, the performer can then approach the mysterious aspects of his/herself in relationship to an image, a classical or contemporary text, or a memory. The drumming and the singing also begin to stir up impulses and embers deep within the body of the actor. This stirs up the Spirit and develops the vigour and life force of the performer.

It is from this awakened, tender and volatile place in the body that the performer meets the text, the music, the dance, the literature, from any cultural source.

When the performer has elaborated a score of actions through this investigation, you have the possibility of articulating this action further. Maybe you add a text from *The Cherry Orchard,* or you add a fragment of Vivaldi's "Four Seasons." It is dependent on what you are working on. The main point is that the performer is working from their cultural source, through indigenous "creative structures." I have seen on videotape Hijikata dancing to a bagpipe version of "Amazing Grace." The anarchic relationship between the music and the dance would've not been possible without Hijikata's intensive investigation of, and grounding in, the Japanese body.

The Japanese have this word, *Ma. Ma* is the interval, the pause, in music and in dance. Butoh artists say that the ancestors and spirits dwell in this interval and pause. It is this we are talking about when we say the dance is in the intervals between the wave, between the movements of the duck from one wave to the next, between the drumbeats.

Working in this manner we begin to move away from an aesthetic that is the result of a "Métissage of forms", and not penetrate beyond this tempting veil to the terrain of impulses and sources which is what a theatre methodology needs to concern itself with.

One simple example of this is when a performer dances a traditional dance to contemporary world music (i.e. Cree Grass Dancer dancing to Jewish Klezmer music, or to a techno beat). Working in this fashion is related to the development of choreography for public presentation and we are remaining only in the area of style. This is valid for its own sake but is not related to methodology.

By reducing the dance to its essentials we move away from attempting to put rituals on stage. Putting the generic physical activity and ritual objects of a ritual on stage (the prayer, the sweetgrass, the actual dance, ritualistic behaviour) is a misguided attempt at developing a native aesthetic and only trivializes traditional actions which have a profound important purpose to our Nations. This leads to a pseudo mysticism and exoticism.

I had a dream where I and a group of people were working in a studio; our director told us that our work had no centre, and so we must find a centre. The director went away so we could have time to complete our task. The actors then placed an artificial tree in the middle of the stage as we understood that in many Native ceremonies, there is often a central votive image, like a fire or a tree.

The director came back to see the results of our work. Horrified, he said, "No, the centre should be invisible."

From this dream I think that, when we put aspects of our rituals on stage we are putting up artificial trees. The tree has no roots, and no animating spirit.

By working in the manner which we have indicated, I believe we can preserve the heart of our ceremonial life, by never revealing or showing it, yet be revitalized and transformed by it. In this way we can touch the spirit of the dance, and the souls of our ancestors which live in the fibres and sinews of our bodies and in the pauses and intervals.

It is not for nothing that our old shamans say, "This is not for show, do not sell this."

It is because of these words that we need to seek a way of working which follows these precepts. This precept stabbed me in my heart when I attended a ceremony in my home area a few years back. Groups of people were going towards the lodge and many of them were sick and pitiful. Their condition made it clear that this is all they have, this is their faith.

How empty and childish it would be for us artists to take elements of this and put them up for show and sale.

"We want essence in action. Freedom. It's not about executing traditional dance forms. We're for the basic embers, the skeleton. Those structures are the doors which will open into ourselves and the universe."

We can apply this understanding of how to work with the Plains Cree Round Dance to other dances and songs from other Native Nations.

For example, there is this Inuit song sung and drummed to a specific rhythm. The singer/dancer/drummer tells a story about a Raven who is flying and flying over a vast ocean. This raven begins to get tired and begins to sink into the water. The water reaches the Raven's feet, knees, waist, chest, neck, then the Raven drowns.

We transformed this traditional act into a creative exercise for the performer by:

1. Having the group sing the melody, and someone keep the drumming rhythm on a drum
2. A single actor then does the Raven's role
3. With his/her voice and personal internal body process, they must communicate the trials and process of the Raven
4. They communicate this, by improvising a melody line above the base melody of the group
5. The movement and voice is anchored in the specific Inuit song and dance.

Through the technical rules of the rhythm, the position of the spine, relationship to the ground, relationship to the song, the performer not only explores the story of the raven but also confronts inner resistance and fears and approaches the heart of this song and dance. At minimum, this exercise is a vigorous vocal and physical exercise.

Confusion between our native traditions and the world at large can be avoided if we use a model from the Iroquoian Confederacy as a guide. In the Two Row Wampum, made in the 1500s for a Treaty with the Dutch, a Wampum was made. On this Wampum are two blue lines on opposite sides of a belt, separated by an open expanse of white beads and shells. One line is the Law, Language, Religion and Customs of the Natives, and other line is the Law, Language, Religion and Customs of the Europeans. They are separate. If one tries to straddle the two lines, then it is like someone with one foot on one canoe, and the other foot in another canoe. If a storm comes up then the individual falls into the water.

This is how I understand and remember this Two Row Wampum belt. If I have made a mistake in its interpretation, then forgive me.

This image obligates us as Native artists to have a working practical knowledge of our languages, songs, dances, stories, and histories. Further than that, we apprehend and are in active collaboration with the world from our position on the opposite shore in a position of equality, and there is no internal conflict, colonization, or beggary.

Native Performance Culture is not a synthesis or fusion of the "traditional and the contemporary." It is an upstream journey to the source of the river of our culture, country and ourselves.

The concept of a synthesis or fusion between the traditional and the contemporary is a false misleading paradigm, and violates the heart of culture. A culture true to its source can only absorb foreign influences and transform and utilize these influences.

Hopefully these tracks can inspire others by providing some precise guidelines, and to individualize it, to suit their time and place, and take our common search further.

As the leader of the project, I would like to thank the Canada Council Arts Award Service. The other members of the research team are: Monique Mojica, Pura Fe, Muriel Miguel.

(1997)

Note

[1] Editor's note: The author wished to include the following proviso with the republication of this essay: "I also want to stress that there [are] many ways of working, and all are valid, and my essays [included in this volume] are just one aspect of one phase of my career" (personal correspondence, 28 October 2004).

Hybridity and Mimicry in the Plays of Drew Hayden Taylor

by Robert Nunn

> I remember once looking at a video tape of a drum group, shot on a reserve up near Manitoulin Island. I noticed one of the drummers seemed quite fair-haired, almost blond. I mentioned this to my girlfriend of the time and she shrugged saying, "Well, that's to be expected. The highway runs right through the reserve."
>
> —Drew Hayden Taylor, *Funny* (12)

I

For a non-Native academic to write about Native theatre in Canada is fraught with possible pitfalls, which I will not necessarily avoid. Terry Goldie, in his powerful paper "*Fear and Temptation* after Oka," reminded his audience of the risk of explaining or recuperating the productions of Native culture. Goldie concluded by advocating a role for the White critic: not silence, which can be oppressive too, but "a very loud silence, which analyzes the silencing and which provides opportunities, not to speak for the silenced, but to allow the silenced to speak" (17). Perhaps that could be glossed by a further comment Goldie makes in the preface to the *Anthology of Native Canadian Literature in English*, which he coedited with Daniel David Moses: "rather than appropriating the voice, educate yourself so you are ready to read, ready to watch. That's what the White audience should be doing" (Moses and Goldie, "Preface: Two Voices" xxii). Alan Filewod warns that there is an easy way out for a non-Native audience confronted with Native playwrights' postcolonial resistance to the "dominant culture of the colonizer" ("Averting" 18). It is to gloss over the historical reality that the White settler-invader culture of Canada colonized the First Nations, and to align Native plays with the settler culture's own postcolonial resistance to the hegemony of the imperial centre. Speaking of the plays of Tomson Highway, Filewod argues: "not only do we erase our own culpability in Highway's plays, but we reconstruct their cultural patterns to serve our own cultural project—a project that has historically erased the native peoples" (21).

It is crucial to keep this in mind when writing about Native theatre for many reasons, but in what follows one consideration stands out. That is, Native plays seem to be *already* assimilated into dominant White culture. The institution of theatre itself, however marginal it may appear to the dominant culture, is an integral part of it. To write plays, then, is to *appear* to work within the dominant culture. A successful Native play may take a place in the canon of Canadian drama and on the reading lists of Canadian drama courses. What resists this gravitational pull is the difference asserted in not *adopting* mainstream cultural forms but *mimicking* them. The hybrid thus created, I will argue, is not evidence of being half-way toward absorption, but on the contrary is a powerful form of resistance to absorption.

In this essay, I want to examine in some detail, and with especial regard to the plays of Drew Hayden Taylor, a particular postcolonial strategy: the appropriation and mimicry of popular culture, which produces a hybrid rearticulation of the original. First of all, however, I need to talk about the very idea of hybridity.

In *The Empire Writes Back*, Bill Ashcroft, Gareth Griffiths, and Helen Tiffin apply the term "postcolonial" to all cultures affected by the imperial process from the moment of colonization to the present day. The literatures of these cultures "emerged in their present form out of the experience of colonization and asserted themselves by foregrounding the tension with the imperial power, and by emphasizing their differences from the assumptions of the imperial centre. It is this which makes them distinctively post-colonial" (2). The authors discuss four models that have developed to account for the special character of postcolonial texts: national or regional models; race-based models; comparative models of varying complexity; and "more comprehensive comparative models which argue for features such as hybridity and syncreticity as constitutive elements of all post-colonial literatures (syncretism is the process by which previously distinct linguistic categories, and, by extension, cultural formations, merge into a single new form)" (15). They note that there is a vigorous debate about what "decolonization" implies. To some it means wiping away all traces of the colonial period, "recuperating pre-colonial languages and cultures," while "others have argued that not only is this impossible but that cultural syncreticity is a valuable as well as an inescapable and characteristic feature of all post-colonial societies and indeed is the source of their peculiar strength" (30).

Perhaps in Native theatre these positions coexist, not as a debate but as an internal dialogue between seemingly incompatible positions that are both necessary. Both positions, for instance, are visible in Monique Mojica's introduction to the issue of *Canadian Theatre Review* devoted to Native theatre in the Americas. She speaks of theatre "as an instrument of our recovery"; but she also speaks of "taking the language of colonization... and transforming it into a new theatrical language, borrowing the tools and techniques of European theatre to create our craft" (3).

Ashcroft and his coauthors go on to say that it is writers and critics of the Caribbean who have produced the most sophisticated models of hybridity and syncreticity. Caribbean writers such as Edward Brathwaite and Wilson Harris propose cross-culturality, hybridization, and syncreticity as not only inescapable realities but as "imaginative imperatives." The Caribbean playwright and poet Derek Walcott concurs, "describing himself as a 'mongrel', a 'neither proud nor ashamed bastard'" (Crow 20), and describing his writing as a "mulatto of style" (21). Without discounting the great difference between the situation of Caribbean writers and their Native counterparts, there are illuminating parallels. It is by now a well-accepted idea that Native theatre is cross-cultural, hybrid, and syncretic. Sheila Rabillard argues that Highway's plays exhibit postcolonial hybridity in Homi K. Bhabha's sense of the term: "part of the point of Bhabha's coinage is to suggest that the cultural products of the colonizer reappear in the hands of the colonized hybridized, transformed into something partially familiar to the dominant culture and yet new and estranging; still other if not, perhaps, the pure and metaphysically defining Other" (23).

II

The Trickster is a metonym of these energies of cross-culturality, hybridity, and syncreticity. Who or what is the Trickster? Rather than try to define the indefinable, I will simply quote Highway and Mojica. According to Highway,

> The "Trickster," [is] as pivotal and important a figure in our world as Christ is in the realm of Christian mythology. "Weesageechak" in Cree, "Nanabush" in Ojibway, "Raven" in others, "Coyote" in still others, this Trickster goes by many names and many guises. In fact, he can assume any guise he chooses. Essentially a comic, clownish sort of character, his role is to teach us about the nature and the meaning of existence on the planet Earth; he straddles the consciousness of man and that of God, the Great Spirit....
>
> Some say that Nanabush left this continent when the White man came. We believe she/he is still here among us—albeit the worse for wear and tear—having assumed other guises. Without the continued presence of this extraordinary figure, the core of Indian culture would be gone forever. (12-13)

And Mojica describes the Trickster in this way:

> Trickster goes between here and the spirit world, for the benefit of mankind. It represents constant change, transformation, moving on; Trickster becomes a shit-disturber when things get too static and can use sexuality, profanity and lewdness to achieve this. It mirrors us so we can see our follies—pushes us past them, pushes us on. Trickster is neither human nor animal, male nor female, good nor bad.... (qtd. in Cashman, "Toronto's Zanies" 23)

Trickster has been incarnated as a theatrical figure in a complex process of cross-cultural exchange. In the mid-1980s, Native Earth Performing Arts in Toronto ran workshops on the Trickster, recruiting the White performers Richard Pochinko and Ian Wallace as resources. Jennifer Preston writes:

> In the fall of 1984 Highway, Makka Kleist, Doris Linklater, and Mojica held a workshop to learn the tools necessary to approach the traditional Native trickster figures. They learned to use masks and

studied clowning techniques developed by Richard Pochinko and Ian Wallace of Toronto's Theatre Resource Centre.... A performance resulting from the workshop, *Clown Trickster's Workshop*, was produced at the Native Canadian Centre in September 1984.... Phase one of NEPA's history ended with *Trickster's Cabaret*, directed by Richard Pochinko and performed by Mojica, [Billy] Merasty, Kleist and Gary Farmer. For the production each actor developed a trickster figure— different Native cultures have variations on the trickster. (139)

Wallace and Pochinko anticipated (and inspired) Native Earth's hybridization of Western and Native cultures. In particular, Pochinko brought the tradition of European clowning and his training with Jacques Lecoq in Paris to this work with Native Earth. But Pochinko had studied not only with Lecoq but subsequently with "the remarkable American Indian clown, Jonsmith." The European and Native American tradition "came together to form the Pochinko technique. At the core of this approach is the idea that if we face all the directions of ourselves, North, South, East, West, Up, Down, we can only laugh—at the beauty and wonder that is in us" (Cashman, "Collective Tribute" 37). Thus, the six directions of Native cosmology were aligned with the six masks of the Lecoq method (Cashman, "Toronto's Zanies" 22). The *Clown Trickster's Workshop* added a seventh mask, that of the Trickster. Going still further back in time, Pochinko's interest in Native American culture may have grown out of the Toronto production of *Hair*, in which he was assistant stage manager. According to Warren Hartman, my colleague in the Theatre Program at Brock University who worked on the show as a design consultant, the entire company of *Hair* "grooved" on Native culture. They called themselves a "tribe" or a "confederation," referred to the producer as the "Silver Chief," et cetera.

This is a complex story. It begins with hip young people who thought Native culture was groovy, something dangerously close to the "plastic shamanism" that Spiderwoman Theater, the Native women's collective based in New York, took aim at in their *Winnetou's Snake Oil Show from Wigwam City*. The next step is something that still looks like cultural appropriation—Pochinko after all was non-Native and took something from Native culture and incorporated it into his own technique. Indeed, there is substantial evidence that he invented his Native guide, Jonsmith, when he was studying Native traditions and seeking to integrate them with Lecoq's techniques. [1] And then he gave these appropriations back to Native artists—not as he had found them but as he had transformed them into a hybrid of Native and European. To complicate the picture, the other important resource for Native Earth's creation of theatrical Tricksters is Spiderwoman Theater. Muriel and Gloria Miguel (Mojica's aunt and mother respectively) established a close relationship with Native Earth at the same time. Their work also witnesses to the power of the Trickster. And they too are instances of cross-cultural syncreticity: they appropriated cultural forms from White culture (thus doing a Pochinko in reverse) in deriving their theatrical techniques from the Open Theatre (Peter Feldman, Joe Chaikin, and others), whose work in turn was extremely eclectic, appropriating traditions within and outside Western culture. The moral is that the Trickster is too foolish, and too wise, to make clear distinctions between White appropriation of Native voice and Native culture. He/she actually seems to have thrived on a breathtaking spiral of appropriation and counter-appropriation.

This postcolonial hybridity/syncreticity not only characterizes the *process* of developing theatrical forms of the Trickster but also characterizes the *products*: the remarkable series of clowns, fools, and Tricksters that appear in the work of Highway, Mojica, and others: René Highway as Nanabush in *The Rez Sisters,* Billy Merasty as The Fool in *The Sage, the Dancer and the Fool,* Doris Linklater and Gloria Eshkibosh alternating as Nanabush in *Dry Lips Oughta Move to Kapuskasing,* and Mojica as Princess Buttered-On-Both-Sides in *Princess Pocahontas and the Blue Spots.* Or more exactly, the spirit of Nanabush that informs these plays seems to always bear marks of hybridity. For it is important not to play the game of "Spot the Trickster," which Taylor and fellow playwright Moses playfully accuse academics of doing (Taylor, *Funny* 88). What is important is to recognize the Tricksterish spirit "permeat[ing] almost all work presented as Native theatre" (Taylor, "Re-Appearance" 51-52).

Maybe I could name this section of the essay "Raven meets Lecoq."

III

At the beginning of this essay, I cautioned that Native theatre's specific postcoloniality can be neutralized by assimilating it into the broader postcoloniality of the settler-invader culture. But the postcolonial itself can be neutralized. Postcolonial hybridity as a creative dismantling of the colonial privileging of the centre over the margin is one thing. But syncreticity/hybridity from the perspective of the majority White culture can be quite another thing; it can easily be reabsorbed and deprived of its subversive power. That is, it can be absorbed into postmodernism's mania for what Susan L. Foster calls "the shopping mall of cultural exotica" (69). Cultural pluralism, which is one manifestation of Western culture's postmodern crisis of authority, tends to draw expressions of postcolonial hybridity into its own orbit and in effect strip them of difference and re-present them as just so many cultural flavours of the month. As Roger Copeland says of "postmodern impurity" and "the current vogue for the 'multicultural,'"

> Every other day, a press release arrives in the mail announcing some new amalgam of tap and kathakali, of break dancing and butoh. This is the blurring of boundaries (national and otherwise) that Jean-Francois Lyotard describes as the "postmodern condition":
>
> One listens to reggae, watches a western, eats McDonald's food for lunch and local cuisine for dinner, wears Paris perfume in Tokyo and "retro" clothing in Hong Kong. (Lyotard 76) Yes, it sounds terribly fashionable, and at the moment at least, it is. (66-67)

Helen Tiffin likewise warns against a confusion of the postcolonial and the postmodern; she sees the latter term being "applied hegemonically" to assimilate postcolonial works into the very culture from which they are asserting their difference. She remarks that although there are a number of strategies characteristic of both the postcolonial and the postmodern, "they are energized by different theoretical assumptions and by vastly different political motivations" (172).

This is emphatically true of the Trickster. No matter how syncretic the construction of the contemporary image of the Trickster, he/she/it is not an instance of postmodern impurity. Highway may note, "We grew up with myths; they're the core of our identity as a people. But I'm urban by choice, so I translate that mythology into contemporary terms. The trickster now takes strolls down Yonge Street and goes into bars" (qtd. in Kaplan 31). And although White culture, not to mention White academics, may find Highway fashionable at the moment, what he is talking about is first and foremost a postcolonial "counter-discourse" recovering Native culture in the teeth of still enormous assimilative pressure (see Slemon 3-5).

Perhaps, though, there is a way for non-Natives to view the "impurity" of the contemporary Trickster without clawing it back into the terms of reference of White culture. Perhaps we could see the Trickster as standing for the potential for *mutual* "contamination" (Brydon 191) of Native and non-Native cultures. To quote Ashcroft and his coauthors,

> post-colonial literary theory... like much post-colonial literature... attempts to construct a future.... Both literary theorists and cultural historians are beginning to recognize cross-culturality as the potential termination point of an apparently endless human history of conquest and annihilation justified by the myth of group "purity" and as the basis on which the post-colonial world can be creatively stabilized. (36)

Nanabush seems indifferent to the very idea of "purity"; perhaps she/he/it has a utopian element. Wilson Harris sees the West African Trickster Anancy as an image for the process of escape from the politics of dominance and subservience: "the trickster character of the spider man... offers a narrow psychic space through which radical transformation can occur" (qtd. in Ashcroft, Griffiths, and Tiffin 35).

Although we must keep in mind Tiffin's warning against a too-easy assimilation of the postcolonial into the postmodern, they do indeed share a number of strategies, the most important being the "attack on binary structuration of concept and language" (172). It is generally recognized that one binary structuration attacked by postmodernism is the opposition of high art to popular culture. Frederic Jameson speaks of "the effacement of some key boundaries or separations" in postmodernism, notably the "erosion of the older distinction between high culture and so-called mass or popular culture" (14). The implications of this for Native theatre are considerable. Andreas Huyssens writes:

> A new creative relationship between high art and certain forms of mass culture is, to my mind, indeed one of the major marks of difference between high modernism and the art and literature which followed it in the 1970s and 1980s both in Europe and the United States. And it is

precisely the recent self-assertion of minority cultures and their emergence into public consciousness which has undermined the modernist
belief that high and low culture have to be categorically kept apart; such
rigorous segregation simply does not make much sense *within* a given
minority culture which has always existed outside in the shadow of the
dominant high culture. (246-47)

What Huyssens proposes about minority cultures applies equally to postcolonial
cultures in that both subvert the claim to universality made by the dominant culture,
whether it conceives of itself as a majority or as an imperial centre.

This suggests a complex reciprocal influence of Native and White culture. The far
greater self-assertion of Native culture over the last two decades (a self-assertion that,
it must be noted, would have faced criminal sanctions before the 1950s) has perhaps
played a part in undermining the dominant culture's segregation of high and popular
art; in turn, the postmodern erosion of the distinction between high and popular culture has perhaps opened up a space for those other voices that had been historically
silenced by, among other things, the overwhelming prestige of high culture. This shift
is evident in theatre itself. Certainly in our time, theatre is perceived as high culture;
even mass-marketed theatre such as *The Phantom of the Opera* proclaims the elite
status of those who "resist no longer," as the authoritative and "cultured" voice in the
television ads intones.

Rabillard offers a provocative interpretation of the presence of popular culture
in Native plays:

One could argue that Highway's deliberate flouting of decorum, his
blending of borrowings from high and low White culture also serves
to create the hybrid. In *Dry Lips* he combines mystic juke boxes, country-and-western hit songs, and an amateur hockey league with evocations of Greek drama and Shakespearean comedy. The strategies and
forms of opera are juxtaposed in *The Rez Sisters* with the low excitements
of a monster bingo. Such conjunctions of popular and elite can subtly
derail the schooled responses of a mainstream audience, as can the
unexpected combinations of the most distressing subject matter—rape,
suicide, alcoholism—with sight gags, comic fart effects, and the like.
They also suggest a perspective from the margins of the dominant
society—a somewhat detached point of view from which "high" and
"low" might appear in a different light and with an altered value. While
it could be flattering to the dominant society to see its serious cultural
products sedulously aped, it is another matter entirely to find the songs
of Kitty Wells on an equal footing with evocations of Shakespearean
drama; certainly this is an estranging use that refuses to accept the
cultural products of the dominant society according to that society's
estimations. (19-20)

This is another way of looking at the syncretic nature of the work of Highway, Spiderwoman, and others. A lot of what enters into this work is material lifted from low culture (the literal meaning of "lifted" testifies to my unconscious association of theatre and high culture). The Trickster seems to find all this stuff lying about tempting to play with. There does not appear to be the gulf between traditional Native culture and the popular culture of the mainstream that Theodor Adorno felt existed between Schoenberg and Tin Pan Alley. So Nanabush in *Dry Lips* plays with hockey, "Guitarzan" and other top 40 trash, and Marilyn Monroe, as well as with the Virgin Mary, Greek mythology, and the institution of theatre itself. Nanabush in *The Rez Sisters* is both a seagull and a bingo MC. Princess Buttered-On-Both-Sides, whom Mojica refers to as "Coyote in drag" (qtd. in Cashman, "Toronto's Zanies" 23), is a composite of beauty-pageant contestant, cigar store squaw, Hollywood movie Indian, Marilyn Monroe, doowop group, and the legend of Pocahontas.[2] Floyd Favel appropriates the conventions of film noir in *Lady of Silences*. Beatrice Mosionier in *Night of the Trickster* creates a hybrid blend of karate and Native ceremony. Daniel David Moses cites vaudeville in *Almighty Voice and His Wife* and science fiction in *Kyotopolis*. The question that calls for further work is: what use is made of this material? It may come from popular culture, and popular culture may have been pushed to the margin for a long time, but there are margins and there are margins. Popular culture is still produced by the dominant culture and carries the enormous hegemonic force of the dominant culture's attitudes, assumptions, and myths. Native theatre cannot pick up material from popular culture without reinscribing the unequal relation between Native people and non-Native society. What does the Trickster do with this stuff, which is far from neutral, far from innocent?

I might call this section of the essay (ambivalently) "Rabbit Meets Bugs Bunny"— or "Coyote Meets the Roadrunner."

IV

In the remainder of this essay, I would like to address this question with reference to the plays of Drew Hayden Taylor,[3] which are particularly interesting as hybrid crossings of Native and popular culture.[4] Taylor's body of dramatic writing is unified by a central concern: to restore a sense of laughter as a core element of Native culture. And to do so he appropriates popular culture forms, particularly television comedy, walking a deliberately risky line between borrowing from mainstream popular culture in order to make it speak to the condition of Native peoples, and producing work that mainstream White audiences can enjoy as light comedies employing familiar conventions. Double-edged stuff—although even for a White spectator, the second option is not all that simple. To judge by my experience of Taylor's plays, White spectators are surrounded by Native spectators, and of course vice versa. A White spectator cannot help but be aware that the response from the Native spectators rules out merely enjoying the play as a light comedy. The humour is coming from a very specific cultural frame of reference, which the White spectator does not share but cannot help but be aware of. Taylor explains why he writes comedies:

I think the way I write is a result of my upbringing. Growing up on the reserve, I was surrounded by this marvellous sense of humour. I have a reputation as a humourist, but I'm no match for some of my uncles and aunts. Even in the darkest moments, there were always sparks of humour. I think that's how we survived 500 years of oppression. It was our humour that kept us sane. (qtd. in Lawless)

Taylor's full-length plays come in two flavours. The first is the "Blues" series, of which there are two so far: *The Bootlegger Blues* (premiered 1990, published 1991) and *The Baby Blues* (premiered 1995, published 1997); you could steal a line from Goldsmith and call them "laughing comedies." The other plays—*Someday* (premiered 1991, published 1993) and *Only Drunks and Children Tell the Truth* (premiered 1996, published 1998)—are "sentimental comedies," plays in which Taylor "discovered the power of tears" (qtd. in Lawless). As the chronology indicates, there is not a progression from one series to the other but rather an overlap. But following Taylor's hint that the discovery of tears came after the discovery of laughter, I will consider the "Blues" plays first, concentrating on *The Baby Blues*, since for the purpose of this essay, a lot more is going on in it than in the earlier *The Bootlegger Blues*, in which the hybrid crossing of Native humour and the conventions of situation comedy is relatively uncomplicated.

The Bootlegger Blues has a situation (a good Christian woman has bought far too much beer for a fundraising event, cannot return it, must get rid of it somehow, and turns to bootlegging), stereotypical characters (the protagonist's madcap daughter and her common-law husband, the Indian yuppie; the young lovers; the drifter who dances at powwows), a tidy ending with one loose end promising further situations, and the steady procession of funny lines that is a defining characteristic of sitcom.

The Baby Blues, like its predecessor, is a cross between Native humour and the conventions of a television situation comedy. Its situation is essentially the same as before: a powwow and the odd group of people it brings together. It features type characters: Pashik, the rebellious teenage girl; Jenny, her equally strong-willed mother; Noble, the fancy dancer from the earlier play, a little long in the tooth now; Skunk, his rival, an up-and-coming young dancer; Amos, the wise older man who runs the snack bar; and Summer, the White wannabe who proudly claims to be one sixty-fourth Native. The play has the insistent driving logic of sitcom: keep 'em laughing, make the lines funny. Its plot revolves around the aging dancer Noble's discovery that he is the father of the pretty teenager he has been trying to seduce (17 years ago, he succeeded with her mother). Jenny insists that he stay a while and give his daughter a chance to get to know him, making sure he will by stealing a few parts from his truck. In true sitcom style, the play ends with a punchline promising more to come: Amos, the wise elder, a fancy dancer in his youth, discovers that he is Noble's father. The play ends as both men faint dead away from surprise.

What makes this play rich is its double, contradictory take on the relations between White and Native cultures. Noble's ludicrous struggle to deny that he is aging is aligned with White culture's obsession with staying young, while his eventual acceptance of maturity and fatherhood is aligned with Native acceptance of what the Creator gives you. In moving from the former to the latter position, Noble gains wisdom in accordance with his Native heritage. But at the same time, the play mocks the notion of uncontaminated Aboriginal authenticity and celebrates the syncretic and hybrid.

At the beginning of her essay on Highway, Rabillard examines the anthropologist Paul Radin's introduction to the famous collection of Winnebago Trickster myths as told by Sam Blowsnake, in which he insists that they are uncontaminated by contact with White culture; that, in Rabillard's words, "in their authentic Otherness [they are] markers of the division between White and Native North American cultures" (17). To do so he must discount their possible contamination by the semi-Christian peyote cult to which Blowsnake's father belonged, and any alterations Blowsnake himself may have made—that is, their origin must be pushed as far back in time as possible. Goldie underlines the irony of such a position: the shaping of the indigene into a "historical artifact" is a "commodity in the semiotic field of the indigene" constructed and constantly reproduced by White discourse. It is in effect Whites, not indigenes, who test indigenous culture for authenticity: "A corollary of the temporal split between this golden age and the present degradation is to see indigenous culture as true, pure, and static. Whatever fails this test is not really a part of that culture" (*Fear* 17). Taking this logic to its limit, the only authentic Indian is a dead Indian. As Goldie notes, "There are, of course, some Indians who are not dead. But are they Indians?" (168). If that is too harsh, the words of Trinh T. Minh-ha are only slightly less so:

> Today, planned authenticity is rife; as a product of hegemony and a remarkable counterpart of universal standardization, it constitutes an efficacious means of silencing the cry of racial oppression. We no longer wish to erase your difference. We demand, on the contrary, that you remember and assert it. At least, to a certain extent. (89)

The Baby Blues makes great fun of Whites in search of authentic Indianness, confronting the White search for the true (that is, vanishing) Indian with thoroughly hybrid real Indians—who are signified metonymically by Amos's famous "Fortune Scones," the recipe for which was included in the program notes at the production of the play at Theatre Passe Muraille in Toronto in November 1997:

NOBLE: Making some bannock?
AMOS: Kinda. It's a special kind of bannock. I call it Fortune Scones.
NOBLE: Fortune Scones?
AMOS: Got the idea in a Chinese restaurant. I fry them with little philosophical Indian sayings in the middle. People love them.
NOBLE: You're kidding?!
AMOS: No, it sells. White people will buy anything. (24)

"Sort of a vision quest in a bun," remarks Noble. The play is full of wise sayings, inside and outside of the Fortune Scones, coming from a wonderful hodgepodge of sources and often playfully labelled as wise: "all that glitters is not gold, and all that's black is not coal" (25); "sometimes the yellow brick road ain't all it seems to be" (36); "seize the day" (37); "a child makes mistakes. A man corrects them" (42); "never trap on another person's trap line"; "eat, drink, and be merry, for tomorrow they may put you on a Reserve"; "check the authentic Native totem-pole for a 'Made In Korea' label" (49); "life is a circle. Try not to get lost" (61).

Summer is disconcerted to find that Amos and Noble are not fluent in Mohawk or Ojibway and in fact know more French and Latin (Latin picked up in a residential school): "Wait a minute. This isn't how it's supposed to be!"

> AMOS: There is something you have to understand about Native
> people. Just because we're proud of who and what we are, doesn't
> mean we can't appreciate the rest of the world out there.
> I personally think there's no better food than a wild-rice casserole
> with deer meat. However, I also get a hard on for a good lasagna. It
> doesn't have to be one or the other.
> SUMMER: Oh, you are so wise.
> AMOS: *(aside to NOBLE)* They love stuff like this. (26)

Indeed, Summer's search for authentic Indians is driven by her sense of sharing White guilt for the destruction of the pure Indian culture of the timeless past, and her desire to do her bit to atone. But as Goldie points out, that very thing actually reinforces the White ownership of the criteria for authenticity: "the sincerity of the guilt felt for the mistreatment of the Aborigine in the past does not allow the Aborigine to be other than of the past" (*Fear* 149).

This combination of White guilt and White ownership of the yardstick for measuring authenticity is held up to mockery in lines like these: "Oh, listen to the children of nature playing, being one with the lake. Oh, it is bliss, sheer bliss. The harmony I feel in this place. Here I am, surrounded by trees, flowers, grass, squirrels, and Native People. Tree to tree. First Nations. Aboriginal people in their natural environment" (*Baby Blues* 4). It is exactly here that I think the Trickster intervenes. I think his presence can be sensed in the following exchange:

> SUMMER: You were going to tell me some Indian legends. I do so
> want to get in touch with my ancestral heritage.
> NOBLE: I'll help you touch whatever you want. Okay, legends. Oh yes,
> legends. Okay. There were these three little pigs.... (32)

Trickster dekes around White criteria of Aboriginal authenticity with ease, as I tried to suggest in my discussion of Native Earth's Trickster workshops. Trickster is both as authentically Aboriginal as they come and utterly indifferent to notions of authenticity. If Trickster can turn himself into a woman by borrowing an elk's liver for a vulva and an elk's kidneys for breasts (Rabillard 3), it is child's play to borrow the Three Little Pigs.

The Baby Blues takes this Trickster hybridity a step further, in a direction whose meaning is clarified by Bhabha's analysis of postcolonial mimicry. In the person of

Summer—the White wannabe, so proud of being (possibly) one sixty-fourth Native, proud of driving a "wonderfully symbolic" Thunderbird, immensely pleased with herself for having taken a first-year university course in Native Studies, thrilled to be at her first powwow—the play mocks the romantic notions of the "authentic Indian" prevalent in popular culture. Summer has lines such as "he's being one with Mother Earth and Father Sky" (39), derived from White romanticization of that "vanishing Indian." As with Radin, it's a White voice uttering authoritative statements drawing a clear-cut line between White culture and what constitutes true Indianness. For a Native dramatist to play such statements back is an act of mimicry that questions their authority. For Native characters in the play to do so doubles the mimicry. As Bhabha argues, "Hybridity is a *problematic* of colonial representation and individuation that reverses the effects of the colonialist disavowal [of the oppression of the colonized Other], so that other 'denied' knowledges enter upon the dominant discourse and estrange the basis of its authority—its rules of recognition" (98, emphasis in original). And further, "The display of hybridity—its peculiar 'replication'—terrorises authority with the *ruse* of recognition, its mimicry, its mockery" (99-100). [5] Throughout the play, we hear the White discourse concerning the "authentic Indian" being mimicked by the Native characters themselves:

> SUMMER: Excuse me, but, if you don't mind me asking, where are
>   you going with the towel. A sweatlodge maybe?
> SKUNK: A swim.
> SUMMER: Oh.
>   *SUMMER looks disappointed, and SKUNK catches this. His attitude*
>   *changes.*
> SKUNK: Ah yes... I'm going for my... morning purification...
>   cleansing swim, in the lake... Mother Earth's lake... the tears of
>   Mother Earth.
> SUMMER: Really?!
> SKUNK: Yes, I do it every morning... to greet our brother the sun.
>   Right around that bend is a secluded bay where I... reveal myself to
>   the world; pay homage to the land, the water and the sun. And
>   wash.... (6-7)

And later in the play:

> AMOS: ...Summer, I'm Amos and this here is Noble.
> SUMMER: Noble?! Is that the English translation of your Native name,
>   like "Noble Warrior" or "Noble Eagle that Flies Across the Blue Sky
>   to Greet the Coming Dawn"?
> NOBLE: Actually... no, that sounds good. I'll go with that. (27-28)

Some of the funniest moments in this play have to do with Native mimicry of White discourse about the authentically Native, or, to paraphrase Minh-ha, "making up" one's mind and painting oneself thick with authenticity (88). The laughter in the mixed audience is probably rather complex. For the non-Native spectator, there is the uncomfortable feeling that his or her stereotypical and/or New Age notions about

Native culture are picking up a peculiar echo, that we are the "We" impersonated by Minh-ha: "We came to listen to that voice of difference likely to bring us *what we can't have* and to divert us from the monotony of sameness" (88). Perhaps Bhabha speaks for the Native spectator:

> Culture, as a colonial space of intervention and agonism, as the trace of the displacement of symbol to sign, can be transformed by the unpredictable and partial desire of hybridity. Deprived of their full presence, the knowledges of cultural authority may be articulated with forms of "native" knowledges or faced with these discriminated subjects that they must rule but can no longer represent. (99)

Native mimicry of White pronouncements on authentic Indianness is easy to talk about compared to the more difficult matter of Native mimicry of the conventions of the most popular genre on television, situation comedy. I have said that the whole play is a hybrid of Native humour and sitcom. How do you catch that mimicry in the act? I will address this question obliquely by examining a related instance of postcolonial hybridity and mimicry in the first of Taylor's sentimental comedies, *Someday*.

Someday was adapted by Taylor from a Christmas story he wrote for *The Globe and Mail* (24 December 1990). It concerns a Native woman, Anne Wabung, whose daughter was taken from her and put up for adoption thirty-five years ago at a time when thousands of Native children in Canada were seized by Children's Aid workers from "unsuitable" Native parents and placed in non-Native families, a time now referred to as "the scoop-up"; the daughter, born Grace, now Janice, who has grown up in a White middle-class family and become a lawyer, having traced her birth mother, comes to see her. The reunion is brief and painful; finally, the daughter cannot bear recognizing that a member of the culture she grew up in took away an Indian woman's child out of arrogance and stupidity. The play is written in the style of a heart-warming Christmas television special, but with subversive effect. The situation—Christmas, a homecoming—is played for sentiment and humour in order to provide a disarming frame for the recognition scene. Another element out of television sitcom—the mother discovers at the beginning of the play that she holds a lottery ticket worth five million dollars—provides a powerful irony: arbitrariness imposed the loss, and since it is the publicity around the lottery win that puts Janice on the trail of her mother, arbitrariness governs the return.

The cosy familiarity of a television Christmas special is evoked throughout the play. The set's dominant feature, a large picture window, is foregrounded by Rodney, who is the perennial boyfriend of Anne's younger daughter, Barb, and who has the clown's ability to pass back and forth between the fictional world and the world of the audience:[6] "Kind of looks like a big television set, doesn't it? Or a movie screen. Oh, the drama of it all" (3-4). References to "How the Grinch Stole Christmas" and "It's a Wonderful Life" abound. But this is not a Christmas special, it is a mimicry of one. In Taylor's hands, the Christmas special's ideological agenda, reinforcing the perennial optimism of the dominant middle class, promising a warmhearted resolution of all problems in individualistic terms, is made explicit as one of the "cultural products of the colonizer" (Rabillard 23) and then wrecked by the stunning inability of the form to resolve the "problem" of cultural genocide.

At the end of the play, Rodney watches what is unbeknownst to him a heart-rending farewell embrace in silhouette through the picture window-cum-television screen.

> Ah, isn't that touching? Looks like there'll be three stockings over the fireplace for sure. This year, Santa came in a Saab. If I was sentimental I'd say all this was what Christmas was all about. It's a good thing I'm not. Forty-five minutes to the Grinch. And the nog. The sun has set over the lake and it's really starting to get cold, but I don't care cuz I feel warm inside and all is well with the world.
> *JANICE walks down the driveway.*
> JANICE: Ah, finished?
> RODNEY: Yep, it's all safe and sound. The car's up the road. Figured I'd give the driveway a going over quickly before I head home. No sense in you getting stuck again. I see things are going well reunion-wise. *(beat)* You've really made their Christmas. God, what a week—millionaires, long lost relatives—has the makings of a great made-for-tv movie.
> [Janice tells him she's leaving.]
> RODNEY: But what about Anne and Barb? It's not supposed to end this way. This should be a happy movie like "It's a Wonderful Life."
> JANICE: Don't tell me about movies. I'm an entertainment lawyer. Movies are my life. Ironic, isn't it? (78-79)

The Christmas special is the dominant instance in this play of the culture industry's apparatus of representation, and the main target of Taylor's mimicry and mockery. Bhabha suggests a further thought: the sentimentality of the dominant representations offered to the public in popular culture *must* function as a way of writing over the actual history of how the dominant culture got here in the first place—through bloodshed, conquest, forced expropriation, and systematic oppression of the conquered. Bhabha argues that the discourse of the colonizer *must* be an *Entstellung*, Freud's term for the

> overall effect of the dream-work: the latent thoughts are transformed into a manifest formation in which they are not easily recognisable. They are not only transposed, as it were, into another key, but *they are also distorted in such a fashion that only an effort of interpretation can reconstitute them.* (105)

When the postcolonial subject interrogates the discourse of the colonizer in his own context, something drastic happens to that overwriting: "The hybrid object... retains the actual semblance of the authoritative symbol but re-values its presence by re-siting it as the signifier of *Entstellung – after the intervention of difference*"(99, emphasis in original). As Jenny Sharpe observes, "The trajectory of Bhabha's work has moved him increasingly closer toward situating the slippages of colonial author-ity in a native appropriation of its signs" (101).

Further ironic references to movies and television occur throughout the play. Anne and her husband Frank's first date was Anne's first movie—Hitchcock's "Rear Window":

> It took me a while to get into it. You gotta understand, I'd never seen a movie before, or even been in an apartment building. So it took me a while, but pretty soon I got to like it. I even found it funny. Reminded me of home, those people looking out their windows at other people's business. I loved it. (35)

Anne rewrites a text from the colonizers and transforms it into a postcolonial text marked by hybridity—Hitchcock meets the Rez.

> ANNE: ...From then on, we practically lived in that theatre. We were married a year later and spent our wedding night there.
> RODNEY: Your wedding night?
> ANNE: It was a double feature. (35)

Anne named her firstborn child Grace after Grace Kelly, ultimately producing the irony of an adoptee originally named after Grace Kelly ending up as an entertainment lawyer who says "Movies are my life."

Native appropriation of the movies is a political act. As Anne recalls, "Nobody in the village went to see movies, but Frank wanted me to go with him. We had a hard time convincing my parents to let me go" (34).

> Well, Friday came and he arrived in his pickup truck with different coloured doors on it. In town there was a whole line-up of White people right around the corner. Some of them looked at us funny. I just looked down. I still have trouble looking White people in the eye. But not Frank. He looked right back. They didn't look much longer. (34-35)

The movie theatre, the movies, and the whole apparatus of representation belong to the Whites and are soaked through and through with their cultural myths, attitudes, and assumptions. Natives do not belong there. Frank says "move over." Frank and Anne sit there and what they watch ends up traced through and through by Native experience.

So is Native culture traced through by the pervasive narrative patterns of White culture.[7] And not just at the ending where Rodney is distressed that the Christmas special is coming apart, but earlier in the play when Rodney warns Anne that returning an adopted child to its birth family and community does not guarantee a happy ending. He tells her about a Native girl taken from her parents at age four and returned after a ten-year legal battle:

> Think about it. This teenager, raised in the city, forcibly taken from the White family she grew up with and loved, shipped off to this isolated

reserve way up north, where she didn't know anybody, or even the language. She was living in poverty for the first time in her life. She didn't know how to relate, make friends, how to live. She didn't fit in. She was gang raped by a group of boys on the reserve. Nobody likes an outsider.

ANNE: Where was that girl's mother? Where was her family? That story should have been a happy story. (15)

Only Drunks and Children Tell the Truth is a sequel to *Someday*. Anne has just died. Barb and Rodney, joined by Rodney's adopted brother, Tonto, come to Toronto and persuade Janice/Grace to come back to the reserve to say a proper farewell to her birth mother. Once there, with the help of a great deal of alcohol (hence the title), she overcomes the vast distance between her actual life and the life she might have lived and grieves for her mother. The extremes—a vaudeville drunk act (and hangover act) and the deep sorrow that for one reason or another all four characters share—meet to produce a complex and powerful effect.

Running through the play as a surreal counterpoint to the lost and found story of the protagonist is a brilliant Native mimicry of one of the mainstays of popular culture: the supermarket tabloid. Rodney, Barb, and Tonto casually reveal to Grace that Amelia Earhart did not die in a plane wreck on 3 July 1937. By 21 November 1937, she had found her way to the Otter Lake Reserve where she has been living incognito as Amy Hart for the last fifty-five years. She is now an old lady in her nineties, in a wheelchair, speaks fluent Ojibway, and is the godmother of Grace. One can picture the headline: "Missing Aviatrix Found on Indian Reserve."

Another even sneakier mimicry of popular culture is that Rodney's adopted older brother is nicknamed Tonto. For quite a while, the audience is allowed to assume that the name comes from the Lone Ranger movies and television series. But it turns out to be derived from his pronunciation of "Toronto" as a small child, although at one point he does answer to his name with "Kemosaabe." The name is a Native mimicry of a White representation of a Native, with—surprise, surprise—"nothing at all" to do with the original.

What do I call this section of the essay? "Weesageechak meets the Great Blob"?

V

To return to the complex relation between the postcolonial and the postmodern, Taylor's plays clearly show both the affinities and the striking differences between them. Taylor's mimicry of White discourse about Natives and of commercial television ambivalently acknowledges *and* undermines their authority; the "typical, post- modern paradoxical form" of parody, as Linda Hutcheon has argued, functions in exactly this way (8). Postcolonial mimicry, postmodern parody—what's the difference? Perhaps we could put it this way. The postmodern artist paradoxically acknowledges and challenges the centre of his/her own culture by assuming a "marginal or ex-centric position" (Hutcheon 3). The postcolonial artist does not assume such a position. It has been imposed and maintained by the imperial centre, and his/her mimicry/parody of its authoritative discourse is an urgent matter of survival and resistance. As Adam and Tiffin argue,

> Pastiche and parody are not simply the new games Europeans play, nor the most recent intellectual self-indulgence of a Europe habituated to periodic fits of languid despair, but offer a key to destabilisation and deconstruction of a repressive European archive. Far from endlessly deferring or denying meaning, these same tropes function as potential decolonising strategies which invest (or reinvest) devalued "peripheries" with meaning. (x)

Likewise, the effacement of the boundary between high and popular culture distinguishes the postmodern and is ubiquitous among plays by Native playwrights. But, as I have tried to argue, Taylor's plays do not just parody discourses of popular culture, they mimic them, in Bhabha's use of the term; they *interrogate* them. The mutual "contamination" of Native and popular culture is not just a fact, but a golden opportunity for the disruptive and explosive energies of the Trickster.

Fundamentally, the difference between postmodern parody and postcolonial mimicry has everything to do with who is speaking, and to whom. The mere existence of a play written by a Native playwright and produced by a Native theatre company such as NEPA identifies it with the political aims of the First Nations of Canada. And when, as is almost always the case, such a play is seen by a mixed audience of Native and non-Native spectators, its reception is also inevitably political. For the Native spectator, a play by a Native author is an affirmation and celebration of indigenous culture and an act of resistance. The non-Native spectator is almost inevitably obliged to engage in the "effort of interpretation" of which Bhabha speaks, rereading the (parodied) texts of his/her own culture, whether high or popular, as signifiers of the massive *Entstellung* of the colonizer.

(1998)

Notes

1. Flora Wellsman quotes Ian Wallace and Eileen Thalenberg, close associates of Pochinko, on Jonsmith. Both accounts clearly identify Jonsmith as a kind of spirit guide or dream image created by Pochinko. In an e-mail correspondence with me, Filewod asks whether this "spirit quest… enabled [Pochinko] to claim his understanding of aboriginality as authentic."

2. See Joanne Tompkins's discussion of postcolonial parodic mimicry in *Princess Pocahontas and the Blue Spots* (48).

3. Taylor is an Ojibway from the Curve Lake First Nation in central Ontario. A writer of many disciplines, he has produced work for television, movies, theatre, short stories, commentaries, essays, and whatever else he can get paid for. He has also taught workshops in scriptwriting/playwriting for Native people and visible minorities. He is the recipient of the Dora Mavor Moore Award in 1996 for *Only Drunks and Children Tell the Truth*, the University of Anchorage Native Playwriting Award in 1996 for *The Baby Blues*, the Floyd S. Chalmers Canadian Play Award in 1992 for *Toronto at Dreamer's Rock* and the Canadian Authors' Association Literary Award, Best Drama, in 1992 for *The Bootlegger Blues* (material taken from *Who's Who in the Playwrights Union of Canada* [Toronto: Playwrights Union of Canada, 1997], 132.)

4. Taylor himself calls attention to the hybridity written on his own body in his collection of essays *Funny, You Don't Look Like One: Observations of a Blue-Eyed Ojibway*.

5. Helen Gilbert and Joanne Tompkins advance a similar argument about Derek Walcott's *Beef, No Chicken* (1981): "while *Beef, No Chicken* seems to suggest that many Caribbean people have little alternative but to imitate the systems which are offered to or imposed on them, the play enacts not only a critique of American culture but also a subversion of its authority. In particular, Walcott's emphasis on mimicry turns the gaze of the colonising media back on itself in a movement which undermines all claims to representation" (282).

6. Let's play "Spot the Trickster."

7. Indeed, in Native Earth Performing Arts' production of the play in 1994, the entire set was covered in newspapers, signifying a thorough saturation of Native culture by the dominant White culture.

Works Cited

Adam, Ian, and Helen Tiffin, ed. *Past the Last Post: Theorizing- Post-Colonialism and Post-Modernism* Calgary: U of Calgary P, 1990.

Ashcroft, Bill, Gareth Griffiths, and Helen Tiffin. *The Empire Writes Back: Theory and Practice in Post-Colonial Literatures.* London: Methuen, 1989.

Bhabha, Homi K. "Signs Taken For Wonders: Questions of Ambivalence and Authority under a Tree outside Delhi, May 1817." *Europe and Its Others.* Ed. Francis Barker et al. Proc. of the Essex Conference on the Sociology of Literature, July 1984. Colchester: U of Essex, 1985. 89-106.

Brydon, Diana. "The White Inuit Speaks: Contamination as Literary Strategy." Adam and Tiffin 191-203.

Cashman, Cheryl, comp. "A Collective Tribute: Richard Pochinko 1946-1989." *Canadian Theatre Review* 67 (1991): 37-38.

———. "Toronto's Zanies." *Canadian Theatre Review* 67 (1991): 22-31.

Copeland, Roger. "Is It Post-Postmodern?" *The Drama Review* 36.1 (1992): 64-67.

Crow, Brian, with Chris Banfield. *An Introduction to Post-Colonial Theatre.* Cambridge: Cambridge UP, 1996.

Filewod, Alan. "Averting the Colonial Gaze: Notes on Watching Native Theatre." *Aboriginal Voices: Amerindian, Inuit, and Sami Theatre.* Ed. Per Brask and William Morgan. Baltimore: Johns Hopkins UP, 1992. 17-28.

———. E-mail to the author. 10 June 1998.

Foster, Susan L. "Postbody, Multibodies?" *The Drama Review* 36.1 (1992): 67-69.

Gilbert, Helen, and Joanne Tompkins. *Post-Colonial Drama: Theory, Practice, Politics.* London: Routledge, 1996.

Goldie, Terry. *Fear and Temptation: The Image o f the Indigene in Canadian, Australian, and New Zealand Literatures.* Kingston: McGill-Queen's UP, 1989.

———. "*Fear and Temptation* after Oka." Assoc. of Canadian College and University Teachers of English Annual Conference. Queen's University, May 1991.

Highway, Tomson. *Dry Lips Oughta Move to Kapuskasing.* Saskatoon: Fifth House, 1989.

Hutcheon, Linda. *The Canadian Postmodern: A Study of Contemporary English-Canadian Fiction.* Studies in Canadian Literature. Toronto: Oxford UP, 1988.

Huyssens, Andreas. "Mapping the Postmodern." *Feminism/Postmodernism.* Ed. Linda J. Nicholson. New York: Routledge, 1990. 234-77.

Jameson, Frederic. "Postmodernism and Consumer Society." *Postmodernism and Its Discontents.* Ed. E. Ann Kaplan. London: Verso, 1988. 13-19.

Kaplan, Jon. "Translating the Spoken Word to Native Theatre Writing." *Now* 27 Nov.-3 Dec. 1986: 31.

Lawless, Jill. "Humour Is Drew Hayden Taylor's Release." *Now* 4-10 Apr. 1996.

Lyotard, Jean-François. *The Postmodern Condition: A Report on Knowledge.* Trans. Geoff Bennington and Brian Massumi. Minneapolis: U of Minnesota P, 1984.

Minh-ha, Trinh T. *Woman, Native, Other: Writing, Postcoloniality and Feminism.* Bloomington: Indiana UP, 1989.

Mojica, Monique. *Princess Pocahontas and the Blue Spots.* Toronto: Women's Press, 1991.

———. "Theatre Diversity on Turtle Island: A Tool towards the Healing." *Canadian Theatre Review* 68 (1991): 3.

Moses, Daniel David, and Terry Goldie, ed. *An Anthology of Native Canadian Literature in English.* Toronto: McClelland, 1992.

———. "Preface: Two Voices." Moses and Goldie xii-xxii.

Preston, Jennifer. "Weesageechak Begins to Dance: Native Earth Performing Arts Inc." *The Drama Review* 36.1 (1992): 135-59.

Rabillard, Sheila. "Absorption, Elimination, and the Hybrid: Some Impure Questions of Gender and Culture in the Trickster Drama of Tomson Highway." *Essays in Theatre/Études théâtrales* 12 (1993): 3-27.

Sharpe, Jenny. "Figures of Colonial Resistance." *The Post-Colonial Studies Reader.* Ed. Bill Ashcroft, Gareth Griffiths, and Helen Tiffin. London: Routledge, 1995. 99-103.

Slemon, Stephen. "Modernism's Last Post." Adam and Tiffin 1-12.

Spiderwoman Theater. *Winnetou's Snake Oil Show from Wigwam City. Canadian Theatre Review* 68 (1991): 54-63.

Taylor, Drew Hayden. *The Baby Blues.* Toronto: Playwrights Union of Canada, 1997.

———. *The Bootlegger Blues.* Saskatoon: Fifth House, 1991.

———. *Funny, You Don't Look Like One: Observations of a Blue-Eyed Ojibway.* Penticton: Theytus, 1996.

———. *Only Drunks and Children Tell the Truth.* Vancouver: Talonbooks, 1998.

———. "The Re-Appearance of the Trickster: Native Theatre in Canada." *On-Stage and Off-Stage: English Canadian Drama in Discourse.* Ed. Albert-Reiner Glaap and Rolf Althof. St. John's: Breakwater, 1996. 51-59.

———. *Someday.* Saskatoon: Fifth House, 1993.

Tiffin, Helen. "Post-Colonialism, Post-Modernism and the Rehabilitation of Post-Colonial History." *Journal of Commonwealth Literature* 23 (1988): 169-81.

Tompkins, Joanne. "'Spectacular Resistance': Metatheatre in Post-Colonial Drama." *Modern Drama* 38 (1995): 42-51.

Wellsman, Flora. "Richard Pochinko's Clowning Process: An Integration of Jaques Lecoq's Mime Technique and Amerindian Traditions." M.A. Thesis. U of Guelph, 1991.

Selling Myself: the Value of an Artist [1]

by Yvette Nolan

In my first year of university, about a hundred and fifty years ago, I received an English Literature paper back from my professor, with this comment on it: *Yvette, you have what Yeats has called "the fascination of what's difficult."* It was a prophetic comment. It turns out I do indeed have "the fascination of what's difficult;" I am an artist, by profession. Which in some circles is an oxymoron, an artist by profession.

Much of the work that I do is unpaid for much of the time. I am first and foremost a playwright. The actual writing of plays that I do is largely unpaid work. Occasionally I am commissioned to write a play, but usually the commission does not cover the actual work, but it is enough to start, usually to get a first draft. In relative terms, it is often enough to pay my rent for a couple of months. But there are a lot of playwrights and very few commissions. So mostly I write plays and then look for a theatre to produce them.

Or else I produce them myself, as I did this past year, with my play *Annie Mae's Movement.*

I have another job. I am the President of the Playwrights Union of Canada (PUC), which is an organisation that serves a membership of some three hundred and fifty playwrights from across Canada. In my role as President, I am the public face of the Playwrights Union of Canada. I correspond with the members, with funding agencies, with the office which is in Toronto, halfway across the country. The week before I came to Germany, I wrote a letter to Dr. Shirley Thomson who is the head of the Canada Council for the Arts, a major funder, asking her to restore funding to all the arts service organisations who lost their funding due to a new fiscal responsibility; I wrote job descriptions for Board Members of the Playwrights Union of Canada; I spoke to clerks in the government about presenting a paper to a committee of members of parliament about cultural policy in the 21st century; I wrote to the new head of The Writers Union of Canada to explore a possible alliance; I exchanged about fifty e-mails with Angela Rebeiro, the Executive Director of PUC, who is in Toronto; I wrote a letter to accompany this, the new catalogue of Canadian plays; I wrote to the National Council to keep them up to date on what was going on in the office. This past week, I spent about four hours a day working on PUC business. It is an unpaid position. There is no honorarium, and I absorb a lot of the costs myself, phone calls and postage and such. When I am in Toronto on PUC business the Union usually buys me lunch.

Playwrights Union of Canada recently began a re-visioning process, a self-examination of where we are now as an organisation and where we would like to be in the next five-ten-fifteen years. Our Vision, as defined by the working group who came together is "to be a leader in defining Canadian Theatre, now and in the future." The number one means, the number one goal stemming from that Vision is "to achieve greater stature for playwrights." To achieve greater stature for playwrights implies that we do not have much stature right now. Well, we don't. When I discovered at dinner last night that you have writers and composers and architects on your money, I almost lost my mind—cultural figures on your currency! In Canada, we have politicians on our currency—or the Queen of England. There's no way the Bank wants to let artists and money get together in the same place. We might get used to it, and then where would we be? We might have to start paying artists as professionals, with professional wages. But I digress. With all of this unpaid work, this *pro bono* work, who has *time* to make a living? How could I make a living?

There are easier ways to make a living—but the cost of making a living is often extreme, often debilitating.

Sometimes, the cost of success is the loss of the title of Artist.

If you choose to continue to write for the theatre, and you write something commercially successful, especially if it is a comedy, you are almost certainly stripped of your status as artist, because there is a perception that you can't reap financial reward and be an artist. And once you do write something commercial, well, the expectations have changed, and you are limited because you are expected to always be commercially successful.

If you want to really make a decent living, you pretty well have to do something other than write for the theatre. Something like television and film work. There is a lot of money in film and television, if you can sell a script. Unfortunately, especially if you are just starting out in television/film, there is often a corresponding loss of control over your work. Story editors often know better than you what your story should be about. I have been asked to change the sex of the protagonist from a girl to a boy. I have been asked to change the age of the characters, from teenagers to adults. Suddenly, my story is not the story I started to tell. A friend of mine, a Native writer who wrote a story about the reconciliation of a Native father and two sons who had left the reserve to go to the city, found by the time his story hit the television screen that he did not even get a writing credit. His story editor, a White woman, got the writing credit.

There is radio, which I find a kinder, gentler medium to writers who come from theatre, but—ah, this is a huge BUT—you see, there's a lot of radio opportunity right now, especially for Native writers, what we call First Nations writers. Now I use these words interchangeably—Native, First Nation, aboriginal and with apology to Himani Bannerji, Indians. We were named Indians and the names you are given often stick a lot harder than the ones you choose.

But there's a cost. For me, it is a more personal cost. There is a huge market for First Nations—or Native—work. Now I am Native—a halfbreed, to use a term that Maria Campbell reclaimed for us. My mother is Algonquin Indian from the province of Quebec. She met and married my father, an Irish immigrant, at residential school, where he was her math teacher. Residential school was where they sent Indian children to learn English, to be assimilated. They were punished for speaking their language, their hair was cut off, they were taught a European view of history, both of the world and of their own country, that had nothing whatever to do with what they came from. They were taught they were savages, and heathen and they were indoctrinated into a religion that was totally alien to thousands of years of their own history. So when my Indian mother married my white father and they moved to the prairies of Canada to raise children, we—she and all of us children—lost our connection to our Native roots, to our Native families, to our Native culture.

But my mother is Native, and over the years, she found her way back, like thousands of other Natives in Canada, to her roots, and her culture. And my brother and I have had similar journeys. Despite being raised "white," white schooling, white communities, my white skin—my brother is much more Indian looking than me—we are—I am—Native. And I am a writer. And that makes me a commodity these days in Canada. In fact, my whiteness makes me a much more valuable commodity because I am articulate and accessible and acceptable. I am the perfect person to be a cultural informant, to interpret the ways of Indian people to white people.

And there is the rub.

You see, the appetite for Native stories, for Native experience, is tempered by a certain set of expectations. The mainstream audience in Canada—and, as far as I can tell, in the United States too—is for the most part willing to accept only certain representations of Native people. These are they:

- the wise Indian. The late great groundbreaking Chief Dan George exemplified the wise Indian;

- the quaint Indian—this is the "Dances With Wolves" Indian—he is a non-threatening Indian, because he is placed in history, in a time that is gone. This is also presented as the noble savage. Some of the "Dances With Wolves" Indians are noble savages;

- the funny Indian. These are often the characters in Drew Hayden Taylor's plays;

- the funny but wise Indian. This is a character who appears to be dumb or foolish, but often says wise things. This is much like the role of Shakespeare's fools—they are often the wisest characters onstage, and their job is to truth-tell. But they have to sugar-coat the truth in cleverness and humour to make it palatable or else they risk banishment, exile or death.

There are more and more representations of Indians being accepted these days. The drunken Indian is a representation you will see presented more often both onstage and in the film, because it has now become fashionable to tell the truth about Native people in popular culture. Indian as victim. Indian as child.

I don't have anything against those writers, those works. I was an early champion of Ian Ross, we were in University together. I count him as a friend. I direct Drew Hayden Taylor's plays. I honour and respect the late Chief Dan George for his work in getting First Nations into popular culture.

But because *those* representations are now acceptable, the door should be squeaking open to allow other Indians through. Functioning First Nations. Fallible First Nations. Healing First Nations. But generally, those representations are still missing.

Here's the thing. The people who make the decisions about what gets onstage, on film or on radio want certain things from First Nations writers. They want certain representations of Indians. They want you to write Indian. There is a radio series on Canadian Broadcasting Corporation radio in Canada right now called the *Dead Dog Cafe*. It's a very funny series, populated by very funny but wise Indians, and they all talk with accents, what Canadian people have been trained to know as Indian accent. "They talk like this, eh? And they all seem a little slow, but really they're wise." Ian Ross—the First Nation writer from Winnipeg, where I come from—won the 1997 Governor General's Award for *fareWel*, which is a play about a dysfunctional reservation. It's a play that essentially confirms what white folks have been saying all along: that Indians cannot take care of themselves. Ian also regularly does radio spots on CBC with a character called "Joe from Winnipeg," who is a funny but wise Indian.

There is a character in literature called Uncle Tom. I tried to think of a definition of Uncle Tom, but could only come up with metaphor, belly-showing, shit-eating— I guess the appropriate word would be pandering, a character who panders to the dominant culture. Well, there is a similar phrase in First Nations circles: Uncle Tomahawking.

We have to be careful to not become Uncle Tomahawks. We have to be careful to not only present representations of Indian people that are palatable to the mainstream audience, or else we risk losing our authenticity. If we only offer certain types, if we agree to offer only that which is palatable, we are in danger of making invisible all those others. Not all Indians are quaint. And for many, many First Nations people in this country, English is our first language, maybe not by choice but by default, and that means many of us do not have an Indian accent. Many of us will not put on an Indian accent either. Not all Indians are funny, either. Some of us are mad.

But that is not a current acceptable representation. Mad is uncomfortable. Mad is threatening. Mad is passé. Get over it.

If one does not fulfil certain expectations, if one does not offer a currently acceptable representation, if you are not willing to write funny but wise Indians, then it gets difficult to get those jobs, to make a living telling your stories.

Let me tell you a story. My first play, *Blade*, which I wrote in 1989 and produced in 1990, was very successful at the Winnipeg Fringe Festival. It sold out completely, standing ovations, nice critical response in my home town. The production ran in Best of the Fringe, and then was invited to the Women In View Festival in Vancouver.

Blade is the story of a young woman—Angela—who is killed by a man who is killing prostitutes, and so, through the media coverage after her death, she becomes a prostitute. Her friends and family try "to clear her name," but the power of the media is much greater than a few voices.

So, we went to Vancouver, and we opened at the Women in View Festival to a full house, a very live house, you know what I mean, a house with expectations. And about two or three scenes into the play, the audience started getting restless. You see, in the Festival program, the organisers to whom I had submitted my play, described *Blade* as being "about a young Native girl who is murdered by a 'hooker-killer'." And this audience, this very full very attentive audience had come to see a Native woman killed. Well, the problem was, the woman who played Angela, the woman, is not Native. She's white, she's blond. She bleeds red, but she's not Native, and this audience was expecting Native blood. They'd paid for Native blood, and they were angry. After the performance, there was a Question & Answer (because there is always a Question & Answer at Women's Festivals), and the audience wanted to know why I hadn't cast a Native woman in that role. I explained that I had not intended the character to be Native, and then they got really mad. Why, as a Native woman, didn't I write about Native women? Didn't I feel it was my responsibility to give my voice to the Native community?

There was an expectation of what kind of story I would tell, as a Native writer. And the story this audience came to hear was about Indian as victim.

What is ironic is that *Blade* is very much about aboriginal invisibility—the central character, who was white, is the last of the women killed by the man who is killing prostitutes, because, you see, she is white. This is from the opening monologue:

> ANGELA: I knew that hookers were being killed—everyone in the
> country knew it and we here knew it better than anyone because
> it was splashed all over the front page—with pictures usually. I
> knew better than most, 'cause I actually knew one of the girls who
> had been killed. Well, not really knew her but she was in my intro
> History class at University. Cindy Bear, her name was—you know,
> like Yogi Bear's girlfriend. She was Native, and very quiet, but
> I think she did quite well in that class because I saw her get back
> a test once with an 88% on it. I only got about 75 on that test.
> It was about colonialism in South Africa and I just couldn't get
> interested. So anyway, when Cindy Bear—no one ever called her
> just Cindy, it was always Cindy Bear—when Cindy Bear got killed
> by the hooker-killer, some people at school said "Oh, I never knew
> she was a prostitute—I never would have guessed" and others said

"I always thought she was a whore—where else would she get the
money to go to school? They usually are, you know." I thought it
was a little funny that Cindy Bear should be a hooker because
I knew she was going to school through some special program,
and she was always prepared for class, so when did she have time?

Blade, my first play was about things I knew about. About the invisibility of Natives,
especially in Winnipeg, my home town, and about how nobody really cares if a Native
woman dies because she must have been doing something to deserve it, something to
bring it on herself. Like being a prostitute. But *Blade* was also about the role of women
in society, and the assumptions about women in the media.

The killer of the women, Jack, is finally caught because the police finally begin to
wonder if he is actually killing prostitutes. In the final monologue, Angela's mother,
Mrs. Erhart, says:

> MRS. ERHART: I know you're all so willing to believe that my daugh-
> ter was a whore, that she was taking money for sex, makes a better
> story I know, and I've been guilty of it too, but now, the police are
> saying it looks like this last girl was not a prostitute either.... So
> I've been thinking about this, very early mornings when I wake up
> and realise my daughter is gone, and I'm beginning to think that
> maybe if the police had been looking for a man who was killing
> women, instead of a man who was killing whores, maybe he'd have
> been stopped a lot sooner. I don't know.

So with my first play, I began to learn what was acceptable. People wanted me to
write the Native experience, but my experience has been in this skin, as an invisible
aboriginal. So the first discrimination I face, the first -ism, in this skin, is sexism.

Much of my work deals with gender issues. *A Marginal Man*—a man takes a
stand against violence against women and becomes a target of violence. *Video*—a
woman who every day puts on her wedding dress and watches her wedding video.
Hilda Blake—an opera libretto about the only woman ever hanged in Manitoba. *Two
Steps Forward, One Look Back* was a work commissioned to celebrate twenty years of
Women's Studies at three Manitoba Universities. Even *Job's Wife*—which does have
a Native character onstage (actually after the *Blade* episode I kind of overcompen-
sated and made him God) is really about how this young woman, this young white
woman, discovers that she has relinquished all personal responsibility and her whole
life has been ordained by her father, her lover, and Big Daddy in the form of the
Catholic church. Which is why an aboriginal god comes to her—she prays for a kinder gentler spiritual relationship. And oh yeah, and because the child she is carrying is
a halfbreed. See, there I am again.

Women's work. My work is women's work, and very often *about* women's work,
what artistic directors refer to disparagingly as "women's issues." And they also tell
me that plays about women's issues are not very interesting to their theatregoers. So
what I need to write about, about women's roles in society, about power and respon-

sibility, about struggling to wrest some of that power away from those who hold it, about striving to take responsibility for our lives, those things are "women's issues" and not interesting to theatregoers.

So I produce my own work. The play I produced this year, is ironically, finally, my Indian play, the play that would make me a commodity, the play that confirms me as a Native writer. It is called *Annie Mae's Movement*. It was produced in Whitehorse in September, 1998, travelled to Winnipeg and was presented by Red Roots and Hardly Art for two weeks; in May it goes to the On The Waterfront Festival in Nova Scotia. In May, there will also be a different production of it in Toronto, produced by Native Earth Performing Arts.

Annie Mae's Movement is about Anna Mae Aquash, a Micmac (now Mi'q mak) Indian from Nova Scotia who became deeply involved with the American Indian Movement (AIM) in the United States during the 1970s. She ran goods into occupied Wounded Knee, she worked in the AIM offices in St. Paul and Los Angeles. She became the only woman warrior in what was essentially a male-dominated organisation. Most importantly, she raised money for them. In February 1976, her body was found on the Pine Ridge Reserve in South Dakota. The FBI moved in and stated that she died of exposure, her hands were cut off and sent to Washington, and she was buried as a Jane Doe. Her family in Nova Scotia heard about this body and they had it exhumed. A second autopsy established that she had died not of exposure but from a bullet in the back of the head (which I guess can be easily mistaken for exposure if you're the FBI). Her story was told in the Hollywood movie *Thunderheart* and Buffy Sainte Marie sings about her in *Bury My Heart At Wounded Knee*: "My girlfriend Annie Mae/Talked about uranium/Her head was filled with bullets/And her body dumped/The FBI cut off her hands/And told us she died of exposure…"

So. We produce the play in Whitehorse, where I now live. Opening night is sold out two days before. Second night is sold out before opening night. By the time the CBC review happens on second night, the run is completely sold out.

The CBC reviewer says this: Great acting, great set, great music, great posters. The play, well—

> Well, I think overall, Yvette Nolan both the playwright and the director of this piece, has created a very provocative piece, and also an important work. Um, however, the message was not subtle at all. As we were confronted with life as Annie Mae saw it. Both the discrimination she felt within the Indian movement and outside it in the larger privileged white world. But at times, I have to say, I felt like the message was overstated a bit. That as the audience we were witnessing a political dissertation rather than watching a play.

In other words, I did not fulfil my end of the bargain with this white reviewer. I broke the covenant. This is not a funny but wise Indian. This is not a drunk Indian. This is not a quaint Indian. In fact, although she gets herself killed in the play, this is not even an Indian as victim. No, Anna Mae is none of those things. Though there is much humour in the play, there is also anger, there are tears. Another reviewer in the *Winnipeg Free Press* said "Nolan's play did not flinch for a minute in naming the atrocity as it affects Native people, government powers and women" and later "Nolan's play was a brave work of naming the horror of racial and gender injustice." Interestingly, the headline of the article was "Quest For Connection" and it was not in the Arts section of the paper, but on the Faith page, the religion page.

I would like to read from *Annie Mae's Movement.* The play is bracketed by two monologues, both Annie Mae's.

Beginning

> ANNA MAE *is isolated onstage in a pool of light. She is wearing
> jeans, and a "host shirt". On her wrist is a large turquoise bracelet.
> She is doing karate moves.*

ANNA: There are all kinds of ways of getting rid of people. In Central America they disappeared people. Just came and took them away in the middle of the night, whoosh gone, and then deny everything. Very effective. Well, here they disappear people too.

They disappear them by keeping them underfed, keeping them poor, prone to sickness and disease. They disappear them into jails. In jails they disappear their dignity, their pride. They disappear our kids, scoop 'em up, adopt em out, they never see their families again.

Our leaders—the leaders of the American Indian Movement—said that we should learn to fight. And because we'd never get enough firearms, we had to use the only thing that they couldn't take away from us. We had to train our bodies, turn our hands into weapons. Alright, I said, right on, and I got up at dawn to train with the rest of them. Well, they didn't mean me, did they? They didn't mean the women. They meant the men, the warriors, the dog soldiers. Not you, girl, fighting's not for you. But my first husband, Jake, he ran a martial arts school...

I guess I got it from my mother, she used to fight with the Indian Agent. This one time, he brought us bunch of clothes, *donations*— army coats and what do you call those pants they wear riding horses?—all moth-eaten, full of holes. I couldn't have been more than four, but I remember she sent him packing, with his crummy rags. After that, he finally started sending us better stuff. After that, she'd write letters to Halifax, to Ottawa, every time he pissed her off.

You gotta stand up, you gotta fight for what's important, no matter who wants to shut you up. We have to fight, even if seems like we're fighting ourselves. Or else we will disappear, just disappear [...].

At that AIM meeting in Wisconsin, when Myrtle waited all morning for her turn at the mike, waited through all the leaders, all the big boys recounting all the victories for Indian people, when she finally got to the mike, they called for lunch, for LUNCH. And she stood there and she started to talk anyway, and our leaders took the mike away from her, covered it up with their hands so she couldn't be heard, all she wanted was to ask where are our children? How many of us have lost children, or know someone who has lost children this way? [...] They wouldn't even let her speak. No business here, they said.

Our children disappeared and our women silenced.

It's so easy to disappear people in this country, especially Indian people. Scoop 'em up here, drop 'em off there. Whoosh, gone. Then just deny everything.

Anna Mae? Anna Mae Who? Never heard of her.... Whoosh...

She is gone.

***

ANNA: I started survival schools in the States. The idea was, if we could give kids the tools to live in the white world, but not let them lose their Indianness, give em a sense of pride in who they were, where they come from, we could help to rebuild an Indian Nation that was self-sufficient, autonomous, healthy and whole.

I started survival schools. Those who can, do. Those who can't, teach. Those who can't, can't. Don't. Don't.

FBI Guy has entered and is watching her. She becomes aware of him. As he approaches her, her "don'ts" become more agitated, pleading, angry, anguished. As he rapes her, she stops begging and begins to say:

ANNA: My name is Anna Mae Pictou Aquash, Micmac Nation from Shubenacadie, Nova Scotia. My mother is Mary Ellen Pictou, my father is Francis Thomas Levi, my sisters are Rebecca Julien and Mary Lafford, my brother is Francis. My daughters are Denise and Deborah. You cannot kill us all. You can kill me, but my sisters live, my daughters live.

You cannot kill us all. My sisters live. Becky and Mary, Helen and Priscilla, Janet and Raven, Sylvia, Ellen, Pelajia, Agnes, Monica, Edie, Jessica, Gloria and Lisa and Muriel, Monique, Joy and Tina, Margo, Maria, Beatrice, Minnie, April, Colleen...

You can kill me, but you cannot kill us all. You can kill me.

There is a gunshot. She falls, curls into a foetal position. Blackout.

Annie Mae is a very successful play, by my standards. It has had productions in Whitehorse and Winnipeg, it goes to a national festival in May, it gets a different production in Toronto. There are several academics who have written about me and about the play. Two have done thesis work on Annie Mae—Val Shantz out of University of Alberta and Christy Stanlake out of Oklahoma University. One PhD candidate from University of Toronto recently called me to ask some questions about *Annie Mae* for a paper she is writing, and she told me that I am the only Native woman currently writing for the theatre in Canada. I told her I didn't think that was true, but I couldn't prove her wrong. I don't know if it's true, but even if it is not, it's pretty scary that she can say so. And it begs the question, why?

Well, maybe it's because the value of the artist is so—small. Maybe it is just too hard to make a living doing the work you need to do. I produced *Annie Mae*, I raised the money to produce the play in Whitehorse, I made an agreement with a theatre in Winnipeg to present my production, I sold the show to the Halifax festival, I employed actors and stage managers, and designers and carpenters, I rented a theatre, I printed posters and programs thereby contributing to the economy. I personally made about $2500. Which is enough to pay my rent for almost four months. The play took me about two years to write. I write fast.

Why do I do it? Why do I bother? I can teach, I do occasionally teach at University, I teach Intro Native Theatre to all Native classes at Brandon University, I teach Intro Acting. I am a terrific administrator, a good organiser. I have a facility with words, I could probably put words together for other people for money. But no, still I insist on this devotion to theatre.

I believe in theatre. I *believe* in Theatre. Theatre is my faith, my church, my spirituality. And all the things I do in the service of theatre, that is my way of witnessing, of proselytising.

I once saw an interview with the great great Canadian theatre artist Robert Lepage in which he said that theatre was vertical, it was about this relationship, about the relationship between human beings and a greater power, be that god or the gods or the creator or the fates. It's about asking the big questions: why do these things happen to us? *Hamlet*: "To be or not to be"—what happens after death? *Waiting for Godot*: is there a god and what is our relationship to that God? He said that film, that movies, is horizontal, like this. It is about the mundane, about the details, about a slice of life. The details ground us, literally. They bind us to the ground, to the earthly questions.

But theatre, from morality plays to *Angels in America*, from *Oedipus* to *Hamlet*, from *Lysistrata* to *Dry Lips Oughta Move To Kapuskasing*, theatre plucks the moral imperative of a society, saying *this is so*, why *is this so?* I was reading, in the middle of the night, Jason Sherman's new play. Some of you will know Jason Sherman from last year. This is from his new play, *It's All True* which is about Orson Welles's non-starter production *The Cradle Will Rock*.

> BLITZ: …anybody could do that, live the life of a provincial artist,
> taking in the shekhels and "believing" in yourself. It's the easiest
> thing in the world to write down to the audience—just give 'em the
> time-tested crap they've been humming for years, a little ditty that
> triggers the memory of childhood, the flotsam and jetsam of a life
> already lived—then you keep that audience in the past, keep them
> wishing they could get back there, back to what they had, instead of
> looking to the future, trying to find a way to make this better.

Artists are the creators and the chroniclers of culture. That makes us vital, contributing members of the societies in which we live, regardless of whether or not the society chooses to acknowledge that. But part of my proselytising is to be visible, to be vocal, to champion playwrights and plays. So I accept the responsibility of being the president of the Playwrights Union of Canada because it gives me profile, and by extension, other playwrights, other artists, other women and other First Nations individuals. I accept non-paying work because as a Native woman who is successful, I am a role model. But mostly it is to do the work—there is in me a desire to serve an idea larger than myself—that idea is Art, and in my case the Art is theatre. It is the idea that, as Tom Stoppard said in his play *The Real Thing*, "if you get the right words in the right order, you can nudge the world a little."

(1999)

Note

[1] Editor's Note: This essay was originally presented at the Association for Canadian Studies in German-Speaking Countries (ACSGSC) Conference, Grainau, Germany, 1999.

Translators, Traitors, Mistresses, and Whores: Monique Mojica and the Mothers of the Métis Nations [1]

by Ric Knowles

Monique Mojica's play *Princess Pocahontas and the Blue Spots* has been well and widely discussed in criticism, though rarely at very great length. The play has been variously cited and analysed in parts of articles and chapters in which it is dealt with as one among several examples of postcolonial metatheatre or hybridity, cultural cross dressing, canonical revisionism, dialogic monologue, the use of the trickster/ clown figure, or transformational performative dramaturgy. [2] What has been less thoroughly considered—though it is usually acknowledged—has been the revisioning performed by both *Princess Pocahontas and the Blue Spots* and Mojica's radio play published with it, *Birdwoman and the Suffragettes*, of the representation of a very specific group of Native women throughout the Americas across several centuries: the mothers of Métis and Mestizo nations, who have been both celebrated and cursed for their roles as the translators, guides, mediators, and mistresses of early European explorers, settlers, traders, and conquistadors.

The omission is not accidental or incidental, since what is at issue for Mojica in these plays, among other things, is a contestation of ownership over the representation of Native women by those who have exploited those representations for political purposes ranging from the colonialist and the nationalist through to the feminist and the academic. And for a not unrelated series of historical reasons rooted in colonialism, [3] most academics writing about these plays, myself included, have been non-Native women or men whose potential complicity with that exploitation—for academic advancement, if nothing else—represents a very real danger. Indeed, the very analytical tools used in the academic analysis of Native plays are seen by many to be grounded in European theorising and thinking which themselves marginalise or colonise indigenous ways of knowing, and remain in any case rooted in the lived, material realities of the colonising cultures. Mojica makes clear in *Princess Pocahontas* her own struggles, as "Contemporary Woman #1," with Western "feminist shoes" that fail to fit her "wide, square, brown feet" (58). Moreover, like many women and men of colonised cultures, she rejects with considerable derision the very term "postcolonial" and its implications [4]—however much academic discourse may define the postcolonial moment as beginning with first contact and continuing uninterrupted into the present. And of course, the history and practice of cultural analysis, literary and dramatic criticism, ethnography, and anthropology have naturalised the positions of the knowing academic subject versus the passive and static object of his/

her knowledge; and those of (European) master discourses versus those of "native informants"—positions that reinscribe colonial relations within the academy, as well as between the academy and its "objects of study."

This cultural gap applies to my own analysis here. In attempting to write about the work of a playwright who aims to "return the [imperial] gaze" (Bannerji xxii-xxiii), and to write from the cultural position of the (white, male) imperialist, I run the risk of reinscribing the colonial and gender relationships and power differentials that Mojica's work interrogates and exposes, since I am in danger of appropriating—in the styles of Cortes, John Smith, or Lewis and Clark—the work of Monique Mojica as (unlikely) "Indian Princess and guide" for my own advancement and sense of "discovery." Not to undertake this type of analysis, however—to retreat into more comfortable (and structurally continuous) analyses of plays and dramaturgies from the Western canon, without opening spaces within the academy for alternative modes of both creation and analysis (and for the consideration of alternative dramaturgies)—would simply amount to "disappearing" the cultural work that plays such as Mojica's can do in shifting power relationships in society, in the theatre, and in the academy. Such an attitude would also entail participation by omission in the colonial project. The following analysis, then, is offered less as an attempt to determine what these plays essentially *are*—to formulate definitive truth claims about them, to "place" them within a Canadian dramatic canon, or to police aesthetic (and therefore political) standards—than as a consideration, made with respect and without claims of cultural authority, of the cultural work which they might perform in shifting power relationships within contemporary Canadian and "American" (in its broadest senses) societies. [5] My analysis, therefore, begins with and focuses on sources, inspirations, genealogies and intertexts identified and enacted by Mojica herself in the published and performed versions of the plays. Moreover, this study tries to take into account the caution delivered by Paula Gunn Allen, the Native American woman whose work, *The Sacred Hoop*, contributed significantly to the writing of *Princess Pocahontas and the Blue Spots*:

> I would caution readers and students of American Indian life and culture to remember that Indian America does not in any sense function in the same ways or from the same assumptions that western systems do. Unless that fact is clearly acknowledged, it is virtually impossible to make much sense out of the voluminous materials available concerning American Indians. (7)

***

My essay begins by attempting to place and contextualise the cultural moment of the plays' production. *Princess Pocahontas and the Blue Spots* and *Birdwoman and the Suffragettes* emerged in the late 1980s and early 1990s, at the intersection of several historical forces. [6] These years marked the beginning of a First Nations *political* resurgence in Canada, as registered in the staking of Native land claims across the country, the mounting of protests and blockades over the ownership or exploitation of sacred Native sites and old-growth forests from Temagami, Ontario, to Clayoquot Sound on the coast of British Columbia, and, most obviously, the so-called "Oka Crisis" in 1990 over the expropriation of sacred Mohawk land near the Quebec-Ontario border for a golf course—a standoff between Mohawk warriors and the Quebec police and Canadian army that attracted international attention. In the arts, and most notably in drama and theatre, as Barbara Godard noted in 1990 citing examples primarily from the theatre, "Native Canadian Culture had never before received such public attention as it did in Toronto in the spring of 1989" (183). In 1990, Penny Petrone published her book *Native Literature in Canada: From the Oral Tradition to the Present,* in which she noted that "the most exciting development in the 1980s has taken place in Drama" (170), providing a nine-page survey as evidence (170-79).[7] And Monique Mojica was a central figure in much of this activity: as a writer, she contributed to TV Ontario's "Many Voices" antiracism series; as an actress, she played the title role in the Maria Campbell/Linda Griffiths collaboration, *Jessica,* as performed at Theatre Passe Muraille in February 1996, created the role of Marie-Adele Starblanket in Tomson Highway's *The Rez Sisters* in 1986, and played Ariel in the Lewis Baumander/Skylight Theatre postcolonial production of *The Tempest* in 1987 and 1989.

A large percentage of this activity in Native culture, and in Native drama and theatre in particular, was nevertheless undertaken by, or acknowledged as the work of, Native men. In fact, its most prominent "mainstream" manifestation—a 1989 production of Tomson Highway's *Dry Lips Oughta Move to Kapuskasing* at the venerable Royal Alexandria theatre and the National Arts Centre, and a subsequent production at the Manitoba Theatre Centre—came under attack from Native and non-Native women as misogynistic.[8] Marie Annharte Baker, in a special issue of *Canadian Theatre Review* on Native Theatre edited by Mojica in 1991, confessed to being made "Angry enough to Spit" by the representation of Native women in the Manitoba Theatre Centre production (88-90). This gendered division in the Native community in the late 1980s and early 1990s is not necessarily new. Race and gender in Native and other communities have long been split, divisive, or overlapping issues, and the division at the moment of production of Mojica's plays echoes what some—mostly non-Native—writers have seen as gendered division in response to first contact among many of the Native communities that Mojica was researching at the time when she was writing *Princess Pocahontas* and *Birdwoman and the Suffragettes.* According to many of her identified sources, the arrival of Europeans in the Americas, and in particular the arrival of European technologies that introduced such things as "kettles, knives, awls and woollen cloth," was more welcome, at least at first, among Native women than men, insofar as it made their lives easier—even as European expectations of the gendering of strength and endurance quite literally lessened the burden of women who, in their own cultures, were often expected unceasingly to haul, toil, and carry to an extent that far exceeded that of their male partners (Van Kirk 6). Sylvia Van Kirk argues of the fur trade society in Canada—and the argument to some extent applies to the *other* central subjects of Mojica's plays and research—Pocahontas in colonial Virginia, Sacagawea on the Lewis and Clark expedition in the American West, and Doña Marina/La Malinche, the translator and mistress of Cortez in sixteenth-century Mexico[9]—that "the notable instances that can be cited of the Indian woman acting as ally or peacemaker to advance the cause of the trader [or coloniser] suggests that it was in the woman's interest to do so" (6). "To become the wife of a fur trader," Van Kirk argues, "offered the Indian Woman the prospect of an alternative way of life that was easier physically and richer in material ways" (6). This to some extent, if controversially and debatably, explains the willingness of the Native women who are the subjects of Mojica's plays—and who are celebrated within the myths of the colonisers, as "trusty little Indian guides" or "faithful interpreters"—to act as translators and guides, and to become the sexual partners (wives "*à la façon du pays*" in the Canadian context of the fur trade, or mistresses and apparent objects of exchange in Mexico and elsewhere) of European colonisers. It also perhaps explains why these women have so often been demonised in the mythologies of their own cultures as traitors and whores.[10]

Mojica's research also reveals, however, that the cultural difference that promised technological advancement and decreased subjection to Native women also ultimately restricted their freedom (particularly their sexual freedom), and finally eroded or destroyed their positions of power in tribal and other societies. Paula Gunn Allen, in a 1986 book upon which Mojica draws extensively (31-42), traces the "chaos" caused by the European introduction of patriarchal philosophies and cultures into Native colonial societies, and the direct and specific destruction of matriarchal and gynocratic structures that had flourished in many pre-contact cultures. She points the way both in spirit and specific wording for Mojica's rallying "call to arms" (60) to Native women "Word Warriors" in *Princess Pocahontas and the Blue Spots* (Mojica 59; Gunn Allen 51-183) to reverse that history, and to claim for Native and mixed-blood women, in a passage quoted from Gloria Anzaldúa, "the freedom to carve and chisel my own face, to staunch the bleeding with ashes, to fashion my own gods out of my entrails" (Anzaldúa 22, qtd. in Mojica 59).

At the same time as the resurgence of First Nations political, cultural, and theatrical activity of the late 1980s and early 1990s was taking place, and at the same time as concerns were being voiced about the gendering of that resurgence, feminist criticism and theory were under attack from a range of locations for purported biological (and other) essentialisms, and for their own elisions of racial and cultural difference. Just as 1960s and 1970s movements from the political left had reinscribed patriarchal privilege in "universalist" fights for social justice according to class (see Hale 77-99), so concern was being expressed by the mid-to-late 1980s that the contemporary feminist movement had reinscribed white privilege in its fights for gender equality and what in *Birdwoman and the Suffragettes* is called "the eternal womanly" (Mojica 83). The phrase is used by Mojica to parody and critique contemporary transcultural and universalising feminism, but it is drawn directly from a speech, quoted at length in the play, that was originally delivered in 1905 by Dr. Anna Howard Shaw to the National American Women's Suffrage Association at the unveiling in Portland, Oregon, of the first of dozens of statues dedicated to Sacagawea (Mojica 83).[11] It is not incidental or accidental that in 1989, between the first workshopping of *Princess Pocahontas and the*

Blue Spots and its first production, and in response to contemporary debates, Toronto's feminist Nightwood Theatre, the show's coproducer, inaugurated its new, corrective mandate to focus on work by women of colour.

Many of the acknowledged sources for Mojica's plays are selected from among the writings by Mestiza women and women of colour (which she calls "Poetry, Narratives, Testimonies," as opposed to other entries by non-Native authors on "Biography and History") to which Nightwood and other feminist groups were attempting to respond. Throughout the 1980s, while Mojica was researching and writing her plays, women such as Gloria Anzaldúa, Chrystos, and Cherríe Moraga explicitly contested, on the basis of race, culture, and sexuality, the transcultural claims of contemporary feminisms. [12] It is the cultural work performed by the writings of these women, largely, like Mojica, of mixed race, [13] in which Mojica's plays most directly participate, and they do so—to an extent largely unremarked upon in the critical writing about the plays by non-Native academics—by linking together in a kind of oppositional transnationalism—also very much a product of the late 1980s cultural climate—the stories of legendary women *across* the Americas: Pocahontas, Sacagawea, La Malinche, and Mojica's "Marie/Margaret/Madeleine," representative of "the hordes of Cree and Métis women who portaged across Canada with white men on their backs" (15)—not to mention the alternative stories of the separatist Peruvian Women of the Puña, the murdered Nova Scotian AIM (American Indian Movement) activist Anna Mae Aquash, and other stories that *Princess Pocahontas* also tells. [14] The plays' transnationalism is important, at a time when Native political struggles were increasingly against the governments, legislative bodies and armies of Nation States, together with their constructions of national histories, identities, and, (often coercive or exclusive) "imagined communities" (Benedict Anderson). This was also a time when, on the one hand, political gains were increasingly made either through international courts or appeals to international (bad) press, and, on the other, resistance was proving effective through the creation of transnational Native communities through the Internet. The instant international circulation of information through email, for example, saved at least one Native community—the Chiapas peoples of Mexico in 1995—from extinction by armies under the command of national governments. [15] And it is worth noting that Mojica's partner is Chiapan, and with her, an active activist networker through email and the Internet with Native communities throughout the Americas.

Interestingly in this regard, the similarities *across* settler/invader cultures in the Americas of the symbolic significance of the various "Indian Princesses" who are Monique Mojica's subjects are rarely acknowledged in writings by non-Natives, for whom National identity is forged through the supposed uniqueness of each of these women, both as *different from* and *naturally superior to* their tribespeople, *and* as "National heroines" at the foundational moment in historical narratives that are framed as the teleological histories of distinct (colonising) *nations*. [16] Thus, for example, one children's version of the Pocahontas story from 1946, which treats her as the saviour of the fledgling Nation, presents her as being "as sweet and pretty as he[r father] was ugly and cruel" (d'Aulaire and Parin 11), confirming the natural superiority of the colonisers, their culture, and their values; and George Washington

Parke Custis's 1830 play, *Pocahontas or The Settlers of Virginia* is subtitled "*A National Drama.*" A popular 1979 biography/historical romance of epic proportions (1359 pages), Anna Lee Waldo's *Sacajawea*, is described on its front cover as "THE HEROIC STORY OF A GREAT WOMAN WHOSE LIFE TELLS THE STORY OF A NATION." The back cover blurb is even more explicit in its construction of the heroine's solitary uniqueness and mythic National significance: "Clad in a doeskin, alone and unafraid, she stood straight and proud before the onrushing forces of America's destiny." And La Malinche is similarly celebrated in non-Native accounts of the conquest of Mexico, notably those of the prolific web-apologist Shep Lenchek in articles with titles such as "La Malinche, Unrecognised Heroine," or "La Malinche—Harlot or Heroine?"[17] More scholarly non-Native sources—particularly Clark and Edmonds, Hebard, Howard, and Fehrenbach—differ from these popular accounts only in degree of subtlety: each treats its particular heroine as at once unique among her race, exemplary, heroic, and foundational for her respective (colonial) National narrative.

All of these sources, of course, come under Mojica's withering satirical gaze in such sequences as her parodic 1950s doo-wop song, accompanied by the back-up group, "The Blue Spots" ("If I'm savage don't despise me,/'cause I'll let you civilise me./Oh Captain Whiteman, I'm your buckskin clad dessert") (26-27), and her Troubadour ballad of Pocahontas (28-32), with its refrain of "Neigh-ho wiggle-waggle/wigwam wampum,/roly-poly papoose tom-tom/tomohawk squaw" (32). But in many ways the play's real subversions come less from direct parody than from linking together the histories of these women, presenting those histories *as* representations, and implicitly or explicitly noticing the similarities among them as constructs, ideologically coded through the discourses of colonisation. For, of course, these similarities do not emerge from considering or contesting the "actual" histories or biographies of these women. The (*written* and therefore *authoritative*) materials that might serve as the bases for such revisionism, considered by Western history to be "primary sources," are exclusively European: Captain John Smith's dubious accounts of his "adventures" (dubious because they were written long after the fact, and long after his early accounts, in which Pocahontas did not appear); Bernal Diaz's "eyewitness" account of *The Conquest of New Spain*; the clearly interested "discovery" journals of Cortes and of Lewis and Clark; and so on. The *linkages* emerge, for Mojica as for other Native writers, from considering these women less as "actual" figures in history than as subjects of Western colonialist historical *representation*. The similarities among their stories emerge, that is, through resistant transliteration that foregrounds and denaturalises the ways in which the stories have been *mobilised* as agents in the subjectification of Native women through colonialist historical discourses.[18]

Unlike non-Native authors, Native, Métis, and Mestizo writers, particularly women, frequently group Pocahontas, La Malinche, Sacagawea, and the fur-trade women together.[19] They treat their stories as ideologically coded representations; and they do so more or less explicitly, as Mojica does, by considering those figures to have been variously constructed in history as archetypal princesses, "squaws," translators, traitors, mistresses, and whores. Finally, they foreground the cultural role that is played by so representing the women who ultimately became the mothers, actual or symbolic, of Metis and Mestizo nations—women whose roles and reputations, internalised by their descendants, need to be rehabilitated for the sake of the psychic health of those descendants and those nations. As Gloria Anzaldúa argues, in a passage from which Mojica quotes,

> Not me sold out my people but they me. *Malinali Tenepat,* or *Malintzin,* has become known as *La Chingada*—the fucked one. She has become the bad word that passes a dozen times a day from the lips of Chicanos. Whore, prostitute, the woman who sold out her people to the Spaniards are epithets Chicanos spit out with contempt. The worst kind of betrayal lies in making us believe that the Indian woman in us is the betrayer. We, *indias y mestizas,* police the Indian in us, brutalise and condemn her. Male culture has done a good job on us. (Anzaldúa 22)

And she calls for "an accounting with all three cultures—white, Mexican, Indian" (22)—as she calls for the dormant spirit of the *mestiza* to "fight for her own skin and her own piece of ground to stand on, a ground from which to view the world" (23).

It might be useful, in understanding the double-bind of Native women caught between cultures—as it plays itself out in Mojica's performative history of their representation from Pocahontas, La Malinche, Sacagawea, the Women of the Puña, and the women of the fur trade in Canada through to tortured Chilean women, Anna Mae Aquash, and Contemporary Women #s 1 and 2 in *Princess Pocahontas and the Blue Spots*—to invoke some of the insights of recent feminist and postcolonialist translation theory, where the traditional Italian proverb, "to translate is to betray," is at issue—together with the traditional *gendering* of translation as a service role. In almost all of Mojica's recommended historical sources—together with those sources which she lists as "not recommended" except as "good source material for satire" (Mojica 85)—the images of her Indian Princesses circulate around a cluster of associations involving translation and faithfulness (or lack of it), associations that link cultural mediation with variations on linguistic, representational, racial, and sexual impurity—including, of course, *métissage* and hybridity—and conflating, more or less explicitly, translation, miscegenation, and cultural betrayal. As Tejaswini Niranjana phrases it, in traditional discourses of colonialist humanist translation the dilemma has generally been whether a translator should be "literal or licentious, faithful or unfaithful?" (54), which raises the crucial question for women caught between cultures, of, in Suzanne de Lotbinière-Harwood's phrasing, "who are you going to be faithful to?" (101).

In the introduction to *Siting Translation: History, Post-Structuralism, and the Colonial Context,* Niranjana points to the political value, in undoing hegemonic representations of colonial subjects, of Derrida's insight that translation, like other representations, "does not re-present an 'original'; rather, it re-presents that which is always already re-presented" (9). She also points to the post-structuralist critique of historicism, "which shows the genetic (searching for an origin) and teleological (positing a certain end) nature of traditional historiography":

> [O]f immediate relevance to our concern with colonial practices of
> subjectification is the fact that "historicism" really presents as *natural*
> that which is *historical* (and therefore neither inevitable nor unchange-
> able). A critique of historicism might show us a way of deconstructing
> [in her example] the "pusillanimous" and "deceitful" Hindus of Mill and
> Hegel. (10)

It might also show us a way of deconstructing the "warlike," "primitive," and equally
deceitful "savages" of colonial Virginia, of sixteenth-century Mexico, and of the nineteenth-century North American West. What Western legal and epistemological systems construct as deceitful—such as the shifting use of multiple names (and therefore *identities*—or multiplicities?) that notably characterise all of the women about
whom Mojica writes, versus the "capturing" through definitive naming that her character Sacagawea (or Grasswoman, Birdwoman, Phoenaïf, or Porivo [Chief Woman])[20]
eloquently resists—Native cultures might consider to be natural, evocative and
liberatory.

In any case, what Niranjana ultimately proposes, drawing on the work of Gayatri
Spivak and Homi Bhabha, is a Subaltern transliterative historiography that resonates
with Monique Mojica's project, in that it is "concerned with revealing the discursivity
of [Western] history," (43) and in that it "tries to show how... [h]istory and translation function, ...creating coherent and transparent texts through the repression of
difference, and participating thereby in the process of colonial domination" (43). Set
against this in Niranjana are Walter Benjamin's critical strategies of citation, quotation, or montage (which pre-echoes Derrida's double inscription), Homi Bhabha's
notion of hybridity ("the revaluation of the assumption of colonial identity through
the repetition of discriminatory identity effects" [Bhabha 154]), and Nirnanjana's
own attempt to initiate "a practice of translation that is speculative, provisional, and
interventionist" (Niranjana 173).

All of this motivates theorists of resistant translation to veer away from gendered
conceptions of faithful re-production toward genuinely *productive* theorisations that
involve, on the one hand, "'enabling' discursive failure" and "affirmative deconstruction" (Spivak qtd. in Niranjana 24-42) and on the other hand, a taking advantage of
the *liberatory* possibilities of *multiplication* and *choice*—what de Lotbinière-Harwood
calls "*deux mots pour chaque chose*" (75). In these configurations, translation, transliteration, and the slippages in meaning they involve, do not suggest duplicity but multi-
plicity; they do not suggest *lack*—of purity, of faithfulness, or of unitary meaning (or
epistemological authority)—but *abundance*, fecundity, endurance, and sustenance.

One task of the women Word Warriors that Mojica invokes, then, consists in
replacing the harmful, internalised representations of their roles as translators and
mediators with more positive translations, metaphors and material practices. And
central to this task, in the work of Mojica and that of her Chicana, Mestiza, and Métis
sisters, it seems, is corn. When I first began thinking seriously about Mojica's work,
I was puzzled by what seemed to be the pervasiveness, and flexibility, of images of
and references to corn in *Princess Pocahontas and the Blue Spots*—many of which are,

well, *corny*: corn adorns the cover of the published text, where "The Blue Spots" are represented as cartoon images of dancing cobs of corn, and in performance the winning by Princess Buttered-on-Both-Sides of the "Miss Congeniality" prize at "the 498th annual Miss North American Indian Beauty Pageant" is marked by the awarding of a *"tablita-style corn 'crown' and ear of corn 'bouquet'"* (52):

> *Screaming; jumping up and down flatfooted as the Host presents her with her "bouquet" and "crowns" her with a headdress covered with small ears of corn which light up. She begins her triumphant walk down the runway, weeping and blowing kisses, while HOST throws popcorn at her feet singing "You Light Up My Life," in true lounge lizard tradition. When PRINCESS BUTTERED-ON-BOTH-SIDES reaches upstage centre she strikes the pose of the Statue of Liberty, and the ears of corn on her headdress are fully illuminated. (52)*

And more seriously, early in the play, CONTEMPORARY WOMAN #1 provides a commentary on Mojica's riff on "Redskin Princess, calendar girl,/Redskin temptress, Indian Pearl," by quoting Cherríe Moraga: "...the concept of betraying one's race through sex and sexual politics is as common as corn" (103; qtd. in Mojica 21). It is interesting to note, in this context, the centrality of corn in Native stories as reported in Paula Gunn Allen's chapter on "the ways of our Grandmothers." For the Keres people of the American Southwest, for example, corn "holds the essence of earth and conveys the power of earth to the people" (Gunn Allen 22). And corn—as metaphor, but also as a *material* and *nurturing* fact of life and sustenance, both mundane and magical, "common" (as the quotation from Moraga indicates), but also transformative—might usefully replace the less savory images of hybridity and *métissage* in ways articulated most clearly by Gloria Anzaldúa, who describes herself and other *mestizas* as

> Indigenous like corn, like corn, the *mestiza* is a product of crossbreeding, designed for preservation under a variety of conditions. Like an ear of corn—a female seed-bearing organ—the *mestiza* is tenacious, tightly wrapped in the husks of her culture. Like kernels she clings to the cob; with thick stalks and strong brace roots she holds tight to the earth— she will survive the crossroads. (81)[21]

It is, then, the *mestiza*, Métis, or half-breed woman herself who is the lived, *material* embodiment—as opposed to the metaphoric representation, no matter how suggestive—of what often represents in postcolonial theorisings a purely *formalist métissage*, or purely *discursive* hybridity, most of which draw upon Homi Bhabha—and more importantly upon Gayatri Spivak and the emerging field of Subaltern studies—but which nevertheless tend to shift discursive analysis away from the material to the (purely) textual.[22]

In the brief biography that concludes the published text of her plays, Monique Mojica aligns herself directly with the women who are the historical subjects of her theatrical works *and* with the women of the 1980s—Anzaldúa, Chrystos, Moraga, and others—who provide her with her poetic, narrative, and testimonial source material—her lived theoretical frame. Identifying herself as "a Kuna-Rappahonnok [the Nation of Pocahontas, a] half-breed, a woman word-warrior [like Anzaldúa, Chrystos, Gunn Allen, and Moraga], a mother [like Pocahontas, La Malinche, Sacagawea, and the fur-trade women] and an actor" (86), Mojica constructs for herself and other women (as did the women of the Puña) a living lineage: a nation, an alternative "imagined community." And as a mixed-race woman who in *Princess Pocahontas* performs her *own* rewritings of the revisionist histories of that lineage, she quite literally and visibly embodies it, even as she embodies, as an actor, the characters whom she performs. These women and their histories *are, in fact,* embodied in her. Her acting, then, becomes genuinely *performative.* She is, in Niranjana's terms, "*living* in translation" (42; emphasis added) inhabiting what Susanne de Lotbinière-Harwood calls (in reference to *her* own position between Canada's founding cultures as signalled by her double-barrelled, bicultural name) "the *body* bilingual" (75; emphasis added),[23] when she moves, at the end of *Princess Pocahontas,* towards the *actual* bilingualism (in this case Spanish and English) that also characterises the work of Anzaldúa, Moraga, and others. In *Princess Pocahontas,* then, Mojica *enacts* a move from Western teleological historiography, with its claims to represent originary realities and to translate the past "faithfully," to a *performative, embodied* genealogy that might be considered to be less Western history's cataloguing and controlling of the dead and their meanings than a First Nations project of keeping the ancestors alive and granting them agency in the present. Thus, Mojica takes part—as actor, activist, and mother—In the (ongoing) *creation* of the nation of women Word Warriors for which she literally "stands in," for which her plays are constitutive, and for the members of which they function as a call to arms.

(2001)

Notes

[1] I would like to thank Patricia Tersigni for gathering an immense body of research material for me, without which I could not have written this essay; my thanks also go to Christine Bold for reading and making her typically perceptive and helpful comments on an earlier draft.

[2] For discussions of the play as postcolonial metatheatre, see Tompkins, "Spectacular" 48, and "Story" 150-53. For an examination of the play's postcolonial hybridity, see Nunn 4-5. For interpretations of the play as cultural cross-dressing, see Brydon, "Empire Bloomers" 33-35. For readings of the play in terms of canonical revisioning, see Brydon, "No (Wo)man is an Island" 54-55. For studies of the play as dialogic monologue, see Harvie and Knowles 207-08. For analyses focusing on the use of the figure of the trickster/clown, see Cashman. For interpretations of the play as resistant performative dramaturgy, see Knowles, *The Theatre of Form* 148-50, and Gilbert and Tompkins 208-9.

[3] There continue to be few First Nations people in the academy, particularly in drama and literature departments.

[4] She did so in public presentations at the "Gender/Colonialism/Postcolonialism" conference at the University of Guelph (5-8 November 1992) and at the annual conference of the Association for Canadian Theatre Studies in Ottawa (June 1998).

[5] Like many First Nations writers and activists, Mojica resists the geopolitical boundaries established by late-coming colonialist Nation States, and prefers to discuss the first peoples of either the Americas (including South America), or of "Turtle Island" (North and Central America). See Mojica, "Theatrical Diversity" 3.

[6] *Princess Pocahontas* was first workshopped in Toronto in the Spring of 1988, received a second workshop by Nightwood Theatre in co-production with Native Earth Performing Arts in May 1989, and was given a work-in-progress presentation in November of that year. It received its first full production at the Theatre Passe Muraille Backspace in co-production with Nightwood in February-March of 1990. It was first published in *Canadian Theatre Review* 64 in Fall 1990 and republished by Women's Press, together with *Birdwoman and the Suffragettes*, in 1991. *Birdwoman and the Suffragettes* was first broadcast in 1991 for CBC Radio Drama's *Vanishing Point* series, *Adventure Stories for Big Girls*.

[7] It is also worth noting that in 1984 The Women's Press published Beth Brant's *A Gathering of Spirit: A Collection by North American Women* (reprinted in 1988); in 1987 ECW Press published the Thomas King, Cheryl Calver, and Helen Hoy collection, *The Native in Literature*; and in 1990 *Canadian Literature* published a special issue on *Native Writers and Canadian Writing* edited by N. H. New, in which the Godard article appeared.

8 See, in particular, Fraser, and see my discussion of the controversy in "Reading Material."

9 The best accounts of these women, all of which (except Cypess) are cited as "recommended" in the published versions of Mojica's plays, are Barbour (which should, however, be read with the articles by Green and Young); Clark and Edmonds (which Mojica, though she recommends it, suggests should be read "with a historical grain of salt" [85]); and Cypess.

10 It is startling how vehemently this demonisation continues, even in websites that are clearly attempting to reclaim pride among what Anzaldúa calls "the new Mestiza." One site, for example, "a tribute to my native culture" by a self-identified "Mexica (NOT HISPANIC, NOT LATINO)," which sets out to celebrate "a beautiful history" and culture, nevertheless feels obligated to preface its comments on La Malinche by saying, "as horrible as a traitor as she was, she didn't do this alone" (see "Nimexihcat!!!," <http://www.hooked.net/~mictlan/mexica.html>). Sites by non--Natives, -Mexicans or -Mestizas, on the other hand—especially men—tend to defend or celebrate "Doña Marina" (see, for example, Lenchek, "Harlot" and "Unrecognised, <http://www.mexconnect.com/mex_/travel/slenchek/ slmalinche. html>), picking up on the "standard" non-Native representation of her (and of "her own race") in Fehrenbach's 1973 history of Mexico, which in some ways echoes Van Kirk's account of the Canadian "fur-trade wives":

> If there is one villainess in Mexican history, she is Malintzin. She was to become the ethnic traitoress supreme. The modern Mexican view, however, is totally emotional rather than accurate. Malintzin was not a symbolic traitress, but an unfortunate and intelligent Amerindian girl, who made the best of the situations life handed her. She was made a slave by her own race and presented to the Spaniards as a concubine, and as Doña Marina, Cortes' mistress, she enjoyed more prestige and consideration than almost any woman of Mexico had ever had. (Fehrenbach 131)

11 According to *Colliers Encyclopedia*, as quoted by Clark and Edmonds, "there are more statues dedicated to her [Sacagawea] than to any other American Woman" (95-96) The authors provide (155-59) an appendix listing these "Sacagawea Memorials" which in itself is almost comic, and on which Mojica draws extensively.

12 Chief among these are Anzaldúa's (significantly) bilingual book, *Borderlands/La Frontera* (which includes on pp. 22-23 Anzaldúa's rejection of the Chicana's internalisation of the role of betrayer, quoted below, in which she compares herself to La Malinche); Chrystos's *Not Vanishing* (which includes her poem, "I am Not Your Princess" [66-67]), which Mojica cites in *Princess Pocahontas and the Blue Spots*, and which would seem to have been inspirational); Moraga's *Loving in the War Years* (which includes the important essay "A Long Line of Vendidas" [90-144], in which Moraga presents herself as a "traitor" to her people, and compares herself to La

Malinche); Anzaldúa and Moraga's important edited collection, *This Bridge Called My Back* (which includes a major section on "Racism in the Women's Movement" [59-101]); Beth Brant's edited collection *A Gathering of Spirit* (which is dedicated to murdered Native Nova Scotian Anna Mae Aquash, whose story comes at the end of *Princess Pocahontas and the Blue Spots* and which includes Paula Gunn Allen's poem to Sacagawea, "The One Who Skins Cats" [19-24]); Diane Burns's *Riding the one-eyed Ford*, and Paula Gunn Allen's *The Sacred Hoop*, already cited as both essential and inspirational.

[13] As the published script of the plays indicates (86), "Monique Mojica is a Kuna-Rappahonnock half-breed," the daughter of a Native mother and Jewish father born in New York City, of which more below.

[14] Because my focus is on the mothers of mixed-race nations and their descendants, I am not considering in detail here the important role in history or in Mojica's play of the (bleakly) alternative stories of the Women of the Puña or of Anna Mae Aquash. For historical accounts of the former, see Silverblatt 197-210; for historical accounts of the latter, see Brand. The Women of the Puña appear in *Princess Pocahontas and the Blue Spots* in Transformation 7 (35-38), "betrayed by our own fathers brothers uncles/husbands," but refusing to weep, and setting up their own separatist society. The murder of Anna Mae Aquash is treated near the end of the play, in Transformation 11, which also deals with the interrogation of Chilean women through the insertion of live rats, wired for electric shocks, into their vaginas.

[15] The best account and analysis of the Chiapas' use of technology in their struggles is Cleaver's article "The Zapatistas and the Electronic Fabric of Struggle," published on the web as listed in the Works Cited. A shorter version appeared as a chapter in John Holloway and Elofna Pelaez, ed., *Zapatista! Reinventing Revolution in Mexico* (London: Pluto, 1998). In (only) apparent contradistinction to this internationalist thrust, Native peoples in Canada achieved much of their success in these years through the tactic of calling themselves "First Nations." This title implicitly denied the nineteenth-century retroactive authority of the Canadian Nation State and its right to legislate on their behalf, and also constructed "Nations" that crossed later-day political and geographical boundaries. This is most noticeably the case in the instance of reserves/reservations that straddle the U.S./Canada border and cause perennial headaches for legislators and politicians concerned with everything from tariffs and taxes to smuggling.

[16] Barbour is to some extent an exception to this rule, pointing out as he does parallels between the colonisation of Virginia and Mexico (6, 23). In spite of the fact that his book is called *Pocahontas and Her World*, however, Barbour presents these as general cultural parallels or lines of historical influence without mentioning links between the stories of Pocahontas and La Malinche.

[17] See <http://www.mexconnect.com/mex_/travel/slenchek/slmalinche.html>.

[18] There are also, however, various websites mounted by Natives that do offer contestatory accounts of the Western histories of all of these women, but attacks on distorted "facts" in Western representations have been as ineffectual, it seems to me, as were offers from the Powhatan Confederacy to "assist Disney with cultural and historical accuracy" in the making of their 1995 film, "Pocahontas" (see "Pocahontas Myth").

[19] See, for example, Allen 282. She notes the reputation of traitress shared by these women within their own cultures, and the fact that they all bore sons to their imperialist partners—both things crucial to Mojica's interrogations, and to the subsequent histories and lives of their descendants.

[20] There is a considerable literature on the naming of Sacagawea, which Mojica capitalises on by stressing the non-Native obsession with naming (understood as pinning down, entrapping, and limiting). See, for example, Irving W. Anderson's representative web article "Sacajawea?-Sakakawea?-Scagawea?: Spelling- Pronunciation-Meaning," <http://www.lewisandclarkgnet.org>.

[21] Even the Disney film version of "Pocahontas" nods in the right direction, when Pocahontas responds to John Smith's description of gold—"you know, it's, it's yellow. Comes out of the ground. It's really valuable"—by showing him a fat and glistening cob of corn. Ironically, of course, what she shows him is clearly sweet corn, not what is now known as "Indian corn."

[22] See Bhabha on hybridity. The canonical progenitor of subaltern studies is Gayatri Chakravorty Spivak; see her "Can the Subaltern Speak?" and her earlier "Subaltern Studies: Deconstructing Historiography."

[23] Lotbinière-Harwood begins her chapter entitled "*Deux mots pour chaque chose*" by saying "*Je suis une traduction. Dans mon corps bilingue habitent au moins deux mots pour chaque chose*".

Works Cited

Acosta, Juvenal, ed. *Light from a Nearby Window: Contemporary Mexican Poetry.* San Francisco: City Lights, 1993.

Allen, Paula Gunn. *The Sacred Hoop: Recovering the Feminine in American Indian Traditions.* Boston: Beacon, 1986.

Anderson, Benedict. *Imagined Communities: Reflections on the Origin and Spread of Nationalism.* London: Verso, 1991.

Anderson, Irving W. "Sacagawea?-Sakakawea?-Sacagawea?: Spelling-Pronunciation-Meaning." <http://www.lewisandclarkgnet.org>.

"Anna Mae Aquash Time Line," <http://www.cbc.ca/news/background/pictou_aquash/timeline.html>.

Anzaldúa, Gloria. *Borderlands/La Frontera: The New Mestiza.* San Francisco: Aunt Lute, 1987.

Baker, Marie Anneharte. "Angry Enough to Spit, but With *Dry Lips* It Hurts More Than You Know." *Canadian Theatre Review* 68 (1991): 88-90.

Bannerji, Himani, ed. *Returning the Gaze: Essays on Racism, Feminism and Politics.* Toronto: Sister Vision, 1993.

Barbour, Philip L. *Pocahontas and her World.* Boston: Houghton Mifflin, 1969.

Benjamin, Walter. "The Task of the Translator." *Walter Benjamin: Selected Writings Volume 1: 1913-1926.* Ed. Marcus Bullock and Michael W. Jennings. Cambridge, Mass: Belknap, Harvard UP, 1996. 253-263.

Bhabha, Homi. "Signs Taken for Wonders: Questions of Ambivalence and Authority under a Tree outside Delhi." *Critical Inquiry* 12.1 (Fall 1985): 144-65.

"A Biography of Anna Mae." <http://www.dickshovel.com/bio.html>.

Brand, Johanna. *The Life and Death of Anna Mae Aquash.* Toronto: J. Lorimer, 1978.

Brant, Beth (Degonwadonti), ed. *A Gathering of Spirit: A Collection by North American Indian Women.* Toronto: The Women's Press, 1984.

Brobribb, Somer. "The Traditional Roles of Native Women in Canada and the Impact of Colonisation." *The Canadian Journal of Native Studies* 4.1 (1984): 85-103.

Brydon, Diana. "'Empire Bloomers': Cross-Dressing's Double Cross." *Essays on Canadian Writing* 54 (1994): 23-45.

———. "No (Wo)man is an Island: Rewriting Cross-Cultural Encounters within the Canadian Context." *Kunapipi* 15.2 (1993). 48-56.

Burns, Diane. *Riding the One-Eyed Ford.* New York: Contact 11, 1981.

Cashman, Cheryl. "Toronto's Zanies." *Canadian Theatre Review* 67 (1991): 22-31.

Clark, Ella E. and Margot Edmonds. *Sacagawea of the Lewis and Clark Expedition.* Berkeley: U of California P, 1979.

Cleaver, Harry. "The Zapatistas and the Electronic Fabric of Struggle." <http://www.eco.utexas.edu/faculty/Cleaver/zaps.html>; repr. (shorter version) in *Zapatista! Reinventing Revolution in Mexico.* Ed. John Holloway and Eloína Peláez. London: Pluto, 1998.

Custis, George Washington Parke. *Pocahontas or the Settlers of Virginia: Representative American Plays from 1767 to the Present Day.* Ed. Arthur Hobson Quinn. Century Company, 1917; New York: Appleton-Century Crofts, 1953, 7th ed. revised. 165-92.

Crystos. *Not Vanishing.* Vancouver: Press Gang, 1988.

Cypess, Sandra Messinger. *La Malinche in Mexican Literature: From History to Myth.* Austin: U of Texas P, 1991.

d'Aulaire, Ingri and Edgar Parin. *Pocahontas.* New York: Doubleday, 1946.

Fehrenbach, T.R. *Fire and Blood: A History of Mexico.* New York: Macmillan, 1973.

Fiske, Jo-Anne. "Pocahontas's Grandaughters: Spiritual Transition and Tradition of Carrier Women of British Columbia." *Ethnohistory* 43 (1996): 663-81.

Fraser, Marion Botsford. "'Contempt for Women Overshadows Powerful Play.' Review of *Dry Lips Oughta Move to Kapuskasing* by Tomson Highway. Royal Alexandria Theatre, Toronto." *The Globe and Mail* (Toronto: 17 April 1991). C1.

Gilbert, Helen and Joanne Tompkins. *Post-Colonial Drama: Theory, Practice, Politics.* London: Routledge, 1996.

Godard, Barbara. "The Politics of Representation: Some Native Canadian Women Writers." *Native Writers and Canadian Writing: Canadian Literature Special Issue.* Ed. N. H. New. Vancouver: UBC Press, 1990. 183-225.

Green, Rayna. "The Pocahontas Perplex: The Image of Indian Women in American Culture." *Canadian Journal of Native Studies* 4 (1984): 698-714.

Hale, Amanda. "A Dialectical Drama of Facts and Fiction on the Feminist Fringe." *Work in Progress: Building Feminist Culture.* Ed. Rhea Trebegov. Toronto: The Women's Press, 1987. 77-99.

Harvie, Jennifer and Ric Knowles. "Dialogical Monologue: A Dialogue." *The Theatre of Form and the Production of Meaning: Contemporary Canadian Dramaturgies.* by Ric Knowles. Toronto: ECW, 1999. 193-210.

Hebard, Grace Raymond. *Sacajawea: A Guide and Interpreter of the Lewis and Clark expedition, with an Account of the Travels of Toussaint Charbonneau, and of Jean Baptiste, the Expedition Papoose.* 1932. Glendale, California: Arthur H. Clark, 1967.

Howard, Harold P. *Sacajawea.* Norman, Oklahoma: U of Oklahoma P, 1971.

King, Thomas, Cheryl Calver, and Helen Hoy, ed. *The Native in Literature.* Toronto: ECW Press, 1987.

Knowles, Ric[hard Paul]. "Reading Material: Transfers, Remounts, and the Production of Meaning in Contemporary Canadian Drama and Theatre." *Essays on Canadian Writing* 51/52 (1993-1994). 258-95.

———. *The Theatre of Form and the Production of Meaning: Contemporary Canadian Dramaturgies.* Toronto: ECW, 1999.

Lenchek, Shep. "'La Malinche' – Harlot or Heroine?" <http://www.mexconnect.com/mex_/travel/slenchek/slmalinche.html>.

———. "La Malinche, Unrecognised Heroine." <http://www.mexconnect.com/mex_/travel/slenchek/slmalinche.html>.

Lionnet, Françoise. *Postcolonial Representations: Women, Literature, Identity.* Ithaca: Cornell UP, 1995.

Lotbinière-Harwood, Susanne de. *Re-Belle et Infidèle: La traduction comme pratique de réécriture au féminin/The Body Bilingual: Translation as Rewriting in the Feminine.* Montreal: Les éditions du remue-ménage/Toronto: Women's Press, 1991.

McDonald, Christie V., ed. *The Ear of the Other: Otobiography, Transference, Translation: Texts and Discussions with Jacques Derrida.* New York: Schocken, 1985.

Mojica, Monique. *Princess Pocahontas and the Blue Spots: Two Plays.* Toronto: Women's Press, 1991.

———. Public presentation. Association for Canadian Theatre Studies annual conference. Ottawa, Ontario, June 1998.

———. Public presentation. Conference on "Gender/Colonialism/Postcolonialism." University of Guelph, Guelph, Ontario. 5-8 November 1992.

———. "Theatrical Diversity on Turtle Island: A Tool Towards the Healing." Editorial. *Canadian Theatre Review* 68 (1991): 3.

Moraga, Cherríe. *Loving in the War Years: lo que nunca pasó por sus labios.* Boston: South End, 1983.

Moraga, Cherríe and Gloria Anzaldúa ed. *This Bridge Called My Back: Writings By Radical Women of Color.* Watertown, Mass.: Persephone Press, 1981.

"Nimexihcat!!!" <http://www.hooked.net/~mictlan/mexica.html>.

Niranjana, Tejaswini. *Siting Translation: History, Post-Structuralism, and the Colonial Context.* Berkeley: U of California P, 1992.

Nunn, Robert. "'They Kinda Wanta Play it Their Own Way.' Hybridity and Mimicry in Plays by Three Native Canadian Playwrights." Paper presented at the conference on "Compr(om)ising Post-Colonialism(s)." University of Wollongong, Wollongong, Australia, 10-13 February 1999.

Petrone, Penny, ed. *Native Literature in Canada: From the Oral Tradition to the Present.* Toronto: Oxford UP, 1990.

Silverblatt, Irene. *Moon, Sun, and Witches: Gender Ideologies and Class in Inca and Colonial Peru.* Princeton: Princeton UP, 1987.

Spivak, Gayatri Chakravorty. "Can the Subaltern Speak?" *Marxism and the Interpretation of Culture.* Ed. Cary Nelson and Lawrence Grossberg. Urbana, Ill.: U of Illinois P, 1988. 271-313.

———. "Subaltern Studies: Deconstructing Historiography." *Subaltern Studies IV: Writings on South Asian History and Society.* Ed. Ranajit Guha. Delhi: Oxford UP, 1986. 330-63.

Tompkins, Joanne. "'Spectacular Resistance': Metatheatre in Postcolonial Drama." *Modern Drama* 38.1 (1995). 42-51.

———. "'The Story of Rehearsal Never Ends': Rehearsal, Performance, Identity in Settler Culture Drama." *Canadian Literature* 144 (Spring 1995): 142-61.

Van Kirk, Sylvia. *"Many Tender Ties": Women in Fur-Trade Society in Western Canada, 1670-1870.* Winnipeg, Manitoba: Watson & Dwyer, 1980.

The Beginning of Cree Performance Culture

by Geraldine Manossa

I decided to begin this article with a Cree story because I wanted a Cree worldview to be the basis for my writing. The article explores Native Performance Culture by examining the contemporary sociological significance between the viewer, writer and performer. The sharing of cultural knowledge through storytelling is something that occurred prior to contact and perseveres today and continues to shape the realm of Native Performance Culture.

I have listened to many Cree interpretations of the *Wasakaychak* creation story, and each time the storyteller has insisted on including his or her own twists and experiences into the adventures of *Wasakaychak*. Each time, as well, the storyteller announced before the telling of the story that "this is how it really happened." One of the most memorable occasions I recall was when I was eighteen. I graduated from high school and was admitted into a Native Communications/Journalism course at a local college. Before classes started in the fall each admitted student was required to participate in a cultural camp, held during the summer, near the Rocky Mountains. I was the youngest student among my peers and listened for the next seven days to a lifetime of knowledge from the Elders who taught there. Ten students attended the camp, the head of the Native Communication/Journalism Program, and two spiritual advisors. Eddie Bellrose, one of the spiritual advisors, had done a lot of counselling and work in northern communities. So, there we were, thirteen of us, all of us strangers to each other.

On the first night we gather into a sitting room. Eddie sits down in a brown leather recliner. He weaves his fingers through the holes on the worn armrest. A few of us congregate around the doorway; his eyes give off a soft radiance, welcoming us with a content grin. Eddie's skinny braids rest below the front of his shoulders. He motions us with his shaky hand to come in and sit. "My girl," he says, pointing with his lips, "Sit there." I sit next to him. His gesture of calling me "my girl" brings me home to my family. Relatives older in age and family friends, when visiting our home, would talk to us kids in this comforting manner. Feeling more at ease, I nestle into my chair and scan the room. Two other students, Tom and Harley, continue a quiet conversation with the occasional outbursts of laughter. The rest of us watch Eddie as he quietly rolls a cigarette and then proceeds to roll a couple of extras. I think to myself, "Yep, this is going to be a long night." Eddie looks up as he finishes licking the last of his rolled cigarettes and begins, "Okay, tonight I'm going to tell you about *Wasakaychak*."

Eddie is wearing a plaid shirt neatly tucked into brown pants. He appears at ease with everything he does. He slowly brushes off the leftover tobacco that has fallen onto his shirt and pants while rolling his cigarettes. Eddie focuses his attention on lighting his cigarette; he takes a puff and smiles, "Yes, he was quite the character, that one." I look around the room and everyone has a smile that seems to confirm Eddie's interpretation of *Wasakaychak*. Tom chuckles and elbows an already smiling Harley. Since we arrived at the camp, Tom is either smiling or laughing. Harley, more composed, nods his head a few times in response to Tom's elbowing. I laugh at Harley and Tom and soon the entire group is laughing. I look toward Judy, and she is shaking her head while laughing at the same time. I can tell by the quizzical look on her face that she really has no idea why she is laughing. Then Eddie begins, "This is how it really happened, a very long time ago."

"Okay, this one day, *Wasakaychak* and his brother were floating on a raft. They were not alone and had many of their animal relatives floating with them down this river." Eddie pauses and takes a deep breath and heavily exhales. He hesitates and again takes another deep breath, as if it pains him to go on. "Okay, the earth is flooded because of *Wasakaychak*. He took revenge against the water creatures that had earlier killed his brother." Eddie's eyes solemnly search the room. He tilts his head to the side and shares his pain with us by cupping his chest with both hands. "Even though *Wasakaychak* brought his brother back to life, he still went ahead and killed those creatures." Bewildered, Eddie shakes his head. "Maybe the water spirits took revenge too… cause I just don't know… I…." He stops talking, as if lost in the spiteful actions of *Wasakaychak*. There is a look of puzzlement on everyone's face in the room except Tom's. Tom cannot contain his grin any more and quietly laughs to himself. I want to laugh too because of Tom's flightiness. I also wonder why *Wasakaychak*, even though his brother was brought back to life, decided to kill these creatures. I remember asking my brother, Basil, the reasoning behind *Wasakaychak*'s actions. He didn't really know either, but he did inform me that *Wasakaychak* was warned by a medicine man that a flood would occur if these creatures were killed. It was based on this warning that *Wasakaychak* built a raft; he knew the consequences of his actions.

Eddie's voice lowers and he looks around the room. "Shhhh…" he continues. The room is quiet and still. He captures our attention further by waving his hands toward himself. "Closer," he says. Everyone except Harley leans forward. He sits back, in a reclined position, with his arms folded over his chest and nods his head. The rest of us wait anxiously for Eddie to speak. "You know the one thing he forgot to do?" Eddie asks. Eddie drops his head into his hands and shakes his head in disbelief. "That *Wasakaychak* forgot to do something very important. What was it?" He asks again. Tom confidently blurts, "He forgot to grab a piece of the earth." Cheryl meticulously picks the lint off her cardigan. Yawning, she says, "That's *Wasakaychak* for you."

Not everyone at the cultural camp is Cree, so the entire group may not be familiar with the *Wasakaychak* creation story. I did get the feeling though that the entire group could identify with the excitement, energy, and multi-dimensional personality of *Wasakaychak*'s character. Within all Indigenous communities there exist numerous mythological figures. In general, a trickster character is overly confident, boastful, arrogant and conceited; he seems to ridicule with his shortcomings. Even though *Wasakaychak* is capable of transforming into various beings, his powers are limited, and in the end he is held accountable for his wrong doings. For Cree people he is responsible for the creation of many land formations that exist today. We are part of *Wasakaychak*'s journey and have been since time memorial; we see ourselves in him. This is why Tom found the events leading up to Eddie's announcement of *Wasakaychak*'s misfortune so entertaining; he was familiar and could relate to *Wasakaychak*'s fate.

In all of the adventures of *Wasakaychak* it appears that *Wasakaychak* may succeed in tricking an unsuspecting creature or being; however, an unforeseen event occurs, catching *Wasakaychak* off-guard. Eddie's voice is calm, and once again he is ready to continue. "That's right," he says, "*Wasakaychak* is always ahead of himself... you know... always trying to trick the animals and not thinking clearly. That's why he gets into so much trouble... he tries to do too much at a time." Eddie sits back in his chair and lights another cigarette and comfortably rests his hands on his round stomach. Like Tom, I have laughed or held my breath, anticipating the consequences *Wasakaychak* will face, due to his hasty and careless actions. I laugh because *Wasakaychak*'s character always assumes and believes that everything is going to end up the way he envisioned. However, just when you think this character is going to succeed in tricking or conning someone, his scheme falls apart leaving *Wasakaychak* scrambling for order. Eddie's voice interrupts my thoughts. "So for many days and nights, *Wasakaychak*, his brother and the animals floated on the raft, in search of land or even the tiniest speck of dirt."

Eddie shakes his head and butts out his cigarette. "It doesn't look too good for them. They have no food and the animals are getting tired." Eddie sighs. "So do you know what he does? He calls Beaver over because *Wasakaychak* knows he is a good swimmer," Eddie bolts upright and takes in a deep breath. He unbuttons the cuffs on his shirt and quickly rolls up his sleeves. Still holding his breath, Eddie sticks out his chest. I see the powerful and confident *Wasakaychak* emerge from Eddie's body. With his hands on his hips, he stands unyielding. Eddie's voice deepens. He says, "my brother, Beaver, I need you to dive deep into the water until you reach the earth." Eddie makes out like he is diving, pushing the water to his sides, blowing air out of his lungs. He continues this diving motion like a wave flowing up and down. Still swimming, Eddie turns to Judy and says, "Beaver you are my brother, and I know you can do this." Judy smiles calmly and accepts *Wasakaychak*'s request. Eddie takes another deep breath and continues the diving motion. His arms curve downward and then arc up; the rest of his body follows curving like a snake. Eddie makes his way toward Colleen who is sitting next to Judy. Attempting to discourage Eddie's advance, Colleen curls up her body, hugging her legs toward her chest. She tucks her head into her arms. Tom chuckles loudly, which seems to cheer on Eddie. Even Harley is doubled over laughing. Eddie continues to dive, plunge, rise and swim around Colleen, but now each movement is greatly exaggerated. He sways his hips from side to side, adding some new choreography to the story. By this time, the whole room echoes laughter.

Tom is hysterical, holding his stomach; he laughs uncontrollably, falling off his chair. In a loud, drawn out voice, Eddie instructs Colleen. "You need to grab a speck of dirt and bring it up to me, and then I can make the land appear again." Peeking up at him, she nods, shyly, giggles and drops her head into her lap, hiding her face. Pleased with her response, Eddie relaxes and *Wasakaychak* disappears.

Eddie sinks into his chair and grabs a handkerchief from his pant pocket and gently blots his forehead. By now, he is out of breath but still continues. "The Beaver dived into the water," he announces. Eddie's hand shakes as he carries out the downward diving motion, this time like Beaver's paws dog paddling. He adds, "You know... those animals waited and waited for that Beaver to come up from the water, but it was a long time, and still he didn't show. They gave up, and thought that their brother, the Beaver, had drowned." Eddie's hands and arm movements flow gracefully from side to side, like waves washing upon shore. His upper body follows the wavy trail that his hands and arms are tracing out. His movements remind me of the waves back home in Calling Lake, gently washing against the sand. The sudden sound of Eddie's voice brings me back to the Rocky Mountains. He shouts, "From these waves came Beaver, gasping for air. It was *Wasakaychak* who pulled him from the water." Eddie's voice slows. "He didn't make it to the bottom. He has no dirt." Again, Eddie's body transforms into *Wasakaychak*. Sitting grand, he inhales, and his entire chest protrudes. Carefully, his eyes scan the room, until he finds another capable assistant. "You," Eddie's voice calls. His eyes focus intently on Harley. "It's up to you, my brother, Otter. You must dive deep into the water until you reach the earth. We need just a small speck of dirt, even the tiniest particle will do. It's up to you, my brother." Harley sits up, honoured that *Wasakaychak* calls on him to help in the recovery of the earth. After announcing the dilemma to Otter, Eddie settles back into his chair. It is as if he is waiting for a response. We all wait. The room is quiet. Harley looks toward us with admiration, as if we are the other animals on the raft. He doesn't speak, but nods his head self-importantly, accepting Eddie's request. We anxiously wait for the change in tone and rhythm of Eddie's voice. His voice is the orchestra that dictates the movements of his body. This is how he brings to life all the beings of the story. I look at my fellow listeners and notice that everyone is captivated by Eddie's presence.

He lights a cigarette, takes a couple of long puffs and lets the smoke escape out of the sides of his mouth. He opens his mouth to talk but stops. He rubs his forehead and briskly shakes his head. He is now ready to speak as if whatever he was previously going to say has escaped him. "The Otter really had no choice. His animal brothers were starving. There really was no one else who could do this, who could dive deep into the water and clutch some dirt." Eddie's "matter-of-fact" tone came about because he needed to emphasize how important Otter's actions were for the survival of the entire animal community. In other words, *Wasakaychak* singles out Otter to help shape the destiny of all the animals; therefore, this gesture is not a time for the individual (Harley/Otter) to bathe in his own spotlight. Eddie puffs on his cigarette; he adds, "So, the animals waited and waited for the Otter to return. Things didn't look good. The animals wait for their brother to resurface from the blackness of the water." Eddie shakes his head from side to side, butts out his cigarette and exhales a mouthful of smoke. "Otter's body rose to the top of the water. He, like the Beaver, was breathless. He didn't make it to the earth. He had no dirt for *Wasakaychak*." Eddie carefully scans his audience. He throws his hands up into the air, and asks us, "Now what?" We all sit quietly, waiting for Eddie's cue.

Harley sits in his usual reclined position, legs stretched out and arms folded over his chest. He focuses on the floor; his spotlight is dim. "All of a sudden, *Wasakaychak* and the other animals hear a tiny sound coming from the far corner of the raft." Eddie whispers. "It's coming from Muskrat. I will do it, Muskrat tells *Wasakaychak*. I will dive deep into the water and I will snatch some dirt for you." Eddie looks to us, posing another question. "Do you know what *Wasakaychak* said to Muskrat?" We remain silent. He answers. "Nothing! *Wasakaychak* brushed Muskrat off, by turning his back on his own brother." There is an urgent sound in Eddie's voice; his breath quickens. "And in that moment, a splash shakes the raft and Muskrat is gone. He disappeared into the water." I can hear the deep hollow sound that comes from Muskrat's plunge into the water. I can see the ripples of his dive, reaching the unsteady raft and still reaching outward beyond the deepest and blackest areas of the lake. Eddie quietly adds, "*Wasakaychak* dragged himself to the corner of the raft and sat there, slumped over. That *Wasakaychak* sure could pout… almost as well as he could gloat." Eddie slips in a smile, but then returns to his remorse. "*Wasakaychak* had given up, and some of the animals on the raft started to say their good-byes to one another. It was a very sad moment."

Eddie's exhausted body lazily reclines into the armchair. Again, we wait in silence; we wait for the return of Muskrat. Out of the stillness, Eddie reaches his cupped hand forward, barely having enough strength to steady it. His body holds that pose, and he stares beyond the walls in this room. In one motion, Eddie slowly lifts himself up from the chair, pulling and lifting something heavy toward his chest. It is Muskrat's body. Eddie's body shifts to a neutral stance, and he announces. "*Wasakaychak* was the first to spot Muskrat's body surfacing. He alone picked him up from the water." Eddie repeats the same slow sequence of the pulling and lifting of Muskrat's body. "*Wasakaychak* couldn't help but pity his brother. He laid his brother's lifeless body down on the raft and walked away." Eddie lowers his head, as if he were about to pray for Muskrat. He takes out his handkerchief and wipes along his forehead and around his eyes. As if not wanting to be part of the dialogue, Eddie says: "Now, the animals really began to worry because they had never seen *Wasakaychak* act so lost. He always had a plan or trick for every situation, and he always had a back up plan." Eddie clears his voice. He whispers and pronounces every word quietly as if it were his last. "The raft continued to float on the lake without a word or sound coming from *Wasakaychak* or the animals."

Eddie lights the last of his rolled cigarettes and again leans back into his chair. He lazily blows the smoke from his cigarette toward the ceiling, where his eyes remain focused. "You see," Eddie says, "one of the animals discovered that Muskrat did get some dirt under his claws. *Wasakaychak* didn't even bother to look. He had given up hope on his little brother and didn't even check his claws." Eddie's body remains reclined in the armchair. Still looking up toward the ceiling in a daze, he continues. "*Wasakaychak* came over to Muskrat and blew into his mouth, bringing him back to life. He took the tiny particle of dirt and began to roll it and as he rolled it, *Wasakaychak* blew into his own hand and the dirt grew and grew with each magical breath." Eddie leans toward his audience and manages to smile proudly at each of us, as if we were his own children. I beam back at him.

During the course of his storytelling, some of Eddie's hair slipped out from his braids. His gray hair hangs loose around his jaw, and he clumsily brushes it away, tucking it behind his ear. Eventually, his hair wins out and remains dangling around his face. His performance ends. No longer transformed into *Wasakaychak* or the water, he, like the rest of us, enjoys the decline of the story's events. "Yes, *Wasakaychak* recreated the earth as we know it today. With his breath he grew forests and lakes. *Wasakaychak* wanted to make sure that the earth was large enough for everyone to live on, so he sent his brother the Wolf on a journey to make sure it was. When Wolf didn't return after a long time, *Wasakaychak* knew the earth was large enough." Eddie grins. "You know something? *Wasakaychak* sure missed his brother, and he's been roaming the earth looking for him ever since... really.... Good thing, eh?" he adds, "...'cause us Indians wouldn't have anything to talk about, eh?"

Eddie is referring to the many stories that exist today which continue to be recounted by the storytellers of the community. The *Wasakaychak* stories that we have today are a result of the encounters *Wasakaychak* had with his animal brothers and the land. There is actually a story about *Wasakaychak* misplacing his eyeballs, and about *Wasakaychak* whipping the birch tree, giving the birch its stripped markings. Eddie slaps his lap with one hand and wipes the tears from his eyes with another. Still laughing, he says, "Oh that *Wasakaychak* sure was something." A Cree person just has to mention the name *Wasakaychak* and people grin. How can we not smile when picturing *Wasakaychak* on the ground, clumsily looking for his eyeballs? I recall on many occasions, during a *Wasakaychak* story, thinking "oh no, not again," as *Wasakaychak* was about to trick yet another animal relative. A *Wasakaychak* story always captivates an audience. The listener never really knows how the storyteller will dramatize the story's events. I have seen one storyteller interpret *Wasakaychak* in a more "clown-like" fashion. Rather than portraying *Wasakaychak* the way Eddie does, where *Wasakaychak* appears physically powerful, forceful and strong, he made his physical attributes comical. This storyteller portrayed *Wasakaychak* slouched over with a protruding buttock and arms as limp as spaghetti.

The collective manner through which knowledge, images, symbols, actions and humour are shared from listener to listener and from storyteller to listener is where I believe the essence of Native performance arises. This is also the core of contemporary Native theatre. If someone asked me to imitate *Wasakaychak*, I could do so because he is so full of life, comedy, energy and magic. He comes from Cree land. Through our storytellers, we as listeners are exposed to and witness the movements, songs and dances of water, of trees and of various life beings. *Wasakaychak's* breath is magic; he can breathe life into the dead. Through his breath he created the earth.

For centuries Cree storytellers retained and passed on this knowledge to their community. Today, thanks to the storytellers of Native communities, I, as a performer, can approach my work and training based upon the history of my ancestors.

One story that I heard from my mother about my great-granny has had a profound effect on how I view the ideas around sharing everything from food, to stories, to worldviews. My mother remembers eating a meal with her granny outside of her tee-pee. My great-granny refused to live inside a house after they had been built for the people, and she stationed herself in her tee-pee, outside of her daughter's home. My mother remembers, her granny made this terrific stew full of vegetables. I say terrific because usually granny's stews consisted only of potatoes, turnips and moose meat. However, this stew was different. Not only did it contain its usual blend, but also the stew was full of carrots, peas and beans. Both Granny and granddaughter slowly slurped and savoured each spoonful. A man, yelling and screaming outside of their tee-pee, interrupted them. My mother said that the louder he screamed the more his face seemed to glow red. Clutched in his hand was a piece of string that he kept waving about while he yelled. Based on the anger and anxiety of this man in the long black dress, my mom thought that he was going to take the string to her granny's neck. He didn't.

Earlier, the priest discovered some carrots, peas and beans missing from his garden. The priest had used the string to measure the footprints he found near the missing vegetables. He stood there, clutching the string, an invaluable witness, ready to prove that Granny was the guilty culprit. This man pointed at her feet and continued to scream at her in an unfamiliar language. He wanted to measure her feet. Unmoved by the priest's emotional outpouring, Granny disappeared back into the tee-pee and returned with a pair of non-matching black rubbers. Granny wore the rubbers over her moccasins to protect them, when she journeyed away from home. Granny was infamous for collecting and wearing mis-matched rubbers on her feet. No two pairs of Granny's rubbers matched up. So when the priest began the meticulous procedure of measuring the string to the size of each rubber, his calculations didn't work out as expected. Not exactly your Cinderella story, eh? The man was furious; he knew something wasn't quite right but couldn't figure it out. He took one last look at Granny, pointed his finger at her accusingly, muttered something to himself and stomped off. I'm sure he vowed vengeance, as my mother remembers it, because the two of them continued to share these bowls of hearty stew, and the priest made regular appearances at her Granny's tee-pee with his piece of string.

Granny's relations still came to see her, reminding her that the priest's vegetable garden was his and his alone. They hoped that these visits would stop this stubborn old woman from helping herself to the priest's garden. Like *Wasakaychak*, the stories of Great-granny shared among my family have the listener shaking her head in disbelief. When Great-granny is talked about in a joking manner, she is called crazy and eccentric. I view her, however, as a woman whose life was shaped by her experiences with her surrounding landscapes. Throughout her whole life, the earth had nourished her and her children. So why was the priest's section of land (all of a sudden) any different from the rest of the territory that she knew so well? This story comes from Cree land and from the collective interactions of Cree community members with each other on Cree land. These are some of the origins of Native performance and contemporary Native drama.

Floyd Favel Starr is a Cree from Poundmaker, Saskatchewan; he is a playwright, director and actor. In his article "The Artificial Tree," he defines Native Performance Culture as the "developing practices of our ancestors" (83). Before her death, Great-granny, like *Wasakaychak*, continued to shape the land. Even when it meant defying a priest, a government imposed authority figure within her community. She allowed the land to nourish her because according to her Cree worldview, food is a gift from the creator. In return, Great-granny would be both respectful and thankful in prayer to the land because it provided food for her and her family.

When Eddie tells a story, he acknowledges his listeners, therefore, making them part of his performance. Both the listener and the teller are actively involved in the process of storytelling, an exchange occurs. Eddie feeds off the energy of the listener and something is shared, be it laughter or a new perspective. Sharing is vital to Cree performance because sharing is vital to Cree culture. Great-granny understood everything that comes from these lands has the potential to be shared. That is why she could never understand why the priest scolded her for taking from his garden. Storytelling is a time of sharing. Sharing knowledge, humour, tears, songs and dances. Storytelling is about sharing the history and knowledge of the land, by recounting how beings since the beginning of time have interacted with it. According to Highway, when Native theatre performance is shared on stage, the audience witnesses "treasures that have been there for thousands of years. It [is] like finding a treasure chest filled with diamonds and silver" (2). Native performers are taking "the gems out of those chests[,] ...showing them to a world that never realized what a richness of culture was hidden away just under the top soil" (2).

Favel Starr's article is based on his research of Native Performance Culture over a five-year period (1991-96). In an attempt to develop a working methodology for it, he discovered it was necessary to reduce Native songs and dances to their "bare essentials" and find the essence of what makes them Native (83). He feels this process, which he labels "reductionism," allows the Native performer to "isolate the basic building blocks of the song and dance, [where] these become the starting points for a creative and vital action" (83). These building blocks can then be developed, modified, revised or expanded. But since their Indigenous core has been carefully considered, they retain their Native cultural integrity in the face of artistic change. In order for Native artists to carry this out, we must know our own tribal songs and dances. It is up to us to conduct the necessary research. For the Native performer, the outcome, through the process of reductionism, is the starting point for Native Performance Culture. We need to listen and learn from Great-granny stories. As artists we should be able to be inspired by our land's powerful beings, like *Wasakaychak*, Coyote, Raven and *Nanaboozoo*. Salish writer/performer Lee Maracle reminds us that prior to the colonization of North America, there existed a theatre tradition for Native people:

"Anyone who has seen those story dances knows we have a theatrical tradition. Anyone who has watched Basil Johnston perform a story knows that the Ojibway have a theatrical tradition. We all have theatrical traditions. We all have theatrical tradition in our cultures [and] we haven't been schooled in that" (11).

Favel Starr also points out that the artist's "starting points for creative and vital action" do not "differ in principle from other performance traditions" (83). An important distinction to mention between Western and Native Performance Culture is that for the Native artist his or her "reference points are from Native culture [which] originate in this land. The artistic source is not transplanted and colonial" (83). To reiterate, the idea of working from an Indigenous source through songs, dances and stories reinforces the worldview of a Native performer whose creative starting points would then originate from the land of his or her ancestors.

Favel Starr disputes the idea that Native Performance Culture is a fusion/synthesis of the traditional and the contemporary. He states that Native artists need to continue to develop and maintain a "working practical knowledge of our language, songs, dances, stories and histories" (85). In doing so, as artists we will continue, like Great-granny, to be influenced by a great worldview, reflecting and representing on stage who we are as contemporary Native people.

Through Favel Starr's research into the methodology of Native Culture Performance, he locates where Native artists can find their story, song, dance, rhythm and their spirit, without "internal conflict, colonization or beggary" (85). Native Culture Performance is not about Native people on stage merely imitating Western theatre. As Favel Starr discovered, Native Performance is its own culture, rooted, upheld, suspended and dancing from the magical breath of *Wasakaychak* and from the determination and stubbornness of our great-grannies.

A main distinction between contemporary Native performance and colonial Western theatre is that the roots of Native performance can be traced to the lands of this country. When a Cree storyteller, like Eddie, tells a story, his sounds, words and movements are inspired by the land that he has experienced. When he imitates the sounds of the waves, unfolding upon a shore, it is a body of water that he has visited and experienced. It is a shore where his grandfather or great-grandfather fished from and prayed to, offering thanks. It may also be a body of water that the old people have warned Eddie to stay away from because *Wintigo* (Cree/Ojibway cannibalistic creature) has been spotted there. Native performance theatre comes from a specific source and entails a particular language, which unfolds movements true to the story. These specifics reflect Native performance as distinct from western theatre based on where the creative process arises. That is why Native performers, writers and directors need to do the necessary ancestral research, so they can continually be inspired from these unambiguous and powerful sources.

(2001)

Works Cited

D'Aponte, Mimi Gisolfi., ed. *Seventh Generation: An Anthology of Native American Plays.* New York: Theatre Communications Group, 1999.

Highway, Tomson. Opening Address. "What is the Purpose of Native Theatre." Croft Chapter House, University of Toronto. National Native Theatre Symposium, Native Earth Performing Arts, Inc., Toronto, June 1998.

Maracle, Lee. "Training in all fields of theatre." Croft Chapter House, University of Toronto. National Native Theatre Symposium, Native Earth Performing Arts, Inc., Toronto, June 1998.

Favel Starr, Floyd. "The artificial tree: Native Performance Culture Research 1991-1996." *Canadian Theatre Review* 90 (1997): 83-85.

A Handful of Plays by Native Earthlings

by Daniel David Moses

I

Of The Essence: about Tomson Highway's *The Sage, The Dancer and The Fool*

I remember being bothered, both puzzled and exhilarated, the first time I saw Tomson Highway's stage poem *The Sage, The Dancer and The Fool*. Probably I was puzzled because it was only 1983—if Tomson's dates are right—and I was still in recovery from my education. I was writing poetry but for some reason felt unready to deal with the plays I had in mind. I had learned a lot of things while earning a couple of degrees, one of the most useful of which for an apprentice playwright, one might have thought, should have been some clarity around what makes a play. But one of my unyielding dilemmas, as the detritus of those school years fell aside, making way for art in the so-called real world, was that the only thing I remembered from my education with any definition around the subject of plays was an often repeated credo that the only characteristic essential to a play was conflict. I know I remembered this credo of conflict to the exclusion of a lot of other ideas because it had been one of the most difficult ideas I had tried to get through my thick skull during the whole of my academic career and finally, I must admit, I did not succeed.

Years later I realized my thickness at the time had a lot to do with growing up in the subculture of my family on the Six Nations lands, a partially Christianized but definitely Iroquoian community, where the only activities in which conflict seemed to be permissible, let alone essential, were hockey and lacrosse, neither of which concerned me. I don't remember that the rules for social behaviour were ever actually articulated then, although there are days now when the idea of a book of aboriginal etiquette, especially focussed on cross-national differences, does not seem like a bad idea. (It may be that some part of largely Iroquoian me looked at *The Sage, The Dancer and The Fool* and wondered "Just what are those Cree going on about?") Those days I grew up in, conflicts arising in areas of our community life outside the arena were not encouraged, were seen, I suppose, as evidence of immaturity, rudeness, or a failure of imagination, if not exactly immorality. We are, of course, talking about public behaviour here. What could be more public, if you want to give your life to it, than art?

I was forced, since I wanted to write plays, to come up with another way of looking at that so-called essential characteristic of conflict, a way that might allow me with some clarity to proceed along my chosen path. So let us say that I decided, without knowing it, that my teachers, in an effort to be reasonable within the limits of their own ruling subcultures—they were professors at universities, after all—must all be making the same simple error. They were trying to turn the characteristic of conflict into a universal quality, something they already knew they valued in the structures of their legislatures (calling it debate), in their economic systems (calling it competition), in their religions ("Onward Christian Soldiers!"), and in their institution (calling it tenure). It only made sense of their world to assume the characteristic of conflict in—or to impose it on—art. It just had to be one of the universals.

Of course, as I realised eventually from my discomfort, where I was coming from, it wasn't one of the universals. Essential conflict made no sense to me. It just seemed wrong. And later, as I looked around for explanations and examples, I realised that conflict was common in the dramatic literature but no more essential to any particular successful piece of theatre than, say, characters with Freudian psychology, hit songs, or a smoke machine.

I also later realised that the common sort of conflict I had been taught to recognise was as easy, as interesting and as ritualised as hockey or lacrosse. Yes, to a certain extent, it was a matter of taste, which should be more than the mouth, or why else were we being taught about art? Yes, I was forced, since I wanted to write plays for my own interest—from my own ethnocentricity even, I'd now admit—to come up with another concept to try to pin down and maybe even understand that characteristic of a good dramatic work that caught the attention, suspended disbelief, and got the imagination going. Was it a tension? Texture? Rhythm? Some sort of suspense? Mystery? Activity? Yes. I borrowed from what little I knew of the visual arts (I had taken a course in photography at an earlier point in my university studies, spending hours in a dark room making light from blacks and greys) the concept of "contrast." I inserted the word into the credo—"The only characteristic essential to a play is contrast"—and felt suddenly at ease. And this minor adjustment to my vocabulary allowed me to proceed with my own work, even though I had to admit, and kept expecting, that the majority of theatrical work would be informed, or even deformed by, or in contrast to the academic conflict model. I had after all been taught a certain standard of taste.

So what puzzled me about The Sage, The Dancer and The Fool, despite my own awkward inner struggle, was that it wasn't to my educated taste, didn't illustrate the credo. Where was the conflict? What was the subject, as defined by the conflict? What was I to make of it? The piece seemed more like a poem, an exploration, a meditation, than an argument or battle. Shouldn't the obliqueness of the dilemma of being a stranger in a strange city be abandoned for the directness of good old conflict? Was this contrast between an urban now and a wilderness then and the longing that expressed sufficient to build a successful piece of theatre on? Well, yes—because, as I've said, part of my bother with the piece was that I was also exhilarated by it.

It was an uncommonly rich theatrical experience in the Toronto of 1983 as I remember it. There were a lot of what I had come to refer to as "furniture plays" being produced, even by those venues that prided themselves on being forward looking, politically and/or aesthetically. I remember being offended that the set of one of these plays was actually applauded, audience members being pleased that it looked "so real" in a photographic reproduction sort of way. I felt sorry for the actors being forced to compete with the design. I don't remember the play at all now, the set was so outstanding, and I have to suspect that that set's connection to whatever play it was supposed to be serving was simply wrong. It now seems like those plays and those audiences were trapped in the then television version of naturalism and that their entrapment was not really allowing them that theatrical universal, the suspension of disbelief.

The Sage, The Dancer and The Fool starts out with a set that is not naturalistic at all, starts out with the assumption that the members of the audience have imagination. It then uses a grand piano, that rather archetypical instrument, to create a seductive, sensual music track, and gelatined lights to show the way, and sends the audience off with a Cree man, abstracted into three archetypes representing his intellect, his spirit and his body, to explore the city of Toronto as it appears only through the abstractions of colour, shadow, music, movement, and the words of both English and Cree, also often used as abstractly, as expressionistically as music. So Toronto, the city, is not defined by one "naturalistic" set but is evoked in ways as various as the realities each member of the audience imagines.

This abstract quality, which one is not surprised to find in the work of either a "much lapsed pianist" or a modern dancer when one considers it, surprised me then, because it was not what I had learned to expect, either from the theatre I could afford to attend in 1983 or from school. I may have been taught about such things, had vague memories of being told the roots of the theatre were in ritual performance, in symbolic movement, that such abstraction was itself theatrical, may even have explained to myself my childhood Christian fervour as a response to the Anglican ceremonial version of such abstraction, but as I have related, it wasn't what got my attention. So that night I first saw *The Sage, The Dancer and The Fool*, it either taught or reminded me—that's what the bother was about—that abstraction may well be an essential quality of a play.

It allowed us to see clearly what the play was about. It removed the extraneous particulars, the remainder were evocative. The contrast of the wealth, the torrent of urban detail the play presents, even inundates the audience with, the contrast of all those shoes, office workers, food and lights, with the simplicity of memories of a life on the land only deepens the longing, the nostalgia, the energetic confusion *The Sage, The Dancer and The Fool* expresses. It is this emotional reality, existing, so to speak, between the lines, in the contrast between the elements of the play, that was Tomson's—and René's—theatrical accomplishment.

As I have suggested, in the theatrical ecology of Toronto of 1983, and even again in 1989, *The Sage, The Dancer and The Fool* stood out because of this quality. The play, I believe, even got some Dora nominations. At moments then and now, the eccentric ethnocentric in me is tempted to allow, as a lot of people assumed at the time, that this stand out quality, and not its authors or its content or its point of view, was what made the play a Native play. They seemed to be looking for ways to explain away their exhilaration, to keep the Indian other. But of course such abstraction is a quality of any good art. Even photography, when it reaches for art, tries to represent reality with selected, evocative detail—which is why black and white photographs are still, or even more beautiful, in contrast to mundane, naturalistic colour. And that abstraction is also why *The Sage, The Dancer and The Fool* could go beyond the audience's prejudices about "Indians" to engage their hearts in the Highways' love for our land.

(2001)

II

Tricky Rabbit: about Beatrice Mosionier's *Night of the Trickster*

How innocuous was the guise Nanabush, the Ojibway trickster, chose for his first fleeting appearance in Beatrice Mosionier's play *Night of the Trickster*.

If one of the characters had not eventually mentioned his name and reminded me of his reputation, I might have continued to be taken in by him, by what he was pretending to be for the purposes of the play, a cute domesticated rabbit in a cage. I might have ignored him and the possibilities he represents. And I might have assumed that the struggles of the characters in the play to continue living a normal and loving life despite traumatic pasts, despite the darkness of a long winter in Winnipeg, were simply their personal dilemmas, that they had nothing to do with, for instance, the anguished revelations of that winter's Aboriginal Justice Inquiry.

But hearing his name reminded me that one of the possibilities he represents is that of healing, and that healing is something that comes both from the self and from outside the self, from the community, even the world. But Nanabush did not, while playing that part, look at all like what I have imagined when reading or hearing of his adventures. Those stories, which seemed to be about the time of the creation of the world's spirits—human, animal, vegetable, mineral—had put me in mind of a character who was a sort of adolescent warrior, someone with more power than sense, a teenager in the thrall of hormones or the newness, the strangeness, the beautiful weirdness of that world.

That sort of power, the kind of energy I'm thinking about, might be embodied—to create a contemporary instance—by a young Graham Greene behaving like the early Bugs Bunny. Although I know that Mister Greene is not Ojibwa (neither, I'm fairly sure, is Bugs), I do think it might be worth some consideration, if only to focus on the sort of characteristics usually associated with trickster energy. What if Nanabush's fabled misbehaviours were inspired by a delinquent Iroquois teenager wandering about in the wrong territories? But if that kid's energetic presence resulted in anything close to the myth, let alone the history, of the Confederacy, then the adjectives 'Iroquois' and 'cute' would not naturally arise together in the mind.

But that Nanabush Beatrice Mosionier offered was looking cute, perhaps even more so than usual, what with the contrast between his appearance and the unattractiveness of the content of *Night of the Trickster*. The play, after all, has in large part to do with the consequences of rape. Cute Nanabush was also mute, sitting there, in the production I saw, inside his wire cubical being fed the inevitable carrot by a young and pretty woman—Bugs and Graham would have been envious, if for different reasons.

Appropriately, as part of what his wordless cuteness seemed to be about, and perhaps also inevitably, the rabbit actor chosen for the part was white, the usual colour of domestication. In the context of *Night of the Trickster*, a play about a bunch of what the rapist refers to as "squaws," this innocuous appearance, the perfect bunny, seemed to me empty, spiritless, insufficient to the cause, a rather weak theatrical whimsy on the irreconcilable irony that white is also the ideal colour of sweetness, light, purity and racist power.

Where was Nanabush's magic in this unfair fairness? What kind of pale trick was this? How did pretending to be so reserved help or surprise anybody?

I was expecting and hoping for some sort of healing power. But Nanabush and the other characters in the play seemed to be just going along living out their every day lives as if nothing much was wrong. And it almost did seem as if having jobs and roofs over their heads should protect them from their bad memories and the news. Couldn't they just ignore the pain? Would they not achieve normality by pretending everything was okay? Wouldn't the ache just some day go away?

No, it wasn't working, the memories seemed worse and there was more news— and that dumb bunny seemed as victimised, as powerless as everyone else in the play felt. Something had to give. So far as I was concerned, cuteness wasn't cutting it. We were in the land of the bland here, nowhere near a place of spirits, of healing. Part of me wanted to say to that rabbit something like "Stand up and be a man!" But next in that scene, in response to her friend Roz's rape and maybe in response to Roz invoking the name Nanabush, the character Wendy starts remembering her Kookum, the sound of loons and a lake, a place of healing from abuse she herself had suffered at the hands of a priest. It was mysterious, magical, intriguing.

It was probably another guise of the proverbial carrot. I suddenly felt confident enough to sit back and wait and see, felt that I didn't have to demand immediately that young warrior energy. Here suddenly was a different spirited energy at play, a glimmering lake. Dare I characterise it as a women's version of trickster energy? Where would it take me? Back to something I had forgotten to take into account in the face of so much cuteness: that inevitable carrot and how common some of Freud's ideas about symbolism have become in our popular consciousness.

The next time it appears, the inevitable carrot is, at first, just part of the business of a scene. The women, Eileen, Wendy and Rachel, are as usual preparing vegetables for some sort of community feast. At the same time they're talking about finding more hands-on ways of dealing with rape, particularly since the Aboriginal Justice Inquiry has so charged the atmosphere of the city that the police feel themselves victimized. (Is it not disturbing how little criticism it takes to send the police into the depths of depression? It does seem like work needs to be done on building them a better emotional support system.) The cops are even less likely to help Native people than before. Rachel, the play's central character has been to this point haunted, even terrorised by the memory of her own rape. Now she stands, the carrot in one hand, a knife in the other, and reveals her decision to prepare herself to go out hunting rapists. Eileen and Wendy are not enthusiastic about so radical a course. "What would we do if we did catch a rapist?" asks Eileen. Rachel replies, "Castrate him!" and she chops the carrot in half viciously. "Make him suffer. Give him some long-term damage."

Ouch. When Nanabush is not Nanabush, a carrot is no longer just a carrot.

I'm sure I winced as I laughed. I'm sure most of the other men in the audience did too. And we all probably, in unison, sat up straight with our knees together. Did the women in the audience have a good laugh? Out of concern for carrots in general, I'm sure I wasn't paying them enough attention.

Yes, the scene that Beatrice Mosionier admits first came into her mind when thinking of writing this play about her experience of rape definitely did cut it, definitely played out an old joke that still worked. (May we all be able to say as much when we're as hoary.) There's something about essential differences that sometimes needs repeating. Now we definitely were talking about trickster energy. It was an admirable joke but part of me didn't like it at all. Perhaps it was too powerful, or tasteless, an image of a revenge right out of the depths of emotion, "an eye for an eye" with other body parts substituted. The impulse suggested circumventing our late twentieth century system of justice in favour of a more mythically tribal one. It just wasn't what I and the rest of the men in the audience, I suspect, were up for. Most of the women weren't either, but for them just considering the possibility could be a perverse bit of fun, especially when a part of what the play is about is this dilemma. Most of us guys are usually not well connected to what goes on on the far side of that gender divide. So this joke does force us to at least face up, if only for a stinging moment, to the barest hint of what a visceral violation rape is.

It also suggests that the laws that are supposed to police rape have clearly not been made with women in mind. In the context of a play about a faulty justice system, a system in which women, and Aboriginal women in particular, could count on rape investigations to feel like additional violations, that joke did get right to the rupture in the matter. I also had to admit that neither that ancient "eye for an eye" nor this modern version of justice could heal it. But Beatrice Mosionier has placed this joke at precisely this point in the story for a reason. It permits the trickster energy to erupt and start transforming the play. What seemed a sociological drama with touches of humour shifts into what seems a social satire or comedy of manners.

Rachel carries out her idea, begins to prepare herself and her friends to go trolling for rapists. Her friends humour her, taking martial arts training—yes, Karate Indian Women Warriors!—and going on diets and trying to quit smoking. In the process, Rachel comes out of her isolation and pain and becomes part of her community. She also is able to find the strength to face her husband Sam, to voice her fears about the peril their relationship is in, and forces him to make his own effort to cross the gender divide. Their dialogue is honest, ugly and funny all at once (Politician Sam complains, "I get screwed more by those guys in Ottawa than I do here").

It is this couple, their love, that Beatrice Mosionier places at the heart of her play. This relationship, that emotion, is what is at stake on the *Night of the Trickster*. The rapist had almost, wittingly or not, destroyed it. His act has forced Rachel and Sam to question their trust in one another. It takes a dramatic sleight of hand to bring of this couple and their community together, a night full of the trickster energy of both sexes to restore that trust and heal the love. It also finishes transforming the play into a comedy.

And of course—we guys in the audience were especially thankful—it makes sure, after all is said and done, that carrots are once again just carrots.

(2002)

III

A Bridge Across Time: about Ben Cardinal's
Generic Warriors and No Name Indians

I am thinking of a landscape just north of Saskatoon as I start thinking about Ben Cardinal's play *Generic Warriors and No Name Indians*. I am thinking about Waneskewin, the traditional culture centre there, a place I have been privileged to visit only once. I am dwelling again on that valley because it seems just the sort of place the characters in Cardinal's play inhabit.

I'm remembering my own November day there, the wind and a bright cold sky overhead. I recall making my way alone along a sheltered path among the bare willows on the river bank, my street shoes slipping or printing tracks in the fresh half inch of snow. Had ice begun to grow out from the shore despite the current? The water still had a dark look to it. In that valley below those rounded slopes, there were few other people I met and acknowledged with waves or nods in my hour long walk. Those people and myself were the only evidence of the modern world.

If I had been like Cardinal's contemporary Native family in their house beside such a river, with their music and guns, their word processor and misunderstandings, in the shadow of a railroad trestle, in the eddies of the wind, it might have been simpler for me to begin imagining a meeting around the next bend in the path with an ancestor still alive, a warrior from the battle of Batoche—the battlefield not that far along the South Saskatchewan—or his wife cooking over a smokeless fire.

But I was a visitor there, almost a city slicker, and not until at last, breath short and cheeks glowing with the effort, I climbed up the slope to the prairie, climbed into the wind, and found myself looking over a medicine wheel did I clearly feel or imagine in the light, the cold, the distances, the power of the place. It felt open and eternal, somehow a place outside of time, the essence of possibilities. And all I had done to get there was to follow that river.

Perhaps I ought to try to explain it away and say that obviously I was able to feel that way in part because I had already passed sites where the archeological evidence of ancient villages and a buffalo jump were slowly coming to the surface. Perhaps it is true that because I'd been reassured, thanks to science, that people had inhabited that place for immeasurable times before our current version of history had begun that I was able to respond in that less than straightforward, less than scientific way.

But I was also able to imagine that way in part because I felt like those prehistoric people were family, not only the ancestors of Cardinal's Musk and Mabel, but my own predecessors. I imagine this way not only because, as they say, I identify as a Native person—usually when "they" are trying to bully me into admitting the overly simple, white-washed identity of Canadian—but more immediately because I still had the memory of *Generic Warriors and No Name Indians* in my head.

Seeing the play, even in my far part of the country, in the city, those how many years before, had prepared me for that *déja vu* sort of day when I was actually *in situ* by that river. It had introduced me not only to specific human characters in its foreground but had also given me an abiding sense if not necessarily a clear picture of the characteristics of its literal background. I was ready to meet that place when I arrived because I had already visited there thanks to Mr. Cardinal.

Those many years before, I had felt no need to be introduced to Musk and Mabel, Florence and Sarah, the family the play centres on. Them I recognised immediately, the type of raw comic characters they were. Yes, I knew about the struggle of the men, Musk and Ennis, to be warriors, whatever that means in times of defeat or peace like ours. And I thought I could pretty well predict the course of the impatient love of a woman like Mabel. And there through Florence and Sarah was ye olde generation gap gaping as the times dictate. Oh I thought I knew the heart of this play, thought it was a mere comedy about a family in crisis.

I had not at first been aware of the obvious, the unmentioned landscape, which so often falls into the realm of the untouched if not intangible in plays. Most plays are only about people, about characters. So I had no idea that this family's crisis could be located and focused into possibilities for the personal, the poetic, the political, the spiritual, for common sense, by a railway bridge crossing a river. In Ben Cardinal's *Generic Warriors and No Name Indians*, the landscape is also a character, the deus in machina.

It starts with a river in Saskatchewan crossed by a railroad bridge. What better place to begin talking about a meeting of eternity and history, about natural cycles and progress, about families and warriors?

I suppose my first clue that something more was going on should have been the grand entry across the bridge that erupts out of nowhere (or "sometime"?) at the top of the play, but at first I just took it for a theatrical gesture. This seemed a fair enough assumption in a world where powwow so often seems to mean a big show and most plays are just about characters.

A series of historically and geographically separate scenes took me well into the play. I met the family alive in the here and now of 1990, the soldier Floyd and his "consort" Marlena in Europe in 1944, and finally the warrior Muskwa and his wife Pihew in the here of 1885 and, following that, again earlier that year, as if, confusingly, their story was curling back on itself, an eddy between the current and the shore of a river. (This confusing eddying, spiralling of the narrative will happen again in the love story of Floyd and Marlena.)

Only then when the next scene back in 1990 re-introduced me to the character Floyd did I start to clue in. Musk in 1990 had already told me the man was dead, but here he is in 1990, loud and lively, and funny, lounging on the tracks, talking to his buddy Ennis. He looks old as Ennis, seems hard of hearing—or is it an act like the one my grandad used to put on for dealing with my grandma? I laughed. He's a veteran you would recognise in any Branch of the Canadian Legion that let Indians in. (That injustice, exclusion from the society of warriors, is one he and Ennis do suffer in the now.) You have to shout as if he's a long way off, even when he's right beside you.

And while Floyd is certainly at home in Saskatchewan, he is also out of place, out of time, in the now. How to explain this? The simple answer is that he is only Ennis' drunken hallucination, which would make Ennis a pathetic survivor of the War. But this play is not only about Ennis and his psychology—Cardinal is not very interested in the study of individual psychology: his focus seems to be family and community—so a more complex answer, and something more suitable to a comedy, is necessary. What if he's a ghost, a ghost as haunted by his memories of the War as Ennis is by him?

But before long, it becomes clear that he is even more than a ghost, that he has a reality in the play separate from haunting. He is able to be a young man at any moment and to go running off into the past, more easily than Ennis is able to remember it. For him the past is not some distant land left behind in the flow of time. It seems no more distant than the far side of the river. The character Floyd, appearing on the bridge at a moment where a hand-held lantern is substituted for the headlight of an on-rushing locomotive, a theatrical sleight of hand, was himself a bridge across time.

The landscape of *Generic Warriors and No Name Indians* is one ripe with possibility, with history, or histories, one full of stories not only of this one family stretched out across time but also of characters from sacred tales like Weesageechak. It is a place in which one character's fiction is another's truth—what Sarah thought was just her "story" is the reality of Muskwa and Pihew. It is a stage where the distortions of memory and desire can find true expression in the reprise of a musical number. It is a location where every time seems to exist in familiar proximity. It is the cosmos where an eclipse of the male sun by the female moon is an expression of the possibility of harmony. It is a dream constructed in a way that functions like personal memory or nightmare—pratfalls hard on the images of blood letting. It is a reality that pushes theatre toward cinema with the cutting speed it uses to shift scenes. It has almost no taste, but a lot of laughs. Is it the eternal present tense, surreal, comic, mysterious?

Those many years ago, back in the city, when I had first seen the play, I had found all its qualities both confusing and exhilarating, and finally touching. I had not recognised what it was about, but I had felt so excited by it, it had seemed the best play I had seen that theatre season.

At Waneskewin, to talk to Saskatchewan writers about some ideas I had been playing with about how Native writers write differently from non-Native writers, I saw the reason I have fallen in love with the play had to do with recognising the way it structured reality and the landscape that reality grew from.

As I said, the grand entry that erupts out of nowhere at the top of the play should have been my first clue to understanding the play. I should have known because the talk I was about to give began by considering the image of a grand entry at a powwow, that great circling and spiralling in of dancers, as a ceremonial, artistic expression of family and community, and a celebration of life's non-linearity.

The landscape of this epic comedy *Generic Warriors and No Name Indians* seems to me most comprehensible if we keep those possibilities of the spiral in mind. Out there in the wind, the light, the distances of the prairies, time is no longer the straight and narrow line demanded by the progress of history or the history of progress. It is a spiral that contains the centre of the world, the eternal moment where each of us lives.

From their places, their moments on that spiral, a character like Floyd or a writer like Ben Cardinal can look sideways and find the freedom to escape history and the injustices of the moment, can embrace the members of their family and communities, despite their displacement through eternity.

From that spiral, we can look back at our lives with enough wisdom to love them.

That medicine wheel in Waneskewin made it clear to me just how grand an entry into the theatre *Generic Warriors and No Name Indians* was.

(2001)

IV

Flaming Nativity: about Billy Merasty's *Fireweed*

So have you heard the one about the faggot Indian?

Maybe I should have said "the Indian faggot."

Oh, whichever epithet I might choose to use hardly makes much difference. Your answer is most likely "No." Hey, why use two, both sticks and stones, why overdo it, when either one would be sufficient to the put down? Yeah, either one has always been enough to build a good story around.

Until now, of course, when some of them Indians have begun to ram this damn political—or is it historical or cultural?—correctness down our throats.

Why can't they take a joke? Hell, talk about doing Kawlija. First Nations? Just what is the story there? It sounds like a brand of diapers. Native renaissance, my ass. On second thought, never mind my ass.

"Hey, have you heard the one about the First Nation faggot?" just doesn't work. Oh joke, where is thy sting?

And—wouldn't you know it?—now they're starting to reassert stories about their national identities. It was so much simpler when they all were just Indians. Hey, you can't live in the past. We're supposed to be able to tell that there's something different between that Cree and this Delaware or whatever? Aren't we all just Canadians? Who's doing the coyote calls? And now that they're rediscovering their traditional cultures, some of them are actually trying to do away with that old and trusty set of insults, faggot, fairy, queer, sissy—even the kids can use them!—and replace them with this New Agey sounding "two-spirit" thing. I mean, talk about limp wristed. Aren't Indians supposed to be warriors? Real men? That's the story I'm used to hearing.

And what about their morals? They do not to seem to give an American plug nickel that the Judeo-Christian God might not like this threat to the fertility of the tribe. Yeah, strangely enough, it seems like their *Gitchy Manitou,* their Great Mystery, actually made some people queer so they could serve, in the interest of harmony, as intermediaries between the divisions of the world, women and men, life and death—us and Ottawa maybe.

What next? Jesus and all the apostles notwithstanding, if this keeps up, "gay" is going to start sounding really normal. Oh for the days of yore when it was just something Christmasy, whenever that was...

"Have you heard the one about the two-spirited Cree?" just isn't funny.

So what about this *Fireweed* play by William (Billy) Merasty? What about its cutely ironic subtitle "An Indigeni Fairy Tale"?

Well, okay, okay, if we are to believe what it says, maybe I should have said "Have you heard the one about the two-spirited Cree? It isn't *just* funny." It's also glamourous in the original sense, charming our imaginations with actual magic tricks as well as a full hand of more usual theatrics—fire, light and lightning, sound, character, stories and their telling.

Its central story of a journey toward healing and home is also a story about escaping that dark side of glamour, the curse, which is laid down in this particular plot by, of course, a man in black, a priest. We would be offended by this pitiful church bashing if we were not also being teased by this twist on the usual fairy tale, this seemingly new or at least naughty and possibly even feminist (who knew Native culture would have to do with women too?) point of view—although if we are to trust the teller, it is an ancient way of seeing. No wonder, despite all the anguish of the story's journey, it remains seductive, mysterious, erotic.

Which is of course why, though *Fireweed* may be the first one we here have heard tell of these doubly epitheted individuals, faggot Indians, Indian faggots, it is certainly not going to be the last. Who knew we could get into such bent and effeminate territory by following this Native renaissance movement? Who knew a Native nativity might involve more than feathered headdresses and war paint, and how, yes, how the Hiawatha did they keep quiet about it for so long?

How the heart of Merasty's *Fireweed* aches for lost loves, for suicides and those who are taught by the church to hate themselves, the queers and the Indians. But then it remembers how heart beats go on.

Its central character Peechweechum Rainbowshield, referred to hereafter as Rainbow, thrown into a holding cell in nothing but his underwear, insulted and assaulted by a police officer, somehow pulls a little red dress, lipstick and high heels out of nowhere. The beautiful young man proceeds to do a drag musical number as his version of the great escape act, disappearing, the vanishing Indian, from that Winnipeg jail into the dream stream of the play.

He slips through the iron bars and stones of the white man's law and religion and right into his and our community's mythology much the same way his predecessor, the legendary medicine dreamer, Isiah Iskootee'oo, did in the long ago to the frustration of the Royal Canadian Mounted Police. Isiah Iskootee'oo escaped punishment, the story goes, for setting fire to the bush, destroying Her Majesty's timber. But now that we have recovered the knowledge—the Native renaissance again—that burning was used traditionally to manage forest environments and facilitate hunting, Isiah Iskootee'oo's misdemeanor appears in a more heroic light.

So, the scene in *Fireweed* where Rainbow escapes, theatrically, magically, perhaps—yes—perhaps incredibly (it is early in the renaissance after all), from laws that would punish him for a crime called "Gross Indecency" may just be a first and teasing glimpse of recovered knowledge, an alternative mythology, and some common sense about sexual behavior.

The scene is certainly pivotal to the play, erupting spontaneous theatrical combustion, burning down the fourth wall. The character Rainbow is allowed to step out of the narrative, as well as his cell, and play with and to us in the audience, just like the characters of the Flight Attendant or Reena Lightningway or even the Judge who are all spirits and not limited by flesh and blood bodies or dramaturgical realities.

Fireweed before this scene is a story about Rainbow, a young man haunted and made almost hopeless by the suicide of his beloved twin brother in the inferno of a burning church. He is haunted by the possibility that he, a medicine-minded young Cree, as the object not only of his rather Catholic brother's love but of his sexual desire, may have been the cause of a great sin—is the dilemma faith or homosexuality or incest or all the above? He fears he may have been the cause of his brother's suicide.

This spiritual murkiness is lit only by the presence of the above mentioned guardian spirits (the "fairy god parents" the play's ironic subtitle invokes) and the Manitoba Legislature's Golden Boy, emblem here of the possibility of love. The play suggests a version of Winnipeg that is a sort of hell on earth, streets where sex, drugs, and rock and roll are never expressions of growth, exploration, joy and youth, but always mean meaningless, directionless despair.

Rainbow's little red dress number redresses this. After its performance, like magic, the story, the stories *Fireweed* tells take on a motive, become hopeful, helpful, loving, and shift Rainbow toward reconciliation with his two-spirited self and his family (his most Catholic mother) and his community (his auntish medicine teacher). He is saved at the same time his former lover Raven is lost. It may be that because Rainbow is able to accept and express, even so campily, his own female spirit that he finds his way home.

Rainbow's little red dress number acts like a front door into a strangely familiar house, a dream world, a memory of adolescence when the erotic was more than the body, was what the whole world was about. The drag number is itself the essence of queer, two-spirited, both true and false, male and female, and is the play's intermediary between us (the audience) and them, our forgotten desires, our bodies.

The home Rainbow returns to is a place not only of pristine wilderness but also of ancient stories, a mythology that is a way to wisdom about our lives, about the body and its hungers. No wonder Rainbow needs to hear again the ones about Weesageechak, the Cree trickster, needs to relive one of that great spirit's adventures. The Weetigo, that embodiment of morbid hunger, traps and threatens to eat Weesageechak, much as western civilization does with Indians. Only Weesageechak's own cunning and the help of a weasel who is willing to journey into the Weetigo's body, via its anus and inners, allows Weesageechak to survive—and the weasel to be beautiful. What more visceral, funny, and queer representation of a journey into and through our fears or lives could we ask for?

Hey, shit happens.

Have you heard the one about the Indian faggot and Weesageechak and the Weetigo? Yeah. It proves things have a way of working out in the end.

(2001)

V

The Lady I Saw You with last Night: about Floyd Favel's *Lady of Silences*

Who is she, this "Lady of Silences"? And whatever is a lady, whoever she is, doing in a play about a bunch of Indians?

There is a sequence in T.S. Eliot's poem or prayer, "Ash Wednesday," where the bones of the poet sing of her and name her. In that sequence—which was quoted in early drafts of this play, one facet of its inspiration—the Lady seemed to succinctly embody all of life's anguished contradictions ("Calm and distressed / Torn and most whole") in a silent, final, English, Judeo-Christian beauty ("The single Rose / Is now the Garden / Where all loves end"). It seemed to be an important part of the weird or mystic nature of that beauty, made from the Lady's contradictions, that it was neither quite cancellation or purity, that the consolation it offered was the vibrant, singing nothingness of white noise. And the Lady was wearing white, though she was not the Virgin. The poem informed or reminded its auditor that Mary's colour is blue and that the Lady herself "honours the Virgin in meditation."

Perhaps our silent lady was one of that virgin lady's sainted sisters, a contemplative in a sylvan retreat, or perhaps even Eve, the Mother of Us All, Eve of the Garden before the Fall, still worthy of all the praise a poet, or at least his bones, might chirp about her from his desert. A rose is definitely more than a rose in such landscapes. But that was the lady on the night of Ash Wednesday in 1930. Who is she, that holy nun or first woman, and what does Eliot's song of bones, his poem or prayer, become in the here and now of a play from First Nation Canada called *Lady of Silences* and in this final decade of the twentieth century? How do the song and the lady exist in the world of Floyd Favel's play?

Only as allusions, immigrant glamour, whispers of a foreign song across Alberta and Saskatchewan, translated into, transformed by Cree? The poem appears now only in Cree, imported to be one part of the ceremony of the play. Does it still manage to be a song, a song in a desert? Yes, but since the desert here in this play is the Americas, or at least the Canadian prairies, after the Fall, after Columbus, the Lady of Silences becomes the embodiment ("Calm and distressed / Torn and most whole"), if not the agent, of that event. It is a weird but sure transformation, a magic act, the Lady into the pale Serpent of race. She has become some sort of *femme fatale* full of Native America's anguished contradictions, an alma mater of its aching quietness.

It is no surprise then that in Floyd Favel's *Lady of Silences,* this song in Cree is the song of bones the chorus of women characters, the three "Native females," the voiceless women of the streets, Ruth, Sheila and Lisa, give utterance to.

What better way could there be to introduce that relic of Whiteness, the dress Linda wore, to prelude the reenactment of that white girl's murder, and finally to escape that reenactment and exit the stage? What better way to reframe that murder as a sacrifice? It is also no surprise that this song and its reprise are connected to the reprisal these silenced dark-visaged ladies took against the Lady of Silences who, through the person of Linda, was no longer their once-removed Nemesis, an unengagable absence, but their very present rival in love, their pale-faced sister.

Her presence as the Lady, that normal but strange fusion of the virgin and the mother, at the centre of the ceremony of the play demands from the dark women some contradiction, an imagining of other aspects of the nature and beauty of women. What erupts from their soured innocence, their lucklessness, their loneliness, goes beyond the song of bones into a speech of war uttered by Watatootis, the warrior woman, Our Lady of Noises.

This eruption of war into the world of the play, into the world of Native North America at the end of the twentieth century, is a thrilling if momentary revelation or admission, a breaking through of the great silence about the continuing war against Native people. Women like Watatootis might be sufficient to win at least a truce. Certainly she fills out the role call for any contingent of women. And of course the admission of the continuing war allows the play at least, this war of words, this cultural conflict, to transform its murder again, this time into a justified killing. These ladies have their say, and in so doing, lay this white succubus to rest, at least until the play's next performance.

How does the playing out of the murder of a white woman in a bar in a city on the Canadian prairie compare to the poet's cry to heaven? This song of bones, especially transformed into the prairie wind of Cree, in this play that is largely in English, is even more of a mystery, is still in large part a prayer, a part of a ceremony, even an exorcism ritual as Favel's subtitle insists, and this whitest of white ladies, this fairest of them all, is the body, the corpus delicti this particular ritual, this mystery play, addresses.

For this rich and strange mix Favel and his friends turned to the inspiration of *The Blacks, A Clown Show* by Jean Genet. That play also plays out a ceremony that masks and then reveals and revels in a murder, a sacrifice. That clown show also gave to our gentleman protagonist, Village, his name, and his aura of nostalgia for the lost simplicity of times past. Does our gentleman antagonist and master of ceremonies, Detective Belmondo, derive his monicker and profession from some role of the French film star, Jean Paul Belmondo? Is this a playful way to make sure Canada's other finding empire is also given presence in the performance? Is that the message in Favel's *métissage*?

In Genet's construction of *The Blacks*, he insists its performance is meant to take place before a white audience, imperial France in the flesh, and suggests that an effigy of a white person be given place of honour in any theatre, any audience where no actual white auditor exists. *The Blacks* only makes sense when a white eye can observe the show's blacks playing both the rulers of white colonial governments and institutions—a queen, a bishop, the whole court scene—as well as the blacks those rulers rule, those blacks as the rulers imagine them. Its parody only works when all the roles can be seen reflecting each other's grotesqueries. Do these reflections also act to cancel each other out and leave us with the pale consolation of mere humanity?

No such white observing eye is present or called for in *Lady of Silences*. As much as it likes to be seen at the centre of every story, in Canada, audiences for theatre or other ceremonies are hard enough to come by without getting picky about their make up. So in the world of this Lady, that white eye is assumed to either be blind to or turned away from what goes on in the streets in the poor parts of town, what goes on in what it imagines as the vast empty wilderness of the country. Is that eye blind because all it can see, all it is drawn to is the Lady overseas in her Garden, Belmondo in a film by Jean Luc Godard? That may be why these characters have been asked to appear in this play, even so allusively, as bait for that white, wandering eye, to give it something to fix on, to be nostalgic about, to see, to help it take root or delight from this soil. That's better, isn't it, than the proverbial poke in the orbit? Or it may be that the Indians too, after so many generations of being told that there's nothing worth their while in this country, also need to do a take or two of the presence of the Lady, also long to look in the direction of the Detective's mystery. To that desertified desire, this new dame Watatootis appears like spring water. Or could it be that mostly there are Indians in the audience, that the eye is the one imagined under the visor-hand, jaundiced, blood shot, and that the Lady and the mystery are here for it to fix on in recognition? Do we love her so much? That has to be partly true. Why else does the I in Indian find myself laughing at the serious anguish these folks, my folks, we, are going through?

But there is the laughter of delight too. Just listen to the music in the way these Indian characters talk, mixing up languages, English and Cree, like *habitués* of a multicultural street, like graduates of residential schools, with a rich sense of the irony of high language, both secular and religious, used by low persons, with a sense of the anguish of low persons with hopes higher than is healthy for them. The language becomes more whole and more holy. There is both surprise and thrills in the shift from vulgar language to the sweetest tenderness, from anger to romantic images that still have their cutting edges, that are not quite worn to cliché. There is suspense as we wait for the next shift, the next jab. There is possibility sparkling like jewellery in the indeterminacy. The ladies of the play wear it and thanks, perhaps, to Watatootis or team work (How else do you survive battle but with the help of your sister soldiers?), get away from their crime, the war, the play, at the end, and one longs to follow them off.

But Floyd Favel keeps us, the audience, (and himself?) with the two gentlemen of the play, if we dare call them that, and so we are not satisfied. We stay with the boys, Village and Detective Belmondo, who are lost in the romantic shadows of the mystery story, longing without hope for loves of the past and for the truth of facts, their existence almost European. God does not answer the prayers of these Indians, he may well be dead, but in Village's vision, his lover Linda might well be sufficient, might be stepping out of the Bible, an angel; in Belmondo's vision, he is a wolf of rage, moving beyond his own darkness, beyond good and evil. Unfortunately, this new territory of freedom for both men also seems to be beyond humanity as well. It is a vision of a particular secular hell we are left with, as well as the promise of the truth of our holy war where the Lady of Noises will be victorious.

(2001)

Daniel David Moses: Ghostwriter with a Vengeance

by Rob Appleford

I

My ears are anxious for questions to come from good people who care about meat and how it gets got and what master's voice it gives resonance to.

—Daniel David Moses, "'The Dogs of Free Speech,' 'Adam' Means 'Red Man': A Talk for 'Challenging Racism in the Arts,' a forum at Metro Hall [Toronto] 22 September 1998. 15 September 2001".

Ghostwriting is a barometer of democracy; it thrives only when democracy thrives.

—Douglas P. Starr, *How To Handle Speechwriting Assignments* (5)

Professor Bowman of the [American] University says: "Most of the great speeches we hear are written in whole or in part by someone backstage." Listen, Professor: we know of people who see ghosts where there is nothing, but you are seeing ghosts where there are people.

—Eric Sevareid, "The Professor and the Ghosts" (161)

Before I discuss the dynamics of absence and presence in Daniel David Moses' playwriting—what I call ghostwriting—I would first like to characterize the critical context of Moses' career as reflecting a similar dynamic of absence and presence. In *The Globe and Mail* review of his 1995 play *The Indian Medicine Shows*, Kate Taylor calls Moses "a coroner of the theatre who slices open the human heart to reveal the fear, hatred and love that have eaten away at it" (C3). Two years later, Arthur Milner writes a review of Salteaux playwright Ian Ross' play *FareWel* in which he states that "Ross is in that short line of Canadian Native playwriting that extends from Tomson Highway to, well, Ross" (98). Of course, this is an unfair juxtaposition, since Milner's genealogy is uncontestably flawed. Moses "broke through" as a performed playwright in 1988 with his play *Coyote City*, one year before Highway's own breakout success *Dry Lips Oughta Move to Kapuskasing* (1989). Yet, Highway's critical reputation as a playwright (based largely on two published plays, *The Rez Sisters* and *Dry Lips*, compared to the nine plays published so far by Moses) has become firmly entrenched, and his work is studied widely by students in undergraduate and graduate classrooms and by scholars of Canadian theatre and Canadian literature. My unfair juxtaposition of

Taylor's enthusiasm with Milner's elision raises an equally unfair question: why does Highway enjoy more critical attention than Moses? Putting the issues of aesthetics and production histories aside for the moment, I believe that a provisional answer is suggested by Taylor's analogy of the coroner. Moses' dramatic *oeuvre* is characterized by a fascination with the dead, while Highway's is very much a celebration of the living. And as a "coroner of the theatre," Moses dramatizes the at once fascinating and repellent spectacle of the dead being cut open and studied on stage. I would, however, like to complicate Taylor's analogy. Moses is less a coroner, whose practice requires a necessary forensic distance from (and establishes the absolute deadness of) the cadaver, than a ghostwriter, who engages in the much messier and implicated practice of staging the return of the living dead. The result of this staging is that the audience is placed in a self-consciously awkward position, where it is reminded of divisions that are often elided in public discourses about Aboriginal artistic expression and Aboriginal/non-Aboriginal relations: divisions between actor and character, self and other, subject and subjection, the living and the "unpaid symbolic debt" of the living dead (Z̆iz̆ek 23). In Moses' plays, being alive and being dead are both revealed to be a lot of damned work. In my examination of what this work of living (and being dead) entails, I employ the term *ghostwriter* multivalently, to indicate how Moses writes ghosts, and how this writing of ghosts is also a ghostwriting of subjectivity. In my discussion of Moses' ghostwriting—the writing of ghosts and the ghostwriting of subjectivity—I will suggest the ways in which Moses' plays demonstrate the complexity of Alice Rayner's assertion that "theatre in some sense not only believes in ghosts, it helps create them" (547).

II

To be seen is the ambition of ghosts and to be remembered the ambition of the dead.
　　—Norman O. Brown, opening epigraph from Daniel David Moses, *Coyote City* (6)

BOO: Disembodied. That's the word.
　　—*Coyote City* (23)

At various times in its history, Western theatre has been seen to emphasize either presence or absence as its fundamental defining characteristic. In an age of globalization and culture-as-capital, Western theatre has more recently been championed as an intervention in the "reproductive economy" of images because of its inherently ephemeral practice, where "performance's being [...] becomes itself through disappearance" (Phelan 146). In this sense, theatre is seen as the archetypal haunted space, ghosted by its own immanent absence. Yet, despite this immanent, or spectral, absence, the means of production are stubborn; the set, props, lighting, sounds effects, posters, programs warning of gunshots/smoking/obscene language onstage, and actors are very much a physical presence in the theatrical event. Thus, critical study of Western theatre has also concerned itself with the intensely material aspects of performance, so much so that the space of theatre seems less haunted than numbingly corporeal. Alice Rayner laments that this emphasis—by scholars, practitioners or audience members—on the material presence(s) of performance risks exorcising the haunted space and theatre's necessarily seanced nature: "Theatre so often becomes too real, too familiar, too merely significant, important or meaningful. Perhaps this is why so few actual productions or performances produce the haunting that belongs there. Empirical and rational values more often than not dominate the readiness of theatrical space to be haunted" (540). In part, what helps to underwrite these empirical and rational values in the theatre is an ontological framework for separating absence from presence. To conjure a clichéd example, Hamlet's father is a ghost, Hamlet is not, and both are played by real actors who are "channeling" the words of Shakespeare. Yet, to be haunted requires both absence and presence in an ambiguously contracted and contradicted relationship.

The play *Coyote City* (1990) opens with a lone actor revealed by a spotlight, and right away, the audience is presented with a problem. The actor begins to speak, begging for a drink. The stage directions indicate that the actor is directing his plea to the spotlight itself, whom he personifies as a dismissive bartender (9), and thus, the audience is allowed to view the actor's performance as being contained within the hermetic world of the play, where the actors fill in absence with imagined presence. But then, the actor turns and begins to speak "to the darkness," to the audience, and his plea for alcohol slides into a curse:

> Acting like he [the bartender spotlight] can't see me. Acting like I'm just another drunk Indian. Think he thinks I've had enough? Do you think that too? Do you think I've had enough? Enough. Shit. You think I've had too much. Well who the fuck are you anyway? I don't know you. I don't know you. Shit you're not even real. [...] Hey you're nothing but a bunch of spooks. (10)

The audience, sitting in "the darkness," has now been cast (out?) as the "spooks." It has been recognized by the actor as having no material presence for the character he plays, except as spectres haunting the imaginary world the character inhabits. While this metatheatrical address reverses the typical ontology of performance (Robin Goodfellow's apology in Shakespeare's *A Midsummer Night's Dream* extended from "we shadows" to his audience, "that you have but slumbered here,/While these visions did appear" [5.1.414-17]), it nevertheless provides an ontology that promises a particular relationship between absence and presence: the audience must play the absence, and the actors must play the presence that the audience has been cast to haunt.

But the audience quickly learns that the lone actor revealed by the spotlight is playing a character named Johnny who is himself a "spook," killed in a bar fight. To dispel confusion for the audience, which has been recognized as spectral by another spectre, Moses provides an explicit ontology in the form of a traditional

Nez Percé story involving Coyote's desire to be reunited with his dead wife. Coyote is shepherded by a "shadow man" to the land of the dead, the exact inversion of the land of the living, where day is night, and "it's like they're awake while we're dreaming, living new lives while we're dead to the world" (43). Coyote finds his dead wife and waits every day until dark until he can be with her in the land of the dead, until one day he seeks to take her back with him. In true Orphic fashion, the only precondition for her return is that Coyote must refrain from touching her as they leave the land of the dead until she is fully alive again. Of course, Coyote fails in this simple task (as he must), and his dead wife (and the land of the dead) disappears forever. Unlike Orpheus, however, Coyote is trapped in the scene of his failure, "pretending under the hot sun to be eating berries [...] He tried to taste the sweetness in his mouth. But when night came down, it was just dust" (103). The audience learns that Johnny is the ghost who is trapped in the scene of his own failure, Toronto's infamous "Silver Dollar" bar, where he was stabbed to death while trying to pick up another man's girlfriend. In a reversal of the Nez Percé Coyote story, the dead Johnny is seeking to reunite with his living girlfriend Lena, whom he calls "long distance" and begs to join him at the Silver Dollar. The audience is then, in a sense, freed from its designated role as "spooks" by this explanation, and can see itself as the living presence witnessing the haunting of the theatrical space by the living dead, the ghost of Johnny.

While the Nez Percé Coyote story frames the play's action, it also reminds us of the inherent tension between presence and absence that marks the realist theatrical event. Just as the play's setting of the Silver Dollar represents the thin membrane between the dead and the living, a membrane which is both constituted and threatened by desire, the realist theatrical space is equally a thin membrane of desire separating absence and presence. The undead character Johnny opens the play by trying to cast the audience as undead so he can realize his own presence through opposition to an absence. In this way, Moses signals that the play is less a verisimilar representation of real life (where presence and absence may have an occluded, shifting, but still recognizable relationship) than an urgent repetition of the undead's desire to be alive, *to be* "real life." Johnny's casting of the audience is also a demand, a demand that, according to Rayner, requires "that the ordinary material world take on the strangeness of itself in order to make itself and all its invisibilities visible" (547). Of course, it mustn't be forgotten that Coyote's fate is to be trapped within the material world, desperately seeking to breach the membrane between the visible and invisible yet only able to mime this breach through the repetition of failed actions, the pretence of eating dust as if it was berries. This failure to breach the membrane is also the failure of realist theatre, which predicates its action on the doomed desire to transcend its props. The result is a staging of failure and desire, both on the level of ontology and character motivation.

While the Nez Percé story can be seen to organize the relationship between the actors and their audience, it also necessarily organizes the relationships of the characters to each other. Yet here too, the relationships appear more vexed than explicated by the Coyote story. When Lena and her family make the trip to the Silver Dollar, both to contact and exorcise the ghost of Johnny, the spectral Johnny's power to establish and challenge the identities of the living is made plain. When Johnny appears in the ladies washroom of the Silver Dollar to Boo, Lena's sister who was once in love with Johnny, he repeats the Nez Percé story, and the stage directions again render the division between absence and presence ambiguous:

> JOHNNY: [...] Coyote and this shadow guy in the middle of nowhere, sitting out there, eating dust, pretending to be in some lodge with Coyote's dead wife. *(His spot begins to fade.)* And then, just like that, the sun goes down. And there they are, people all around him. *(Another spot begins to reveal BOO.)* Coyote hears them folks whispering at first and then really talking. All of them living their lives in the land of the dead. (74)

The stage directions suggest that Boo, Lena's sister, is living in the land of the dead, while Johnny is the living Coyote who seeks to connect with her. What this scene also calls into question is the status of Coyote. Coyote, as a mythological figure, is neither living nor dead, but something in between, and if Johnny is attempting to reify his presence through identification with Coyote, his connection to Coyote only further mystifies his own status as living dead.

In Moses' play, what connects absence and presence, spectrality and materiality, is not a stable and fixed ontological relationship but rather the *unrequited desire for such a relationship*. In order to make herself pretty for Johnny, to make herself seen by him, Johnny's girlfriend Lena transforms her appearance so that she resembles a whore. When she enters the washroom and finds her sister Boo conversing with Johnny, Lena finds herself invisible to Johnny. She desperately calls to him, but he does not recognize her and therefore cannot see her. She tries to wipe off her garish makeup, but to no avail, and she can only watch in frustration as her spectral lover shares an intimate moment with her sister Boo. Lena, with her body rendered invisible by artifice in the failed attempt to be seen by, and therefore seduce a ghost, is also a powerful symbol of the actor, a fitting counterpoint to Johnny's self-consciously performative narration. Both characters make manifest the often suppressed, doubled anxiety of theatrical representation, where the actor's performance of a text is, as Daniel Mesguich suggests, the "monstrous division of a text by a body as well as that of a body by a text." This "monstrous division" involves both Lena's attempt to rewrite her appearance with the signifiers of a whore (her body divided by a text), and Johnny's attempt to insert himself into the Coyote story (a text divided by his body), and as Mesguish warns, "this division doesn't quite fit" (113). What connects their attempts at division is the desire to be seen, to be wanted, to be desired through recognition by the Other, which makes the invisible visible through its desire. In this way, *Coyote City* demonstrates with unsettling clarity that a ghost is neither dead nor alive, absent nor present, but is simply what you desire.

III

The specter thus may be said to represent more than the instability of the real; it also represents the ghostly embodiment of a fear and panic provoked by intimations of an impossible state of being. Recognition of the flawed or incomplete nature of being [...] can trigger emotional reactions aimed at denying or exorcising such a recognition.
—Tom Lewis, "The Politics of 'Hauntology' in Derrida's *Specters of Marx*" (140)

INTERLOCUTOR: These fine, kind folks want to know the truth, the amazing details and circumstance behind your savagely beautiful appearance. They also want to be entertained and enlightened and maybe a tiny bit thrilled, just a goose of frightened. They want to laugh and cry. They want to know the facts. And it's up to you and me to try and lie that convincingly.
—Moses, *Almighty Voice and His Wife* (32)

While it is possible to read *Coyote City* (and Moses' later work) as a parable about realist theatre and the necessary failure of its spectral desires, the implications of Moses' ghost writing extend far beyond the limits and ontology of theatrical performance. The notion of haunting is central to discussions of theatrical space and the uneasy relationship between absence and presence within it, but haunting, or spectralization, has in recent decades become a very portable and powerful way to characterize the indeterminacy of social space and social life.[1] My own understanding of this trope of haunting in its various employments is that haunting involves three ideas: the repetition of anachronistic categories no longer useful but nevertheless still oppressive, the inherent subjection of the subject as an object to itself, and the ethical demand of the dead for justice from the living. All three ideas hinge on the return of the spectral or living dead (to use Žižek's term) as an ontological destabilization of strict definitions of absence and presence; while this destabilization sometimes makes possible a redemptive refiguring of subjectivity, it also warns of the risks of failing to negotiate a compromise (or "co-promise," as Rayner coins it [550]) between the dead and the living. I will show how all three ideas play out in Moses' theatre of ghosts.

Just as the ghost is not only an embodiment of individual fear and desire but is, as Avery F. Gordon points out, a "social figure" which can "lead to the dense site where history and subjectivity make social life" (45), Moses' ghost writing reveals Aboriginality as a tautological category which, through historical and ever-present desire, is given illusory heft. In an essay entitled "How My Ghosts Got Pale Faces" (1998), Moses relates an anecdote about his performance of the opening monologue of *Coyote City* at a public reading at York University. A "fair-skinned, dark-haired young man" listened to Moses read the monologue and then asked him angrily "whether I thought I was exploiting stereotypes of Native people" (120). Moses is at first bemused by this response, and later, after being told by a professor that the young man had just recently discovered that his biological mother was a Native woman, "probably Ojibway" (125), Moses realizes that the investment the young man had in positive Native images was intensely personal. But Moses also makes the interesting connection between the angry young man and the character of Johnny:

> [...] in my memory now, he's still fair-skinned, dark-haired, young, but lost like Johnny, my besotted ghost, in some city, not knowing who his people are or where they come from, not even able to be one with that mixed bunch of people who appear as the audience in the dark theatre, both wanting to get spooked and afraid of its happening. (126)

By conflating the young man with a ghost, Moses makes the point that the former's desire for positive images of his heritage is akin to the latter's doomed desire for presence. Like spectres, whose apparition is both uncanny and citational (since the ghost would not be recognized as such if it did not seem familiar or referential in some way [Attridge 224]), the young man's hunger for images that reflected his desire for identity is fed by a system of citations which are at once historical and ideal (ahistorical), and therefore also impossible to realize. Moses affirms that his dramatization of ghosts in *Coyote City* does not simply spook the relationship between absence and presence in a theatrical context, but more importantly, reveals the spectral nature of authenticity and its necessary haunting of social discourse involving Aboriginal peoples. By characterizing Johnny as "a human creature who had to deal with a handicap: being dead but not realizing it" (123), Moses echoes both Žižek's warning about the residual power of state or ideological apparatuses which "although they are clearly anachronistic [...] persist because *they do not know [that they are dead]*" (emphasis in original 44), and the disavowal by the individual subject of the debt of the living dead which makes itself apparent through failed efforts to exorcise or defer it.

Authenticity persistently haunts the interpretation of Aboriginal literatures in the interstitial space between absence and presence. Terry Goldie's early influential study of non-Aboriginal versions of Aboriginal identity (1989) argues that perceived Aboriginal values act as "commodities" which circulate within dominant discourse and serve to buttress dominant ideology. This circulation, in turn, determines what is accepted as authentically Aboriginal in Aboriginal discourses. Goldie critiques non-Aboriginal narratives involving Aboriginal characters not by appealing to ethical arguments involving appropriation of voice, but by asserting an essential qualitative authenticity which non-Aboriginal writers can never capture. Goldie critiques Samuel Hearne's *A Journey* because it "misses the appearance of subjectivity [...] in which, to recall Bishop Berkeley, the character exists because we perceive him perceiving" (45). Later, he makes a similar discursive pronouncement against Thomas Kinsella's construction of an Aboriginal narrator named Silas: "the reader is thus not required to judge [Kinsella's character] Silas's absent thoughts 'Indian' or 'Non-Indian' but is left with the paradox of an Indian narrator and no Indian consciousness" (52). Because Goldie refuses to define what "the appearance of subjectivity" in an "Indian consciousness" might look like (indeed, how could anyone do so?), the evocation of an authentic Aboriginal subjectivity is both substantial in its ability to eliminate inauthentic constructions of Aboriginality and spectral in its limning of Goldie's interpretations, always escaping definition yet underwriting the attempt to reject that which is not consonant with what it could be. Malcolm Page, in his 2001 review of Ian Ross' play *FareWel*, deploys a similar evocation of authenticity, in this case involving a desire for political utility which is as equally solid and ephemeral, to dismiss Ross' play as a failure: "while I don't ask for a wholly positive and therefore untruthful view [of reserve life], [Ian Ross' *FareWel*] does not aid the cause of Native self-government at the time of the Nisga'a treaty" (128). In this way, the spectral nature of authenticity effects both Aboriginal and non-Aboriginal constructions of subjectivity because it can never be grounded in anything but unfulfilled desire.

The symbolic debt the living owe the dead creates a relationship between the two parties. In one sense, the relationship has been characterized as one of possession, where the ghost "provides the vehicle for both a dangerous possession by and an imaginative liberation from the past" (Brogan 11). In this model, the living present risks being overtaken by the ghostly ancestral past, and the past must either be exorcised or incorporated into the living present's project of "healthy" self-possession. Ric Knowles reads Moses' plays in part according to this model. He argues that all of Moses' plays "are replete with ghosts as the *not-seen*, who model a culturally repressed *what-really-is*, the repressed truth that must be revealed beneath an oppressive realism in order to release the *what-could-be*" (190, emphases in original). I, too, first saw Moses' work in this redemptive way, seeing, for example, his 1991 play *Almighty Voice and His Wife* as showing that "the obstacles [to subjectivity] are texts which reify themselves at the expense of bodies which enact them" ("Desire" 26). At the time, my own understanding of Aboriginal theatre presupposed the spectral presence of authenticity as perpetually struggling for immanence through the exorcism of stereotype on stage.[2] But as I look at Moses' work thus far, and examine the recurrent motif of ghosts who are lost and do not realize that they are dead, it seems to me that his plays are less about the spectres of "repressed truth" (and the bodies that reclaim it), than about the awful spectacle of the living dead enacting their eternal subjection.[3] Rather than redemption, what Moses gives us is an old-fashioned ghost story, again and again.

IV

[...] this living *individual* would itself be inhabited and invaded by its own specter. It would be constituted by specters of which it becomes the host and which it assembles in the haunted community of a single body. Ego=ghost.
 —Jacques Derrida, *Specters of Marx* (133)

[a client] will probably present the ghostwriter with a combination of images. An astute observer will see yet another image: the one meant to be projected. You will be successful if you can compare the desired

image with the image that is actually projected and produce a speaking style somewhere between the two.
—Douglas P. Starr, *How To Handle Speechwriting Assignments* (13)

Just as Coyote in the Nez Percé story must eat dust as if it was berries, the audience of a Moses play must make do with spectres of Aboriginality as if they signified something authentic. It is because of Moses' consistent efforts to make the desires of ghosts palpable (and to show that desire makes ghosts of us all) that Moses can be seen to be a ghostwriter in the journalistic sense, a pen for hire who writes a script that rhetorically mimics another's voice. While the perception of ghost writing has always involved a discomfort with the counterfeiting of authentic voice,[4] ghostwriters themselves have seen this counterfeiting as a natural and revealing reflection of an individual's subjectivity. This act of reflection as fully self-possessed is very much in keeping with postmodern ideas about the limits of subjectivity.

In "The Creative Ghost," Warren Bower supplies an extended discussion of the ghostwriter's process, and he suggests that the relationship between the "ghost" and his or her subject is limnal and mutually constitutive:

> The ghost who writes a speech or an article uses his mind for a brief, intense period as a mirror. He catches the reflection of the man he is to impersonate, studies the image, concentrates on the portion of it he is to imitate, and rehearses the role. [...] Then, pretending that he himself is the man, he writes as if that man had taken on, temporarily, his, the ghost's, skill as a writer. (267)

Ghostwriters must lose themselves in the role of amanuensis, and by blurring the distinction between self and Other, ghostwriters can lend the immaterial signs of personality temporary material weight and efficacy in another's script. Bower goes on to suggest that while ghostwriters must suppress their own personalities, it requires "the ability on the part of the ghost to separate the central part of his mind from the process of identification and use it to observe what is taking place in his imagination" (267). This separation entails a self-possession that can permit the observation of oneself as being (always) possessed by an/other, and it is in the imagination where self and Other coexist in a fencing relationship, equal parts riposte and barbed wire. Rather than simply parroting another's mannerisms and verbal style, ghostwriting is the ability to understand subjectivity as a fundamentally haunted space. It is by being ghosted that one can recognize oneself in a spectral revelation of subjectivity's limits. "Subjectivity is formed or named as the proximity to a limit whose crossing is always already required even as it remains in some sense unrepresentable," writes Étienne Balibar, and at this unrepresentable vanishing point "we are dealing with the dissolution of structure—whether it be to the advantage of flux, dissemination, the machine, or the thing" (9-10). In a postcolonial context, we may well fear such a dissolution, and desire an indigenous speaking subject which, spectrally, is both absent (outside of an oppressive anachronistic hegemony) and present (within a recognizably authentic discourse of humanism). What is perhaps most feared is a ghost which refuses to speak, or refuses to speak *authentically* but instead spooks us with its hollow mimicry of what we have always wanted (or feared) to hear. The ghostwriter observes the client and produces a text somewhere between "the desired image" and "the image that is actually projected" (Starr 13). Between these two images is the ghost. What this ghost represents is an occulted subjectivity, based on secrets, mysteries, and the conceal-ment of the body (material and politic) by another interposed in the line of vision.

I have introduced this concept of ghostwriting because I see Moses exploring the ghostwriting of subjectivity on stage, regardless of ethnicity. Just as the ghostwriter plays intertextually between subjectivities, Moses dramatizes how characters on stage continually struggle to negotiate between absence and presence, being dead and being alive, in their desire to matter, *to be matter*. And since the ghost by its very nature is a citation of the past, of a history forgotten or suppressed, Moses' audience must grapple with the citational anxiety of the dead who can only voice their living desires using dead images and ideas. The "fair-skinned, dark-haired young man" in Moses' audience who reacted angrily to Johnny's pleading, "I'm almost empty here. Come on and dispense with the booze," must also reject wholesale what Johnny offers the audi-ence for the booze that can *fill him up*: a knife, a "pretty Indian chick, fresh from the bush," and a traditional story (9). All three are metonymic commodities—violence, sex, and orality—which Goldie argues have circulated within discourse since contact and continue to define authentic Aboriginality. Instead of replacing (or at least pick-ing and choosing amongst) these commodities, Moses shows us how they all continue to manifest a relationship between the living and the dead, a relationship predicated on desire. Just as the ghostwriter must force the "ghostee" to return to the past despite the fact that "he will be reluctant to release his attention from the events and anxieties of his contemporary existence" (Bower 272), Moses pushes his audience to confront the historical legacy of failed repetitious desire which occults both Aboriginal and non-Aboriginal subjectivity.

Ghostwriters cannot afford to be either just themselves or other people in order to successfully channel the intersubjective voice of the script. Similarly, Moses rare-ly presents a narrative in which occulted subjectivity is the provenance of either Aboriginal or non-Aboriginal subjects. One example of this spectral neither-nor can be taken from Moses' 1996 historical drama *Brébeuf's Ghost*. The play tells the story of an Anishnaabe/Ojibway community at Lake Nipissing struggling to survive famine, evil medicine, Iroquois invasion, and insane French missionaries in 1649. One of the central motifs in the play is the Windigo, a cannibal spirit which possesses humans and infects them with the desire to eat human flesh. The Windigo complex, as it is now called by anthropologists, has garnered considerable attention and attendant contro-versy since its identification.[5] Early anthropologists claimed that the "Windigo psy-chosis" (as it was first labeled) was a real manifestation of Algonquin peoples' anxiety over starvation and evil sorcery, and many went so far as to see the complex as a man-ifestation of traditional Algonquin individualism and lack of community solidarity (i.e., it is easier to eat someone if your culture teaches you that your personal survival is paramount, and that others aren't that important in the larger scheme of things).

A later dissenting school argued that the "Windigo complex" (the change in terminology reflecting the change in attitude) was an invention or misapprehension of early-contact settlers, and that any rumour of afflicted Windigo cannibals circulated by Algonquin peoples was meant to frighten these settlers, to obtain alcohol from them as "medicine" for the condition, or to deter other Aboriginal groups from trespassing on valuable fur trapping areas.

What emerges in this debate about the Windigo is the ideological investment in seeing the syndrome as immanent in Algonquin psychopathology or as the result of post-contact material conditions, the psychological implications of a psychosis versus the historical implications of a complex. While many non-Aboriginal writers in the last century have been attracted to the Windigo complex as a fertile subject for creative work, it has only been relatively recently that Aboriginal writers have tackled the subject. A reader might expect that the Aboriginal writer chooses this topic in order to dispel Eurocentric prejudice about traditional Algonquin culture, emphasize the material conditions of this prejudice, or reaffirm the reality of the cannibal condition as an historical fact. In *Brébeuf's Ghost*, Moses chooses all three options, and, key for this discussion, dramatizes the ambiguous ontology that makes the Windigo condition so terrifying.

The play shows the tiny Anishnaabe/Ojibway community beleaguered by hunger, internal conflict and the external pressures of Iroquois and Jesuit encroachment. While all the characters variously display the classical symptoms which precede Windigo psychosis (extreme individualism, community infighting, despair, malnutrition, and fear of sorcery), it is significantly the Jesuit Father Noel who is first afflicted with full-blown Windigo cannibalism in the community. Moses makes the point that the missionary brand of Catholicism, with its twinned emphasis on ritual cannibalism of Christ's body and blood and its need to harvest souls, makes the Jesuit a particularly receptive candidate for Windigo possession. In an important sense, the play can be read as a postcolonial revision of the Windigo story, where non-Aboriginal ideology is shown to be predicated on insatiable hunger and psychotic breakdown. [6] But as in *Coyote City*, where staging calls into question ontological distinctions, *Brébeuf's Ghost* presents a scene which foregrounds the audience's unfulfilled desire for certainty.

During the height of starvation, the character Flood Woman enters the scene carrying, as the stage directions indicate, "*the better part of a large, frozen and peculiar-looking sturgeon*" (84). Once again, the audience is presented with a problem. The designation "*sturgeon*" would indicate that the prop we see in some way resembles a fish. Its peculiarity lies in both in its appearance, but also in the audience's presumption that the object is not in fact a fish, but the disinterred body part of a buried Iroquois warrior, killed in a previous scene. In the dissolute subjectivity of the Windigo-afflicted, human body parts are necessarily misconstrued as animal flesh to permit their consumption. Thus, by describing the ambiguous object borne by Flood Woman as a sturgeon, Moses has the audience share her subjective perception. But by tagging the object as "*peculiar*," Moses also reminds the audience that it cannot entirely accept this psychotic perception as its own. In a grisly sense, the audience desires that the object be recognized as what it "really" is (human flesh), so that the audience can solidly reinvest its own identity as objective observers of a subjective phenomenon. We, as audience members, must deny the subjectivity of the character because to accept it would require us to also accept that our own subjectivity is afflicted by uncertainty. The "peculiar" ambiguity of the object presented to us—which glows "*with a spectral light*" (86)—prevents a comfortable differentiation between subject and object, just as the ghost is an uncanny deferment of certain distinctions between presence and absence, real and unreal. At its icy heart, the Windigo represents the hunger that blurs necessary divisions between truth and rumour, individualism and community, and self and Other. Those who have "gone Windigo" can no longer recognize the difference between being human and being possessed by a spiritual monster, and more importantly for those around them, between being human and being an animal. In this way, the desire for an authentic and real version of experience (the only way to cure the condition is to reject what one sees) is shared by both Aboriginal characters and the audience that observes them. No subjectivity is unalloyed here. The Windigo complex is the breaching of the thin membrane between what can and cannot be known, between phantasmal and material ontologies, and between subjective awareness and its unrepresentable limits. Subjectivity will eat itself.

It must be remembered that ghostwriting is nothing new in the occulting of Aboriginal voices by settlers. Dominant discourse has always put words in Aboriginal mouths, and disavowed the desires that shape the words that come out of these mouths. What is fascinating about Moses' project, threaded through nine plays, is the exploration of this ghostwritten authenticity from the perspective of the spectres, rather than from the living who would exorcise them. Moses' work poses a fundamental challenge to those who would ask for images free from the legacy of colonial oppression and distortion. As an epigraph to his 1995 play *City of Shadows*, a sequel to *Coyote City*, Moses supplies a famous warning from Chief Seattle:

> All night when the streets of your cities and villages are silent and you think them deserted, they will throng with the returning hosts that once filled them and still love this beautiful land. (104)

On the surface, this is a warning from the living dead, "an ethical demand to do justice in light of asymmetrical power relations between the living who do the work and the phantoms of representation, of history, and of the invisible" (Rayner 536). This would be the ideally postcolonial haunting, the demand of repressed and deferred subjects to be afforded discursive rights to subjectivity. But even this straightforward apparition contains further deferred subtleties. Renee Bergland reminds us that Chief Seattle's speech is itself a product of colonial ghostwriting, its content determined by many non-Aboriginal writers who have continually rewritten the speech to reflect their own ideological concerns: "[In Chief Seattle's speech] White Americans and Europeans want to hear their own mythology so much that they put it into the mouth of a dead Indian." Bergland calls this "ghostwriting with a vengeance" (160), and it is this inevitable ghosting of subjectivity that Moses turns to his profit in his plays. The final line of *Brébeuf's Ghost* is a chilling promise that his plays would seem to forestall: "Soon you'll step into your flesh" (141). Indeed, as "that mixed bunch of people who appear as the audience in the dark theatre, both wanting to get spooked and afraid of its happening," we are forced to ask: whose step, and whose flesh?

(2005)

Notes

1 Haunting has become a central trope in cultural studies (Žižek), history (Bergland), sociology (Gordon), architectural theory (Wigley), psychoanalytic theory (Abraham and Torok), theology (Bahti and Klein), postcolonial literary studies (Brogan), gothic studies (Castricano), and philosophy (Derrida).

2 See Appleford ("Desire," "That Almost Present Dream").

3 For want of space, I have refrained from discussing Moses' other plays in which spectrality is foregrounded, especially *Almighty Voice and His Wife* (1991), *Kyotopolis* (1993), *City of Shadows* (1995), and *The Indian Medicine Shows* (1995). For example, the need for a spectral Aboriginal absent-presence is so strong in *The Indian Medicine Shows* that a non-Aboriginal character forces a living Aboriginal character to dress up as a ghost, complete with bed-sheet and dime-store feather headdress.

4 See Sevareid for an example of this discomfort, and Kennedy for the historical trajectory of this discomfort, from the ancient Greeks to 1950s America.

5 For the "psychosis" school, see Teicher; for the "complex" school, see Marano.

6 In an unpublished essay on *Brébeuf's Ghost*, Jillian Garrett argues that "like human flesh to the windigo, history fills us up; it eases our hunger; we need it to survive. [...] Just as the cannibal Jesuits will continue to haunt the Ojibwa group in attempts at conversion, the European historians will always be equally willing to cannibalize significant moments in Native history to feed their own Western historical project" (13-14).

Works Cited

Abraham, Nicholas and Maria Torok. *The Shell and the Kernel: Renewals of Psychoanalysis.* Vol. 1. Trans. and ed. Nicholas T. Rand. Chicago: U Chicago P, 1994.

Appleford, Rob. "'That Almost Present Dream of Tomorrow': Daniel David Moses' *Kyotopolis* as Native Canadian Science Fiction/History Play." *Crucible of Cultures: Anglophone Drama in the New Millennium.* Ed. Marc Maufort and Franca Bellarsi. Brussels: Peter Lang, 2002. 199-208.

———. "The Desire To Crunch Bone: Daniel David Moses and the 'True-Real' Indian." *Canadian Theatre Review* 77 (Winter 1993): 21-26.

Attridge, Derek. "Ghost Writing." *Deconstruction is/in America: A New Sense of the Political.* Ed. Anselm Haverkamp. New York: New York UP, 1995. 223-27.

Bahti, Timothy and Richard Klein. "Introduction to 'The Ghost of Theology: Readings of Kant and Hegel.'" *Diacritics* 11.2 (1981): 1-5.

Balibar, Etienne. "Structuralism: A Destitution of the Subject?" Trans. James Swenson. *Differences: A Journal of Feminist Cultural Studies* 14.1 (2003): 1-21.

Bergland, Renee L. *The National Uncanny: Indian Ghosts and American Subjects.* Hanover and London: UP of New England, 2000.

Bower, Warren. "The Creative Ghost." *How to Write for Pleasure and Profit.* Philadelphia and New York: J.B. Lippencott, 1951.

Castricano, Jodey. *Cryptomimesis: The Gothic and Jacques Derrida's Ghost Writing.* Montreal and Kingston: McGill-Queens UP, 2001.

Derrida, Jacques. *Specters of Marx: The State of the Debt, the Work of Mourning, & the New International.* Trans. Peggy Kamuf. New York and London: Routledge, 1994.

Garrett, Jillian. "*Brébeuf's Ghost* and the Cannibal Project of History." Unpublished essay, 2002.

Goldie, Terry. *Fear and Temptation: Images of the Indigene in Canadian, Australian, and New Zealand Literatures.* Kingston: McGill-Queen's UP, 1989.

Gordon, Avery F. *Ghostly Matters: Haunting and the Sociological Imagination.* Minneapolis: U of Minnesota P, 1997.

Kennedy, George. *The Art of Persuasion in Greece.* London: Routledge and Keegan Paul, 1963.

Knowles, Ric. "'Look. Look again.': Daniel David Moses' Decolonizing Optics." *Crucibles of Cultures: Anglophone Drama at the Dawn of a New Millennium.* Ed. Marc Maufort and Franca Bellarsi. Brussels: Peter Lang, 2002.

Lewis, Tom. "The Politics of 'Hauntology' in Derrida's *Specters of Marx.*" *Ghostly Demarcations: A Symposium on Jacques Derrida's Specters of Marx.* London: Verso, 1999. 134-67.

Marano, Lou. "Windigo Psychosis: The Anatomy of an Emic-Etic Confusion." *Current Anthropology* 23.4 (August 1982): 385-412.

Mesguich, Daniel and Gervais Robin. "The Book to Come is a Theater." *Sub-Stance* 18/19 (1977): 113-19.

Milner, Arthur. Review of *FareWel. Prairie Fire* 18.3 (Autumn 1997): 97-99.

Moses, Daniel David. "'The Dogs of Free Speech,'Adam' Means 'Red Man': A Talk for 'Challenging Racism in the Arts,'" a forum at Metro Hall [Toronto] 22 September 1998. 15 September 2001.

——. *Almighty Voice and His Wife.* Toronto: Playwrights Canada, 2001.

——. *Brébeuf's Ghost: A Tale of Horror in Three Acts.* Toronto: Exile, 2000.

——. *Coyote City: A Play.* Toronto: Playwrights Union of Canada Copyscript, 1988.

——. *The Indian Medicine Shows: Two One-Act Plays.* Toronto: Exile, 1995.

——. *Kyotopolis.* Toronto: Playwrights Union of Canada Copyscript, 1993.

——. "How My Ghosts Got Pale Faces." *Speaking For the Generations: Native Writers on Writing.* Ed. Simon Ortiz. Tucson: U Arizona P, 1998. 118-47.

Page, Malcolm. "Plays Unplaced." *Canadian Literature* 168 (Spring 2001): 126-28.

Phelan, Peggy. *Unmarked: The Politics of Performance.* London and New York: Routledge, 1993.

Rayner, Alice. "Rude Mechanicals and the Specters of Marx." *Theatre Journal* 54.4 (2002): 535-54.

Sevareid, Eric. *In One Ear: 107 Snapshots of Men and Events Which Make a Far-Reaching Panorama of the American Situation at Midcentury.* New York: Alfred A. Knopf, 1952.

Shakespeare, William. *A Midsummer Night's Dream.* Ed. Roma Gill. New York: Oxford UP, 2001.

Starr, Douglas P. *How To Handle Speechwriting Assignments.* New York: Pilot Books, 1978.

Taylor, Kate. "Dark play explores emotions." *The Globe and Mail* 11 January 1996: C3.

Teicher, Morton I. *Windigo Psychosis: A study of a relationship between belief and behavior among the Indians of Northeastern Canada.* Seattle: U of Washington P, 1960.

Wigley, Mark. *The Architecture of Deconstruction: Derrida's Haunt.* Cambridge: MIT P, 1993.

Žižek, Slavoj. *Looking Awry: An Introduction to Jacques Lacan through Popular Culture.* Cambridge, Mass.: MIT P, 1993.

A Windigo Tale: Contemporizing and Mythologizing the Residential School Experience

by Armand Garnet Ruffo

In March of 2001, the CBC announced that my play *A Windigo Tale* was one of three winners of its Performance Showcase Competition for that year. The competition is designed to provide what is called a "calling card" for dramatists wanting to move from stage to screen. In effect, what happens is that the CBC films a couple of scenes from the play and invites a studio audience for a screening and reception. To say that I was surprised to be selected would be an understatement because the competition that year had over two hundred applicants, and the other two winning plays had both won Governor General Awards for Drama. My little play had not even been produced. Furthermore, it was slight, a mere sixty-one pages. What I believe made the judges take notice of the play, despite any shortcomings it may have had, is the interfusion of a contemporary issue, namely, the intergenerational impact of the residential school experience, with traditional Anishnaabe storytelling strategies based on the oral tradition. To proceed, then, I will attempt to illustrate my journey through the creative process of writing the play while coming to understand how the oral tradition could figure into it and provide a culturally appropriate response to the subject matter.

Aside from various "Trickster" figures, like Nanabush for the Ojibway or Weesageechak for the Cree (among other manifestations), no other Aboriginal deity has captured the imagination of western audiences like the Windigo or Weetigo creature. Within the oral tradition of the Anishnaabe numerous stories about the Windigo exist, most having to do with encounters between Windigoes and humans or with other deities, like Nanabush. Over the years, a number of these stories have been collected by ethnologists and writers and can be found in any number of anthologies and collections. For example, in 1965, author and artist Selwyn Dewdney edited a collection of stories, by the great Anishnaabe painter Norval Morrisseau, entitled *Legends of My People*, in which Morrisseau tells the story of Kit-chin-ik-koo (Big Goose) and the Windigo. A few years later, in 1969, Morrisseau again published a collection of stories from the oral tradition under the title *Windigo and Other Tales of the Ojibways*, edited this time by Dr. Hubert Swartz. What makes this collection so unique is that Morrisseau also did illustrations for the book and, for the first time, we are given a glimpse of what this horrific creature may have looked like. Indeed, the Windigo has permeated the imagination of western culture to such an extent that in 1982 John Robert Colombo published *Windigo: An Anthology of Fact and Fantastic Fiction*. Unfortunately, the subtitle of Colombo's book undermines the significance of this

Anishnaabe deity and seems to set it on par with Transylvania's Dracula or maybe the Abominable Snowman of the Himalayas.

Probably the most graphic description of the Windigo appears in Anishnaabe educator and writer Basil Johnson's book *The Manitous: The Spiritual World of the Ojibway*:

> The Weendigo was a giant Manitou in the form of a man or a woman, who towered five to eight times above the height of a tall man... (and) it was afflicted with never-ending hunger. The Weendigo was gaunt to the point of emaciation. With its bones pushing out against its skin, its complexion the ash gray of death, and its eyes pushed back deep into their sockets, the Weendigo looked like a gaunt skeleton recently disinterred from the grave. What lips it had were tattered and bloody from its constant chewing with jagged teeth. When the Weendigo set to attack a human being, a dark snow cloud would shroud its upper body from the waist up. The air would turn cold, so the trees crackled. Then the wind would rise. (221)

What of course all these stories have in common is that the Windigo is always portrayed as an insatiable cannibal with unfathomable power.

Judging from Windigo behaviour, then, one can well imagine that my play would not exactly have people rolling in the aisles with laughter. At the risk of being morbid, or worse, of falling into the horror genre, why did I feel compelled to employ the character of a Windigo? Certainly I had no intention of alienating my audience. Was it because in trying to relate to something as horrific as the residential school experience that I needed to dig as deeply as I could into what might be called primal fear? My own perhaps. I am fortunate that I was not subjected to the Residential School, but, like most Native people in Canada, I too have been affected by its legacy. But then how could I not be? From the mid 1800s to 1969 (the official date when the Church withdrew from running the schools, though some remained open well into the 1970s), First Nations, Métis and Inuit children were, by government decree, forcibly removed from their communities and sent to schools, where they were denied access to their languages and cultures. In *The Circle Game: Shadows and Substance in the Indian Residential School Experience in Canada*, psychologist Rolland Chrisjohn and his colleagues estimate that at one time or another nearly 75% of all Native children in Canada between the ages of seven and fifteen were attending residential schools. They do not flinch from using the words "genocide" (44) and "holocaust" (45) to describe what happened: "In any intellectually honest appraisal, Indian Residential Schools were genocide" (44). It is well documented that these schools were sites of rape, sexual assault, induced abortion and sexual/psychological abuse (27). In no uncertain terms, such violence has been identified as "individual and community dismemberment," in which the state apparatus, endorsing the Christian run educational institutions, functions as a kind of cannibalistic force. In his text *The Manitous*, Ojibway educator Basil Johnston refers to what he calls "modern Weendigoes."

"Actually, the Weendigoes did not die out or disappear," he says; "they have only been assimilated and reincarnated" (235).

To delve deeper into why and how I wrote *A Windigo Tale*, I need to go back a few decades to my hometown of Chapleau in northern Ontario. As a kid, one of my favourite pastimes was walking along the tracks to go fishing at the east-end trestle. My brother and I would usually head there Saturday morning before the sun got too high, eat our lunches halfway there, and spend the day in the shadows of the cool concrete pylons, our feet dangling in the water, while the trains rolled by overhead. Across the tracks was a thin row of trees and an old rusted wire fence and beyond it a cleared out field. Our mother, who was Ojibway, had told us not to go over there, so like most boys our age that's exactly what we did, went over and checked it out. But we didn't stay long. With the sun beating down on us in the clearing, the river was much more inviting. In fact, all I ever saw over there was a stone foundation and scattered remnants of some big old building.

Although I did not know it at the time, I had inadvertently stumbled upon "The Chapleau Indian Residential School," also known as "The Saint John's Indian Residential School." I have to admit that I still don't know much about the school. Frankly, people who went to it never wanted to talk about it. What I do know is that it was run by the Anglican Church, opened in 1907 and closed in 1950. The first time I saw it was around 1960, ten or twelve years after it closed. (Catholic Indians, by the way, were sent to Spanish, about 150 miles away.) What I also know is that the effect of the school on the Native people who went to it was profound. In fact, so profound, they had not only learned their place in the pecking order of the town and larger Canadian state, they had given up their language and many of their traditions, in the process. Is it any wonder, then, that some of these same students could still be seen staggering in some dark laneway despite having been "taught better."

Growing up in a small northern town did have its benefits. For example, in the summer, I could walk down the street to the river and go swimming or fishing any time I wanted. In the winter, there was snowshoeing, skiing, and even snowmobiling. But while these things were great for tourists, as far as I was concerned the most impressive thing about the town was the Fox Theatre. Yes, our little town, stuck in the middle of nowhere, actually had a cinema that showed movies every evening of the week, plus two weekend matinees. For while there was only one pot-holed gravel road leading in and out of town, the CPR had four trains, two eastbound and two westbound, going past every day. Hence, the access to the films. Black and white classics, first run features, we got them all. Always American and always blockbusters. Needless to say, my favourite movies were westerns. John Wayne, you bet. I know what you're thinking, but the Indians are always the bad guys in westerns, always playing the narrative of manifest destiny, enemies of the moving train of progress (Berkhofer 44). True enough. But then who wanted to be an Indian?

Years later, while living in Ottawa, the persuasive power of the colonizer's expansionist fantasy became astoundingly clear to me. I had had a few poems of mine published in the first anthology of contemporary Native poetry in Canada. Entitled

Seventh Generation: Contemporary Native Writing, the anthology came out in 1989 and featured a selection of Native writers I had never read before. The reason being, we simply hadn't had access to each other's work. I distinctly remember receiving my copy of the anthology, tearing open the packaging, and reading a poem by Lenore Keeshig-Tobias that nearly knocked me off my feet. For the first time, I realized my experiences were the experiences of others. In a poem entitled "Indians", she writes:

> When I was
> a kid back home,
> we kids used to
> play cowboys and Indians.
> We never wanted
> to be Indians
> 'cause they were
> always the bad guys
> and lost,
> so we were all cowboys
> back home on the reservation. (Hodgson 70)

By the time I was growing up the persistent theme about Indians was that the successful ones, meaning those with a job and a roof over their heads, assimilated into dominant culture, acted white and gave up their languages and culture, while the rest, the blanket Indians, the ones whooping and hollering in the movies, were exiled to a degraded and doomed no man's land. This assessment of course is itself a variation of the vanishing Indian theme, in which civilization and Indians are antithetical, civilization historical and dynamic, Indians ahistorical and static (Berkhofer 29). Assimilation. Suicide. Alcoholism. Prison. Death. Forget Chuck Connor's Geronimo. Even Paul Newman's blue-eyed Apache "Hombre" died at the end. So much for role models.

What I am trying to get at here is that the movies, like the residential schools, were emblematic of a colonial culture that systematically sought to erase the Aboriginal presence from the country or at best, simply parade Native people when convenient (as when Lester B. Pearson came to town) and then shut them away, preferably, on reserves. While I loved the movies, unbeknownst to me, they were ironically indoctrinating me, like generations before me, and those to come, to reject my Native heritage. To put it another way, while popular media fictionalized and propagated the destruction of the Indian, church and state—the vanguard of western civilization—perfected the mechanism by which it would occur. The residential school became the systematic manifestation of an exclusive and dematerializing culture, a culture that ironically portrayed itself as pluralistic and open as it searched for its own national identity. If Native culture had a contribution to make, it was clear that aside from kids riddled with stereotypes, like I had been, few cared, and even fewer were prepared to listen. What was being told was inaccurate and agenda-driven. It also was evident that what authenticity and power Native culture contained had been drained out of it, to use a euphemism, turned into fluff and feathers. It was time for Native people to engage the Canadian hegemony and push for space, even if marginal, to speak and reclaim their own voice. To tell their own stories.

And they did. Beginning in the late 60s, early 70s, Native newspapers and magazines, like *The Indian Voice, The Ontario Indian, Tawow,* and *The Native Perspective Magazine,* among numerous others, began to publish not only political tracts and news, but also histories, life stories, stories from the oral tradition, fiction and poetry. This was soon followed by books by Native authors, such as Maria Campbell's *Halfbreed,* Wilfred Peltier's *No Foreign Land,* Howard Adam's *Prison of Grass* and Basil Johnston's *Ojibway Heritage,* among many others. (During this period Native filmmakers, such as Alanis Obomsawin and Gil Cardinal, also began making documentaries.) By the late 80s and early 90s anthologies, like Theytus Books' *Seventh Generation* and *Gatherings,* began to appear, providing a forum for fledgling writers, and leading to the active publishing scene we have today. The literary development that garnered the most attention during this period was however in the area of drama. Playwrights such as Tomson Highway, Daniel David Moses, Shirley Cheechoo, Margo Kane and Drew Hayden Taylor, among others, began to make themselves heard and soon found receptive audiences. Interestingly, it was also at this time that playwrights Highway, Moses and poet Keeshig-Tobias along with others formed a loosely knit group called "The Committee to Re-Establish the Trickster." In a quasi cultural manifesto published in 1988 as an introduction to a small collection of poetry and prose, Keeshig-Tobias stated that the aim of the group was to "consolidate and gain recognition for Native contributions to Canadian writing—to reclaim the Native voice in literature. To facilitate the creation and production of literature by Native people" (3).

Just how were they were going to accomplish their goals, and, specifically, reclaim the so-called Native voice? As the name of the group explicitly indicated, for them the way forward was to reclaim the Trickster, and to do so, ironically, it entailed looking back to the oral tradition. Tomson Highway's two plays *The Rez Sisters* (1986) and *Dry Lips Oughta Move to Kapuskasing* (1989) perhaps best illustrate this agenda in that both feature the Trickster Nanabush/Waskesakuk as a central character in the plays. Like Highway, Moses went on to use the Trickster as a character in his 1990 play *Coyote City* while Keeshig-Tobias wrote a long experimental prose-poem called "Trickster Beyond 1992: Our Relationship" which appeared in the catalogue of the *Indigena* art exhibition held at the Museum of Civilization. What the "Committee to Re-establish the Trickster" attempted to do, then, albeit with varying degrees of success, was to integrate elements of the oral tradition with western poetic and/or theatrical convention while addressing contemporary issues, such as domestic violence, poverty, alcoholism, and colonialism. If as Highway implied in an epigraph to his play *Dry Lips Oughta Move to Kapuskasing,* "before the healing can take place, the poison must first be exposed" (6), then, for Highway and the others, it was the Trickster who was just the man, or woman, to do it. By extension, the sacred narratives of the oral tradition would be central to this process.

Considering my own goal to address the intergenerational impact of the Residential School, this observation raised a central question: if the way forward to the

Native voice indeed required a gaze backward to traditional narratives, what did the narratives themselves tell us? Of course, there is continuous, unabated debate among specialists concerning the function of myth (defined here as sacred narratives). Nevertheless, to avoid getting lost in the quagmire of theoretical positions, the Native writer could always turn to the primary source itself. And that is exactly what I began to do: return to the source, the stories themselves. Incidentally, the 1980s also saw a major revival of traditional storytelling as exhibited in international festivals and a myriad of publications. One of the most significant published sources that I came across was anthropologist Alfonso Ortiz and storyteller Richard Erdoes' 1984 collection *Indian Myths and Legends*, consisting of 160 stories from 80 nations offering a magnificent panorama of the Native American mythic heritage. For me, a clue to the role of these traditional narratives for the purposes of the contemporary Native writer was found in the introduction to this collection. The authors write that "By moving often cataclysmic events into the realm of myth or folklore, the storyteller can at once celebrate, mourn, and honour the past—and look ahead to a time when the great heroes may return to their people, bearing powerful medicine to restore former glory" (xv). Cataclysmic is certainly a way to summarize the damage wrought on Native people by the Residential School experience. And, yet, how was I to go about doing this? The task was not to ascribe the event to the realm of the mythic (an obvious impossibility) but rather to use elements of the mythic to get at the act(ion) itself, the underlying level of destruction, or, as I indicated earlier, a form of behaviour that was of itself archetypal. And that was already there in the stories. In other words, was their something in the oral tradition that could help me to understand how to approach the play I wanted to write?

These were my thoughts as I drove north on Highway 17 one fall afternoon. Between North Bay and Sturgeon Falls, overlooking a section of Garden Village Reserve (where my Auntie was born), there is a rest-stop where I often park my car and stare onto the vast expanse of Lake Nipissing. As far as your eye can see you look to an undulating body of water that is more a sea than a lake. For most who stop, it is merely a pleasant view, a nice break from a long drive. But there are stories there that tell of another time, a time long before the arrival of the European to the shores of Turtle Island. Some of these stories tell of the wars, some tell of adventures, hardship and famine, while others tell of the Manitous. One such oral story tells of Nanabush, the great Ojibway cultural hero, and the Windigoes, and I was reminded of it when looking out onto the lake.

It was a time when the evil Windigoes roamed the world in search of human flesh. With jagged teeth and claws, a breath of ice, a voice howling like the wind through rock, they would fall upon an Anishnaabe encampment and tear its victims limb from limb. It's little wonder then that when Nanabush spotted some thirty of them hot on his trail, he began to cry and pray and run as fast as his feet could carry him. So there was Nanabush running and stumbling, praying and choking in fear when suddenly he had to stop dead in his tracks because he found himself on the shore of Lake Nipissing. These foul creatures almost upon him, with no recourse other than certain death, Nanabush called upon The Great Mystery to help him. At that moment, a path of stone rose out of the water, allowing Nanabush to hurry across the great lake. Undaunted the greedy Windigoes continued after him, also running upon the stone path. But deep in the centre of the lake, as soon as Nanabush crossed over, the stone path began to recede, drowning the pursuing Windigoes. Nanabush, of course, carried on to the far side of the lake where he continued his many adventures. As for the Windigoes, their bones rest at the bottom of Lake Nipissing. A simple story that moves both Nanabush and the Windigoes from the pages of a dusty book, or a static museum, out into a living community and landscape.

It did not take me long to realize that there was only one character within the Anishinabek pantheon of Manitous who could express the damage wrought on Native people through the Residential School experience. Furthermore, I realized that to employ elements of these ancient narratives in a contemporary context to address such a cataclysmic event was indeed using them in a traditional manner. As the "Committee to Re-establish the Trickster" had done in their plays and poems, I would re-establish the Windigo, at least in this play. If the mythic can be considered not pre-logical but instead another reading of the world (Dundes 228), or perhaps more accurately another dreaming of the world, then, it is this dreaming that would provide the way into the play. This is not to say that the Windigo had not been used as a literary device in other contemporary work; however, to my knowledge it had always been presented as a physical manifestation of a monster-like creature going around eating unsuspecting campers and the like. As I noted, in coming to stories about the Windigo I was much more interested in behaviour, what made the thing tick, so to speak. Or to put it another way, what had been the traditional role of the Windigo and how could I link it to what went on in the schools and later at home.

It was at that point I returned to the oral narratives themselves to see if they would provide the clue to making the connections between what I was now calling "Windigoness" and the Residential School experience I was interested in portraying. What came to mind in thinking about the stories I had heard, and later those I had read, were the distinct world-views they embodied. If "a world-view may be under-stood as a set of conceptual presuppositions, both conscious and unconscious, artic-ulate and inarticulate, shared by a culture" (Overholt & Callicott 1), then, we can also understand that "there exists a variety of world-views, perhaps as many as there are distinct cultures" (xi). As for Native people to some extent the opposite is also true. It is a given that within the various Native cultures of the Americas there exists certain commonalities among these worldviews. "One thing that Native American people have in common in their traditions of sacred knowledge is the belief in the existence of unseen powers. These powers may take the form of deities (Manitous) or they may be more of a 'feeling' that something exists and is sacred and mysterious" (Beck, Walters & Francisco 9). Power. I rolled the word around in my mouth and pondered the concept. What did it mean exactly? I felt this was the clue I had been looking for.

I remembered a book I had read a few years earlier called *Stories from the Six Worlds*, a collection of Migmaw stories transcribed by Ruth Holmes Whitehead. I opened it to the introduction and immediately found what I was looking for:

"Modern science maintains that all matter is energy, shaping itself to particular patterns. The Old Ones of the People took this a step further: they maintained that patterns of Power could be conscious, manifesting the worlds by acts of will" (3). I turned the page, and I again read another sentence. This was it: "Power is the essence which underlies the perceived universe: it gives rise to it, transcends it, energizes and transforms it. It is everywhere at once, and yet it is also conscious, particulate: it is Persons. Within the six worlds live a number of such Persons. Muini'skw—Bear Woman—is just what her name implies: a Bear Person and a Woman, a human woman" (4). The idea of someone inhabiting the space of both Bear and Human simultaneously appears to be a contradiction for sure if one is trying to understand the concept from outside the Migmaw world-view. Trying to understand it from an etic perspective.

Because my connection lies with Anishnaabe culture, Windigo residing specifically within the Anishnaabe world-view, it was important to me to consider the concept of Power within that cultural belief system. I thought of the story about Nanabush and the stone path rising and then sinking into the water and drowning the Windigoes. A collection of Ojibway stories originally translated by William Jones at the turn of last century immediately confirmed what Whitehead had observed from the Migmaw narratives. In discussing elements of the Anishnaabe world-view, the editors noted that "perhaps one of the most striking features of these stories is that so many of the characters, creatures, and objects in them are pictured as performing actions which from a Western point of view we would consider quite extraordinary. We are confronted with a variety of occurrences without analogue in our world of everyday experience. These aptitudes and capacities of the various actors may conveniently be designated as manifestations of 'power'" (Overholt & Callicott 140).

Returning to the Morrisseau-Schwartz text, *Windigo and Other Tales of the Ojibways*, I reconsidered the details of Morrisseau's narrative, specifically how the protagonist Kit-chin-ik-koo (Big Goose) gains his power to defeat the dreaded Windigo. In this version, Morrisseau elaborates that Bear Medicine Man appears, and functioning as Big Goose's totem or spirit helper, intervenes and blows his spirit powers into Big Goose. As in Morrisseau's earlier version of the story, found in the Selwyn Dewdney edited text *Legends of My People*, Big Goose immediately begins to transform himself into a huge and mighty giant called Mis-sah-ba. After a fierce battle with the Windigo, Big Goose, now Mis-sah-ba, defeats Windigo and sets his people free (11). For me, the intervention of a guardian spirit who was both Man and Bear simultaneously, the transference of Power, and the transformation of Big Goose into Mis-sah-ba were the central motifs in the telling of this variation of the Windigo story and key to understanding the world-view from which the story originated; likewise, they would also be a significant elements in the writing of my play. I now had the clue to how to approach my story.

What I realized from the outset is that mimetically it would be a challenge to stage such conventions for a western audience because, as observed, there is no analogue in our world of everyday experience. To put it another way, as Thomas King recently noted in the Massey Lectures, "The magic of Native literature... is not the themes of the stories… it is the way meaning is refracted by cosmology, the way understanding is shaped by cultural paradigms" (112). One thing I knew for sure is that I did not want a monster-like creature roaming the stage (—as dramatized in recent popular movies). This, I knew, would be far too campy, and would certainly present an inaccurate portrayal of the mighty Windigo. Also, in a practical sense, it wouldn't work. Remember, I am referring to a creature that the oral narratives describe as being as tall as the trees. Okay, you might be thinking that I could have used slight of hand, illusion. Projection, for example. I thought of this option, and, although I didn't totally disregard it, I felt there had to be another method of conveying the Windigo. What about introducing a human sized Windigo? The runt of the litter so to speak. Scale him down. The idea seemed ridiculous. And although I initially dismissed it outright, the more I thought about it the more I began thinking about it in the context of my initial interest: behaviour. What I was now calling "Windigoness."

For the play to work, I knew it would have to present the illusion of western experiential reality and move from there. I would begin with the Residential School experience. I had spoken to survivors myself. I had read numerous reports and books about the schools, which analyzed, historicized and personalized the experience, and it was clear that the schools had been a dismal failure. The project to rid the country of its Indian problem, to educate and imbue them with the values of European culture by severing the bonds between child and family, had in the process destroyed and scarred generations. While there was little consistency among the schools, it appears that to a large extent inadequate funding and gross mismanagement hampered them all (Royal Commission on Aboriginal Peoples 353). Furthermore, from my reading, it appears that because the schools had little or no supervision, the children were subjected to deviants who ended up with unmitigated free reign over them. For example, in sentencing Arthur Plint, the dorm supervisor of the Port Alberni Residential School, who pled guilty to sixteen counts of indecent assault of Aboriginal boys aged six to thirteen between the years 1948 to 1968, B.C. Supreme Court Justice Douglas Hogarth said the former supervisor was a sexual predator. And "as far as the victims are concerned, the Indian residential school system was nothing more than institutionalized pedophilia" (Fournier & Crey 72). Plint, then seventy-seven, far from being remorseful for abusing helpless children, struck out with his cane and cursed his accusers (71). Perhaps this is what I'm trying to get at, I thought, making the link between "Windigoness" and the kind of behaviour that Plint exhibited. For is not sexual abuse a kind of cannibalism? A devouring of the spirit. Justice Hogarth went on to say that "Generations of children were wrenched from their families and were brought up to be ashamed to be Indians" (72). With that I was reminded of the ruins of the old school I had explored as a kid. What had gone on behind those walls I could only guess.

Having my subject, the intergenerational impact of the residential school experience, and my approach, behaviour, I now needed to answer a fundamental question. Who exactly was the play about? Having met a young Native woman who had been sexually abused, my immediate reaction was to model the play after her. Although not having gone to a Residential School herself, as I had suspected, she had been the child of parents who had. When I had cautiously told her that I was thinking about exploring the issue in my writing, she simply told me to go for it. As far as she was concerned, Canada had kept its dirty secret under the carpet for far too long. Looking at this woman, one would never know she had been sexually abused. She had a job and what appeared a normal life, children, and a family. Yet, on further discussion, I learned that she had been in therapy for years, and it had been a long hard road for her to get to a healing place in her life. There had been depression, alcohol and drugs. My main character Lily would also have a career and on the surface appear normal and successful. She would appear to be in complete control. But there would be relapses, the demons that haunted her—the Windigo—was something she would have to contend with daily. She would still be in therapy, taking an array of tranquilizers, trying to dull the nightmares and get on with her life.

The more I thought about Lily though the more I realized the story was not hers. It had to focus on her mother. It had to be her mother's story. A central question had to be answered. If Lily had been subjected to sexual abuse in the home, why had her mother not intervened to stop it? Yes, thematically, the story had to focus on this question. Her mother, whom I now named Doris, would be the central character, the protagonist. Lily would be the catalyst driving the plot. To get the two of them together, something would happen, and under great duress she would return home to confront her mother. Maybe there would be a death. The death of the father. Maybe someone would call her and tell her it was time to come home. Lily would then unknowingly awaken the Windigo spirit, which would manifest itself into something not quite human. She would do something to release it. Open Pandora's box to use a mythic analogy. Or perhaps her presence would be enough to stir things up. It would then be up to Doris to make things right. She would be given a second chance to save her daughter. We all long for a second chance.

To explore why Doris had let such a horrific thing happen to her daughter, I needed to know who Doris was as individual. What had she experienced? I went back to my research and found something on the Internet that jumped out at me. I read the testimony of Vera Hunt of Bella Bella given to Reverend Kevin Annett on 3 March 1998 and my eyes widened in astonishment. In her testimony, Hunt says that she "heard a lot of stories about babies' bodies being found buried at St. Michael's Residential School in Alert Bay." This was it. Doris had been impregnated with Lily in the Residential School and had managed to get her baby out and save her. Then, in a terrible twist of irony, the man she married ended up abusing her child. Why had she stayed with him? Because, as Justice Hogarth alluded to, by the time many of the students left the schools they were completely ashamed of who they were, had no self-esteem, and didn't believe they deserved any kind of a life. An explanation for Doris. Yet, something perplexed me: despite having got the baby out of the school initially, she let the abuse continue to happen at home. I read a report on "Post Traumatic Stress Disorder" and learned that "psychological trauma is an affliction of the powerless" (Turcotte 1). Already emotionally traumatized, the added stress of her husband's abusive behaviour was psychologically just too much for her, and she reverted to persistent avoidance by succumbing to the indoctrination she had grown up with all those years in the residential school. Instead of finding escape in alcohol and drugs, she turned to the church and prayed fervently, setting up her own little altar to the Virgin in the corner of her living room. This would be my Doris. But was this enough? There was still something I couldn't quite put my finger on.

At this point I turned my attention to the husband. Who was he? I didn't know yet. What I did know is that his actions had indeed embodied "Windigoness." Maybe he had gone to the Residential School himself. Maybe he had learned his behaviour. Maybe not. I went back to the traditional oral narratives, and then reread the section on modern Windigoes in Johnston's book *The Manitous*, and thought of them in the context of the husband's behaviour and realized that my instincts were correct; the concept of Windigo was indeed both a noun and a verb. Thing and action. Windigo and "Windigoness" were one and same. Just as "Bear Medicine Man" was both Bear and Man simultaneously. Within a Native world-view it all made perfect sense. I felt as though I was suddenly liberated. By this I mean that I was no longer tied to a specific physical entity. Yes, the husband was indeed dead but his actions lived on. They were still very much alive. Still very much in the house. Lily was now coming home unsuspectingly because she had heard that her father was dead. Little did she know his presence was waiting for her to return.

Okay, but if the father was not in the play, who would embody Windigo? At this point I decided to introduce David, Lily's non-Native boyfriend who has been living with her for three years. A graduate student, David is writing his thesis on Eurocentrism and the First Nations' treaty negotiations. Therefore, he is interested in Native culture, albeit primarily as an academic, meets Lily and falls in love with her. Lily likewise comes to love David and, significantly, comes to depend on him. However, because of Lily's psychological wound, her behaviour is at times erratic. Again, after reading about "Post Traumatic Stress Disorder," I saw Lily either withdrawing from him, as she detaches and numbs herself of any kind of stimuli or, on the contrary, intensifying and replaying the traumatic events in her life. In fact, it is this intensification that becomes a turning point in the play. Their relationship comes to a head when Lily begins to role play her rape and drags David into playing along with her. This leads David to demand that Lily talk to her mother about what happened at home. He can no longer handle Lily's behaviour, and feels that her therapy isn't doing much good. Desperate to keep her relationship, David having become a crutch of sorts, Lily agrees to go up north with him. Once they arrive at Doris' home however things go awry. To solve the problem of introducing and characterizing the Windigo creature, I once again returned to the traditional narratives.

As Morrisseau's retelling of "Windigo" in *Windigo and Other Tales of the Ojibways*, indicates, in receiving spirit power from his totem, the protagonist Kit-chin-ik-koo (Big Goose) transforms into the giant Mis-sha-ba to defeat the Windigo. Employing the principles of transference and transformation, then, two reoccurring motifs in the traditional narratives, I decided that through ritual David would become both the Windigo and the father. To accomplish this I employed the traditional narrative principal of the *many* inhabiting the *one*. The device I used for the transference, or the power object, was the dead father's clothes. Doris would perform a ritual in which David would put on the clothes and transform into the Windigo/Husband and, then, as part of the ritual, she would have to remove them from him and burn them in order to vanquish the Windigo's power. Forced into action to save Lily from the "Windigoness" threatening to claim her, Doris' struggle would be emotional, physical, and spiritual. After much soul searching, David would go along with the ritual for the love of Lily and, in doing so, commit himself to moving beyond his dispassionate gaze of the "other." Of course, there would be additional complication. Once Doris gets the clothes on David, and he transforms into the Windigo/Husband, she is unprepared for his Windigo power and fearfully falls into subservience. Here the challenge would be to make David believable as the Windigo/Husband; unfortunately, as Supreme Court Justice Douglas Hogarth had encountered in the B.C. Supreme Court, such models of behaviour were all too available. Doris would have to overcome her sense of inferiority and powerlessness and regain her dignity and strength by returning to her cultural traditions. She would do this to save her daughter. Thus, in a sense, this ritual would function as a rite of passage for both Doris and David.

The ensuing struggle would be one of life and death, as it had been for so many children in the Residential Schools. Again, I used the motifs of transference and transformation. To dramatize Doris' cultural awakening, I chose to use the "Bear" as both a physical animal and an Anishnaabe totem of strength and courage (Johnston 53). I knew that this would work well since "the cultural significance of the bear is so strong that the elders rely on the Great Spirit to warn them of possible future calamity by sending the bear as a dream visitor" (Spielmann 174). I also knew that Anishnaabe traditionally pay great heed and respect to the dream world, and that the divisions between the dream world and the physical world are blurred. Therefore, I would have the bear come to Doris in both worlds, at home where she would see bear tracks, *and* in her dreams. Bear would come to warn Doris of the impending Windigo, but because of her Catholic upbringing Doris would feel confused and threatened by Bear's intervention. Finally, in the climax of the story, the moment of crisis, Doris would turn away from her Residential School indoctrination and actually call upon the Bear spirit to intervene on her behalf. But unlike in Morrisseau's story of the Windigo, where Kit-chin-ik-koo (Big Goose) transforms into the giant Missha-ba, Doris would transform into Medicine Bear Woman, both bear and woman, an other-than-human-person. In her determination, I saw her lumbering across the living room floor and ripping open the bedroom door to confront the Windigo/Husband and protect her "cub", something she could never do without the strength of her culture, her Bear Medicine power. Every step would be her symbolic journey back to cultural renewal, a journey that many Native people are now making in their journey towards healing. To end the play, I envisioned Lily telling a story about picking blueberries with Doris and encountering an actual mother bear and her cub. This story would serve to bring us full circle so to speak from Doris' mythological journey back to the contemporary world of daily living while emphasizing the instinctual protective nature of both human and animal.

In conclusion, I should mention that although the play has had dramatic readings, at Lakehead University in Thunder Bay and Native Earth Performing Arts Inc. in Toronto, it has not yet had a full production. However, through its healing initiatives, the Aboriginal Healing Foundation has provided funding for a co-production of the play and for development into a film. For me, this is an indication that there are experts in the field of Aboriginal health and healing who see value in the work. I am very pleased with this because when I set out, my goal was to write a drama that would say something about the significance of Aboriginal culture in the context of the intergenerational impact of the Residential School experience. From the report of The Royal Commission on Aboriginal Peoples, there is little doubt that for Aboriginal people to move beyond collective trauma, the restoration and promotion of Aboriginal culture and expression is primary. This of course necessarily takes many forms, theatre being but one of them. Whether or not a full production of "A Windigo Tale" will take place is yet to be seen. Nevertheless, from the research that went into the writing, it is clear that the potential to draw on traditional oral sources to tackle contemporary issues and create provocative theatre (as well as other forms of cultural expression) is only beginning to be realized.

(2005)

Works Cited

Aboriginal Healing Foundation. *Residential School Update.* Ottawa, 1998.

Aboriginal Healing Foundation. *Where Are the Children?* Ottawa: Legacy of Hope Foundation, 2003.

Beck, Peggy V., Walters, Anna Lee and Nia, Francisco. *The Sacred: Ways of Knowledge, Sources of Life.* Tsaile: Navajo Community College, 1977.

Berkhofer, Robert. *The White Man's Indian.* New York: Vintage, 1979.

Chrisjohn, Rolland et al. *The Circle Game: Shadows and Substance in the Indian Residential School Experience in Canada.* Penticton: Theytus, 1997.

Colombo, John Robert. *Windigo: An Anthology of Fact and Fantastic Fiction.* Saskatoon: Western Producer Prairie Books, 1982.

Department of Indian and Northern Development. *Indian Residential Schools (IRS) Data Project.* Ottawa, 1998.

Dundes, Allen, ed. *Sacred Narratives: Readings in the Theory of Myth.* Berkeley: U of California P, 1984.

Erdoes, Richard and Alfonso Ortiz, ed. *American Indian Myths and Legends.* New York: Pantheon, 1984.

Fournier, Suzanne and Ernie Crey. *Stolen From Our Embrace: The Abduction of First Nations Children and the Restoration of Aboriginal Communities.* Vancouver: Douglas & McIntyre, 1997.

Highway, Tomson. *Dry Lips Oughta Move to Kapuskasing.* Saskatoon: Fifth House, 1989.

Hodgson, Heather, ed. *Seventh Generation: Contemporary Native Writing.* Penticton: Theytus Books, 1989.

Jaine, Linda, ed. *Residential Schools, The Stolen Years.* Saskatoon: University Extension Press, U of Saskatchewan, 1993.

Johnston, Basil. *The Manitous: The Spiritual World of the Ojibway.* Toronto: Key Porter, 1999.

———. *Ojibway Heritage.* Toronto: McClelland and Stewart, 1976.

Keeshig-Tobias, Lenore, ed. *Magazine to Re-establish The Trickster.* Toronto: Blackbird Design Collective, 1988.

King, Thomas. *The Truth About Stories: A Native Narrative.* Toronto: Anansi, 2003.

Morrisseau, Norval and Selwyn Dewdney. ed. *Legends of My People: The Great Ojibway.* Toronto: Ryerson, 1965.

Morrisseau, Norval and Hubert Schwartz, ed. *Windigo and Other Tales of the Ojibways.* Toronto: McClelland & Stewart, 1969.

Moses, Daniel, David and Terry Goldie, ed. *An Anthology of Canadian Native Literature in English.* 2nd Ed. Don Mills: Oxford UP, 1998.

Overholt, Thomas, W. and J. Baird Callicott. *Clothed-In-Fur: An Introduction to an Ojibwa World View.* Lanham: UP of America, 1982.

Royal Commission on Aboriginal Peoples. *Final Report, Residential Schools. Volume 1 – Looking Forward, Looking Back.* Ottawa: Canada Communications Group, 1996.

Ruffo, Armand Garnet. *A Windigo Tale.* Unpublished playscript, 2000.

Shohat, Ella and Robert Stam. *Unthinking Eurocentrism: Multiculturalism and the Media.* London: Routledge, 1994.

Spielmann, Roger. *'You're Too Fat!' Exploring Ojibwe Discourse.* Toronto: U of Toronto P, 1998.

Testimony of Vera Hunt, Affidavits of Church Sponsored Abuse. 23 November 2004 <http://canadiangenocide.nativeweb.org/affadavitvhunt1.html>

Turcotte, Shirley. "Post Traumatic Stress Disorder." Unpublished document. 2000.

Whitehead, Ruth Holmes. *Stories from the Six Worlds: MicMac Legends.* Halifax: Nimbus, 1988.

Suggested Further Reading

Andrews, Jennifer. "Framing The Book of Jessica: Transformation and the Collaborative Process in Canadian Theatre." *English Studies in Canada* 22.3 (1996): 297-313.

Appleford, Robert. "The Indian Act(ing): Proximate Perversions in Genet's *The Blacks* (1959) and Favel Starr's *Lady of Silences* (1993, 2003)." *Theatre Research in Canada* [forthcoming].

———. "'No, the Centre Should Be Invisible': Radical Revisioning of Chekhov in Floyd Favel Starr's *House of Sonya*." *Modern Drama* 45.2 (Summer 2002): 246-58.

———. "Making Relations Visible in Native Canadian Performance." *Siting the Other: Re-visions of Marginality in Australian and English-Canadian Drama*. Ed. Franca Bellarsi and Marc Maufort. Brussels, Belgium: Peter Lang, 2001. 233-46.

———. "Natives and the Theater." *Native America: Portrait of the Peoples*. Ed. Duane Champagne. Detroit: Visible Ink Press, 1994. 722-27.

Bolt, Carol. "No Wings Yet." *Books In Canada* 18.2 (March 1989): 24-26.

Brask, Per and William Morgan, ed. *Aboriginal Voices: Amerindian, Inuit, and Sami Theater*. Baltimore: Johns Hopkins UP, 1992.

Braz, Albert. "Nanabush's Return: Cultural Messianism in Tomson Highway's Plays." *Changing Representations of Minorities East and West*. Ed. John Rieder and Larry E. Smith. Honolulu, HI: College of Languages, Linguistics and Literature, University of Hawaii, with East-West Center, 1996. 143-56.

Crew, Robert. "Pocahontas' unique view interesting but uneven." *Toronto Star* 12 February 1990: C7.

Crook, Barbara. "A Few Slips Twixt Audience and Lips." *Vancouver Sun* 25 March 1995: H8.

Däwes, Birgit. "An Interview with Drew Hayden Taylor." *Contemporary Literature* 44.1 (Spring 2003): 1-18.

Gilbert, Helen. "Black and White and Re(a)d All Over Again: Indigenous Minstrelsy in Contemporary Canadian and Australian Theatre." *Theatre Journal* 55.4 (Dec 2003): 679-98.

Glaap, Albert-Reiner. "Drew Hayden Taylor's Dramatic Career." *Siting the Other: Re-visions of Marginality in Australian and English-Canadian Drama.* Ed. Franca Bellarsi and Marc Maufort. Brussels, Belgium: Peter Lang, 2001. 217-32.

———. "Margo Kane, Daniel David Moses, Yvette Nolan, Drew Hayden Taylor: Four Native Playwrights from Canada." *Anglistik: Mitteilungen des Verbandes deutscher Anglisten* 7.1 (March 1996): 5-25.

Godard, Barbara. "Writing Between Cultures." *Traduction, Terminologie, Rédaction: Études sur le Texte et Ses Transformations* 10.1 (1997): 53-99.

Grant, Agnes. "Canadian Native Literature: The Drama of George Ryga and Tomson Highway." *Australian-Canadian Studies* 10.2 (1992): 37-56.

Gray, R.W. "'The nice thing about being two-spirited is it exists despite the patriarchy': an interview with Daniel David Moses." *Arc* 42 (Spring 1999): 29-30.

Hannon, Gerald. "Tomson and the Trickster." *Toronto Life* (March 1991): 28-31, 35-44, 81-85.

Hauck, Gerhard. "Roses on the Rez: Chronicle of a Failure?" *Canadian Theatre Review* 115 (Summer 2003): 47-51.

Hengen, Shannon. "First Tellers of Tales." *Canadian Theatre Review* 106 (Spring 2001): 35-38.

Hunt, Nigel. "Tracking the Trickster." *Brick* 37 (Autumn 1989): 58-60.

Imboden, Roberta. "On the Road with Tomson Highway's Blues Harmonica in 'Dry Lips Oughta Move to Kapuskasing'." *Canadian Literature* 144 (Spring 1995): 113-25.

Innes, Christopher. "Dreams of Violence: Moving Beyond Colonialism in Canadian and Caribbean Drama." *Theatre Matters: Performance and Culture on the World Stage.* Ed. Richard Boon and Jane Plastow. Cambridge: Cambridge UP, 1998. 76-96.

Jonnie, Curtis. "Inside 'In Deo': An Indian Musical." *Ontario Indian* 5.9 (1982): 42-43.

Knowles, Ric. "The Hearts of Its Women: Rape, Residential Schools, and Remembering." *Performing National Identities: International Perspectives on Contemporary Canadian Theatre.* Ed. Sherrill Grace and Albert-Rainer Glaap. Vancouver: Talonbooks, 2003. 245-64.

———. "'Look. Look Again': Daniel David Moses' Decolonizing Optics." *Crucible of Cultures: Anglophone Drama at the Dawn of a New Millennium.* Ed. Marc Maufort and Franca Bellarsi. Bruxelles: Peter Lang, 2002. 187-98.

———. "'Marlon Brando, Pocahontas, and Me'." *Essays on Canadian Writing* 71 (Fall 2000): 48-60.

————. "Reading Material: Transfers, Remounts, and the Production of Meaning in Contemporary Toronto Drama and Theatre." *Essays on Canadian Writing. 20th Anniversary Issue* 51-2 (Winter-Spring 1994): 258-95.

Lenze, Christine. "'The Whole Thing You're Doing Is White Man's Ways': *FareWel*'s Northern Tour." *Canadian Theatre Review* 108 (2001 Fall): 48-51.

Leonard, Paul. "*The Tempest* X 2 in Toronto." *Canadian Theatre Review* 54 (1988): 7-12.

Linklater, Doris. "Linklater responds." Letter to the editor. *The Drama Review* 37 (Spring 1993): 15-16.

Loucks, Brian. "Another Glimpse: Excerpts from a Conversation with Tomson Highway." *Canadian Theatre Review* 68 (Fall 1991): 9-11.

Maufort, Marc. "Forging an 'Aboriginal Realism': First Nations Playwriting in Australia and Canada." *Siting the Other: Re-visions of Marginality in Australian and English-Canadian Drama*. Ed. Marc Maufort and Franca Bellarsi. Brussels: Peter Lang; 2001. 7-22.

————. "Recognizing Difference in Canadian Drama: Tomson Highway's Poetic Realism." *British Journal of Canadian Studies* 8.2 (1993): 230-40.

Methot, Suzanne. "The Universe of Tomson Highway." *Quill & Quire* 64 (November 1998): 1, 12.

Mojica, Monique, ed. *Native Theatre. Canadian Theatre Review* 68 (1991).

Mojica, Monique and Ric Knowles, ed. *Staging Coyote's Dream: An Anthology of First Nations Drama in English*. Toronto: Playwrights Canada, 2003.

Morgan, William. "The Trickster and Native Theater: An Interview with Tomson Highway." Brask and Morgan.

Morrow, Martin. "The Rez Sisters: ATP has trouble with wonderful play by Tomson Highway." *Calgary Herald* 22 Sept 1990: D1.

Nadjiwon, Rolland. "Harvesting the Colonies." *ASAIL Notes* 13.3 (1996): 7-9.

Nothof, Anne. "Cultural Collision and Magical Transformation: The Plays of Tomson Highway." *Studies in Canadian Literature* 20.2 (1995): 34-43.

Nunn, Robert. "Drew Hayden Taylor's *alterNatives*: Dishing the Dirt." *Crucible of Cultures: Anglophone Drama at the Dawn of a New Millennium*. Ed. Franca Bellarsi and Marc Maufort. Brussels, Belgium: Peter Lang, 2002. 209-18.

Perkins, Lina. "Remembering the Trickster in Tomson Highway's The Rez Sisters." *Modern Drama* 45.2 (Summer 2002): 259-69.

Shackleton, Mark and Hartmut Lutz. "Interview with Tomson Highway." *Kunapipi: Journal of Post-Colonial Writing* 25.2 (2003): 74-85.

Shackleton, Mark. "Language and Resistance in the Plays of Tomson Highway." *Postcolonialism and Cultural Resistance.* Ed. Jopi Nyman and John A. Stotesbury. Joensuu, Finland: Faculty of Humanities, University of Joensuu, 1999. 215-21.

———. "'Restoring the Imprisoned Nation to Itself': Resistance, Repossession, and Reconciliation in the Plays of Tomson Highway." *Reconfigurations: Canadian Literatures and Postcolonial Identities.* Ed. Franca Bellarsi and Marc Maufort. Brussels, Belgium: Peter Lang, 2002. 203-14.

———. "Tomson Highway: Colonizing Christianity versus Native Myth-From Cultural Conflict to Reconciliation." *Missions of Interdependence: A Literary Directory.* Ed. Gerhard Stilz. Amsterdam, Netherlands: Rodopi, 2002. 41-51.

Stanlake, Christy. "Blending Time: Dramatic Conventions in Yvette Nolan's *Annie Mae's Movement.*" *Journal of Dramatic Theory and Criticism* 14.1 (Fall 1999): 143-49.

Streed, Judy. "Tomson Highway: My Way." *Toronto Star* 24 March 1991: D1-2.

Taylor, Drew Hayden. "Canoeing the Rivers of Canadian Aboriginal Theatre: The Portages and the Pitfalls." *Crucible of Cultures: Anglophone Drama at the Dawn of a New Millennium.* Ed. Franca Bellarsi and Marc Maufort. Brussels, Belgium: Peter Lang, 2002. 25-30.

———. "There's a Trickster behind every Nanabush." *Toronto Star* 3 June 1995: J8.

Tompkins, Joanne and Lisa Male. "'Twenty-One Native Women on Motorcycles': An Interview with Tomson Highway." *Australasian Drama Studies* 24 (April 1994): 13-28.

Usmiani, Renate. "The Bingocentric Worlds of Michel Tremblay and Tomson Highway: *Les Belles-Soeurs* vs. *The Rez Sisters.*" *Canadian Literature* 144 (Spring 1995): 126-40.

Wasserman, Jerry. "Drama." *University of Toronto Quarterly* 60 (Fall 1990): 69-71.

Wheeler, Jordan. "A Revolution in Aboriginal Theatre: Our Own Stories." *Canadian Theatre Review* 66 (Spring 1991): 8-12.

Wigston, Nancy. "Nanabush in the City." *Books in Canada* 18.2 (March 1989): 7-9.

Wilke, Gundula. "Traditional Values and Modern Concerns: The 'Committee to Re-Establish the Trickster'." *Revista Canaria de Estudios Ingleses* 35 (Nov 1997): 135-49.

Notes on Contributors

Rob Appleford is an Associate Professor in the English and Film Studies Department at the University of Alberta. He has published many articles on Aboriginal literatures and theatre. Currently, he is at work on a monograph study entitled *Caliban's Children: The Politics of Desire in North American Aboriginal Literature.*

Floyd Favel (Starr) is a theatre director, writer and performer. He has travelled to Siberia, Japan, Australia, and northern Canada in his investigation and development of indigenous performance methodologies.

Alan Filewod is a Professor in the School of English and Theatre Studies at the University of Guelph. He is the author of *Performing Canada: The Nation Enacted in the Imagined Theatre* (Textual Studies in Canada 2002) and *Collective Encounters: Documentary Theatre in English Canada* (U of Toronto P, 1987). With David Watt, he is co-author of *Workers' Playtime: Theatre and the Labour Movement since 1970* (Currency Press, 2001).

Reid Gilbert teaches in the Department of English at Capilano College, Vancouver. He is the author, with Sylvan Barnet, of *A Short Guide to Writing about Literature*, now in its second Canadian edition. He has published a play and more than 60 articles and reviews. He has read papers at many national and international conferences. He is a co-editor of *Canadian Theatre Review* and a member of the Editorial Board of *Theatre Research in Canada.*

Tomson Highway is a former Artistic Director of Native Earth Performing Arts Inc., Toronto's only professional Native theatre company. His 1986 play *The Rez Sisters* won the Dora Mavor Moore Award for best new play in Toronto's 1987/88 season, was honoured as one of the runners-up for the Floyd S. Chalmers Award for Outstanding Canadian Play of 1986, and was one of two productions to represent Canada on the Mainstage of the Edinburgh International Festival. It was also a finalist for the Governor General's Literary Award in 1988. His next play *Dry Lips Oughta Move To Kapuskasing* won four Dora Mavor Moore Awards, the Floyd S. Chalmers Award for Outstanding Canadian Play in 1989 and was also a finalist for the Governor General's Award for Drama that same year. In addition, he has written five other plays. In 1998 Tomson Highway's first novel *The Kiss of the Fur Queen* was published by Doubleday Canada and has been published in the U.S. by University of Oklahoma Press. Tomson has also written three children's books published by Harper Collins: *Caribou Song, Dragonfly Kites* and *Fox On Ice.* Tomson was the Barker Fairley Distinguished Visitor at the University of Toronto (1997-99), and he has been honoured by the University of Winnipeg, the University of Western Ontario, and Brandon University in Manitoba with Honourary Doctor of Letters Degrees (LLD). In January 1994, Tomson received the Order of Canada. He is currently at work on his second novel.

Ric Knowles is Professor of Drama at the University of Guelph and general editor of *Critical Perspectives on Canadian Theatre in English*. He is co-editor, with Monique Mojica, of *Staging Coyote's Dream: An Anthology of First Nations Drama in English* (Playwrights Canada, 2003). He is also editor of the journals *Modern Drama* and *Canadian Theatre Review* and author of *The Theatre of Form and the Production of Meaning* (ECW 1999), *Shakespeare and Canada* (Peter Lang 2004), and *Reading the Material Theatre* (Cambridge UP, 2004).

Geraldine Manossa is a member of the Bigstone Cree Nation of Wabasca, Alberta. She completed a Master of Arts Degree from the University of Lethbridge and presently teaches in the National Aboriginal Professional Artist Training Program at the En'owkin Centre in Penticton, BC. She is dedicated to researching and writing about authentic Indigenous performance methodologies and training practices. She plans on pursuing doctoral studies based on kinesiology related programs within rural Indigenous communities.

Playwright, poet, dramaturge, editor and teacher, **Daniel David Moses** is a Delaware, from the Six Nations community lands along the Grand River in southern Ontario. His plays include *Coyote City*, a nominee for the 1991 Governor General's Literary Award for Drama, *Big Buck City* and *The Indian Medicine Shows*. He is also the author of *Delicate Bodies* (poems) and co-editor of Oxford UP's *An Anthology of Canadian Native Literature in English* (the third edition appeared in Spring 2005). His most recent other publications are *Sixteen Jesuses* (poems), *Brébeuf's Ghost* (drama), and new editions of the plays *Almighty Voice and His Wife* and *Coyote City* (included in *Necropolitei: two plays* with *City of Shadows*). His honours include a James Buller Memorial Award for Excellence in Aboriginal Theatre, the Harbourfront Festival Prize, a Harold Award and a Chalmers Fellowship. In 2003, he was appointed as Queen's National Scholar in the Department of Drama at Queen's University.

Yvette Nolan is a playwright, director and dramaturg. Her plays include *Blade*, *Job's Wife*, *Video*, *A Marginal Man*, the libretto *Hilda Blake* and the radio play *Owen*. She has worked from Nova Scotia to the Yukon on new play development. She is currently the artistic director of Native Earth Performing Arts in Toronto.

Robert Nunn was until his retirement a professor in the Department of Fine Arts at Brock University. He is the author of a number of articles on Canadian drama and dramatists, two of which received the Richard Plant Essay Prize. He is on the editorial board of *Theatre Research in Canada/Recherches théâtrales au Canada* and *Essays in Theatre/Études théâtrales*.

Sheila Rabillard is Associate professor of English at The University of Victoria, Canada. She has published articles on modern British, American, and Canadian playwrights; edited *Essays on Caryl Churchill* (1998). She is currently at work on a study of avant-garde theatre.

Armand Garnet Ruffo's work is strongly influenced by his Ojibway heritage. He is the author of two collections of poetry, *Opening In the Sky* (Theytus, 1994) and *At Geronimo's Grave* (Coteau 2001), winner of the Lampman Poetry Award. His poetic biography *Grey Owl: the Mystery of Archie Belaney* (Coteau, 1997) has received wide acclaim and has recently been adapted to the stage. His play *A Windigo Tale* was a winner of the 2001 CBC Arts Performance Showcase competition. He is also editor of a collection of essays, *(Ad)Dressing Our Words, Aboriginal Perspectives on Aboriginal Literatures* (Theytus Books, 2001). Born in Chapleau, northern Ontario, Ruffo now makes his home in Ottawa, where he teaches Aboriginal literature at Carleton University.

Former Artistic Director of Native Earth Performing Arts Theatre, **Drew Hayden Taylor's** plays have been produced throughout Canada, into the United States and studied as far away as Italy, Germany and New Zealand. He has won wide acclaim for his work, including the Chalmer's and Dora Awards. His play for young audiences, *The Boy In The Treehouse* toured cross country with the Manitoba Theatre for Young People, and his latest play, *The Buz'Gem Blues* debuted at Lighthouse Theatre in Port Dover and will be remounted by Trinity Repertory Company in Rhode Island in 2005.